The Atlanta Riot

SOUTHERN DISSENT SERIES

UNIVERSITY PRESS OF FLORIDA / STATE UNIVERSITY SYSTEM

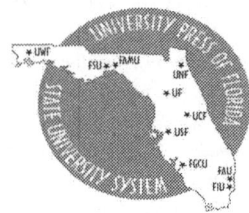

Florida A&M University, Tallahassee
Florida Atlantic University, Boca Raton
Florida Gulf Coast University, Ft. Myers
Florida International University, Miami
Florida State University, Tallahassee
University of Central Florida, Orlando
University of Florida, Gainesville
University of North Florida, Jacksonville
University of South Florida, Tampa
University of West Florida, Pensacola

Southern Dissent
Edited by Stanley Harrold and Randall M. Miller

The Other South: Southern Dissenters in the Nineteenth Century,
by Carl N. Degler, with a new preface (2000)
Crowds and Soldiers in Revolutionary North Carolina: The Culture of Violence in Riot and War,
by Wayne E. Lee (2001)
*"Lord, We're Just Trying to Save Your Water": Environmental Activism and Dissent
in the Appalachian South,* by Suzanne Marshall (2002)
The Changing South of Gene Patterson: Journalism and Civil Rights, 1960–1968,
edited by Roy Peter Clark and Raymond Arsenault (2002)
Gendered Freedoms: Race, Rights, and the Politics of Household in the Delta, 1861–1875,
by Nancy Bercaw (2003)
Civil War on Race Street: The Civil Rights Movement in Cambridge, Maryland,
by Peter B. Levy (2003)
South of the South: Jewish Activists and the Civil Rights Movement in Miami, 1945–1960,
by Raymond A. Mohl, with contributions by Matilda "Bobbi" Graff
and Shirley M. Zoloth (2004)
Throwing Off the Cloak of Privilege: White Southern Female Activists in the Civil Rights Era,
edited by Gail S. Murray (2004)
The Atlanta Riot: Race, Class, and Violence in a New South City, by Gregory Mixon (2004)

THE
Atlanta Riot

RACE, CLASS, AND VIOLENCE IN A NEW SOUTH CITY

Gregory Mixon

Foreword by Stanley Harrold and Randall M. Miller, Series Editors

University Press of Florida

Gainesville · Tallahassee · Tampa · Boca Raton
Pensacola · Orlando · Miami · Jacksonville · Ft. Myers

Copyright 2005 by Gregory Mixon
Printed in the United States of America
All rights reserved

First Paperback Printing, 2006

A record of cataloging-in-publication data is available from the Library of Congress.
ISBN 0-8130-2787-X; ISBN 0-8130-3075-7 (pbk.)

The University Press of Florida is the scholarly publishing agency for the State University System of Florida, comprising Florida A&M University, Florida Atlantic University, Florida Gulf Coast University, Florida International University, Florida State University, University of Central Florida, University of Florida, University of North Florida, University of South Florida, and University of West Florida.

University Press of Florida
15 Northwest 15th Street
Gainesville, FL 32611-2079
http://www.upf.com

Contents

List of Maps   vii
Series Foreword   ix
Acknowledgments   xiii

Introduction   1

PART ONE

Prologue: White Elite Control, Black Urban Mobility,
and Working White Women   7

1. Atlanta: The City of Progress   13
2. "If Folks Don't Treat Me Right": Atlanta's White Working Classes   27
3. African Americans in Atlanta   38

PART TWO

4. "Sowing Dragon's Teeth": Watson, Hardwick,
and Progressive Reform, 1904–1906   53
5. "The Seeds of Incendiarism":
The Gubernatorial Campaign of 1905–1906   64
6. The Summer of 1906   73

PART THREE

7. Riot   85
8. "Off the Streets"   101
9. Reconstruction: The Illusion of Hope   116

Conclusion: Urbanization, Segregation, and Violence   128

Notes   131
Bibliography   173
Index   189

Maps

6.1. Copenhill   82

7.1. Oakland City   96

7.2. Peters Street mob   97

7.3. Alleged assault victim   98

7.4. Bellwood section   99

7.5. Streetcar rioting   100

8.1. Atlanta and Western Suburbs   111

8.2. Intersection of Magnolia and Vine Streets   112

8.3. Militia mobilization   113

8.4. Summerhill   114

8.5. Brownsville   115

Foreword

"Violence is as American as apple pie," said black militant H. Rap Brown in 1967, as he described centuries of violence against black people and justified black violence in response. His remark suggests that race riots in American cities have not been aberrations. Rather, they are a deeply rooted and persistent phenomenon.

In New York City in 1712, a band of enslaved Africans used muskets, hatchets, and swords to kill nine white men and injure six others. Subsequently, white authorities executed twenty-six of the rebels. Beginning in the 1810s and extending into the late 1840s, white mobs led by "gentlemen of property and standing" attacked black communities in such northern cities as Philadelphia, Cincinnati, Providence, and New York. Philadelphia alone experienced seven race riots between 1820 and 1849. In 1863 in New York City, large numbers of Irish immigrants, opposed to the Union's Civil War conscription law, expressed their anger by killing more than 100 African Americans. During Reconstruction, some white residents of Memphis, New Orleans, and other southern cities responded to black freedom with mob violence. In both northern and southern cities, white mobs acted against African Americans to keep them out of work, off the streets, or away from the ballot box.

The Atlanta race riot of 1906 was a pivotal moment in a history of racial violence. It underlined W.E.B. Du Bois's earlier observation that the history of the twentieth century would be the history of the color line. Similar antiblack urban riots followed in Springfield, Illinois, in 1908, East St. Louis and Houston in 1917, Chicago in 1919, and Tulsa in 1921. Although there was a hiatus after the early 1920s, urban race riots reemerged in northern cities during World War II as blacks and whites competed for jobs and housing. During the turbulent 1960s, after urban demographics had changed significantly, the impetus and instigations of riots shifted as African Americans took to the streets in such cities as Los Angeles, Philadelphia, Newark, and Detroit to vent their anger and frustration concerning an institutional racism that led to joblessness, poverty, and police brutality. In 1991, the beating of black motorist Rodney King by several white police officers led some black residents of Los Angeles to react in violent protest after a predominantly white jury acquitted the officers on most of the charges against them.

The riots—their savageness, their complicated causes, and their consequences for public policy and racial and ethnic identity—have attracted the interest of many historians and sociologists. They indicate something fundamental about this country. Yet few such riots have been the subject of detailed historical analysis, and no scholar has probed so deeply as Gregory Mixon into the Atlanta race riot of 1906, one of the more significant in southern history. Much had changed over the nearly two centuries between the New York City rebellion of 1712 and the violence that tore apart this New South city. More would change between Atlanta's racial outburst and the urban mayhem of the latter half of the twentieth century. But a racial component, divergent class interests, and a governmental response marked by conflicting agendas remained constant.

In *The Atlanta Riot: Race, Class, and Violence in a New South City,* Mixon unmasks the New South's progressive pretensions by describing how local boosters pushed Atlanta into the twentieth century by imposing white domination. The modern Atlanta that later boasted that it was "a city too busy to hate" was built on hate. Mixon places the Atlanta riot within the contexts of complicated New South politics, of ambitious local white entrepreneurs, and of an emerging black community that threatened white interests economically, politically, and psychologically. He maps the interrelationships between southern white political Progressivism, economic development, masculinity, and racism.

Mixon demonstrates the volatility of race through his analyses of technological change and of the class and gender divisions within Atlanta's black and white communities. The new mobility of the streetcar, in which black and white people jostled for space, threatened to break down social barriers, as did work in factories where men and women came together. The very success of African Americans in building their own churches and neighborhoods threatened the white demand for control. Other historians have shown how emotional charges that black men lusted after white women were not just excuses for racial violence but also reflections of deeper white insecurities. Mixon goes beyond this to analyze the complex relationship between Atlanta's black and white elites, of the black and white working classes, and of the women of both races. Violence resulted as this multifaceted social tension could not be contained in a fast-growing city whose white leaders used race to propel their political ambitions.

This brutal and disturbing story helps readers to understand a racial cauldron that is still capable of boiling up urban violence. Mixon's fine study is a welcome addition to the Southern Dissent series. It invites further research into each of the other urban race riots that have helped define American character. It demands an appreciation of the ways black aspiration and dissent have struggled against violent repression.

Stanley Harrold and Randall M. Miller
Series Editors

Acknowledgments

This book began as a paper in Herbert Shapiro's graduate seminar on racial violence. The work on that paper led me to conclude that the Atlanta riot was not a spontaneous outbreak but, as the early literature suggested, a complex event involving the histories of both black and white men and women, Georgia, the South, politics, and the growth of the region's urban network. What began at the University of Cincinnati as a graduate course assignment became my dissertation. This monograph brings to a conclusion a study that has been a major part of my professional development. It is a work that many have encouraged me to complete, tempered by the question, "When will you finish?" My thanks to those who stayed the course despite the long and winding road this project has taken.

I would like to thank Bethany Baptist Church of Cleveland, Clayton Missionary Baptist Church of St. Louis, Zion Baptist Church of Cincinnati, Pilgrim Baptist Church of Omaha, First Baptist Church of Lexington, First Baptist Church of Lincoln Gardens, and Friendship Missionary Baptist Church of Charlotte. Each provided aid, nurturing, comfort, and understanding when I needed it most.

The institutions that employed me as a teacher and scholar provided the necessary resources to help complete the project. The Black Studies Department at the University of Nebraska at Omaha enabled me to edit and complete the dissertation. Virginia Military Institute colleagues Donald Thomas and Thomas Davis critiqued proposals for funding from the VMI Grant in Aid program, which funded two valuable research trips to archives in Atlanta and the Southern Historical Collection at the University of North Carolina. They also suggested that I apply for a National Endowment for the Humanities Summer Institute that focused on "Slavery and Freedom in the American South."

This marked the transition from dissertation to a book. Department heads Willard Hays and Blair Turner, along with Superintendent General John Knapp and Board of Visitors members Eugene Williams and Glen Jones, were encouraging and supportive. NEH Seminar director Michael P. Johnson, the University of California, Irvine, and all the seminar participants made a wonderful summer memorable. A Pew Charitable Postdoctoral Fellowship at the Center for Afro-American Studies at Wesleyan University provided me valuable research time and travel support. Erness Brody, Marshall Hyatt, and the faculty and staff made this a productive year. The drafting of this manuscript was made possible with the support of two Rutgers University Minority Faculty Development Awards, a Research Council Grant, and History Department leave from teaching responsibilities.

The research staffs of archives and libraries have been vital in making this work possible. Beginning with the librarians at the University of Cincinnati and Rutgers University's Reference and Interlibrary Loan Departments, especially the late Stan Nash, librarians and archivists have opened their facilities and knowledge to me with warmth and kindness. The Robert W. Woodruff Library and Special Collections at the Atlanta University Center and the Atlanta History Center archives provided a firm foundation for the study. Both institutions allowed me to visit their facilities frequently. The Georgia Department of Archives and History likewise welcomed me and made their collections available for extensive use. The Auburn Avenue Research Library, a new archive, also gave me important assistance by opening its collections. At the University of Georgia, the Library's Special Collection division and the Richard Russell Memorial Library allowed me to examine the personal papers of Georgia politicians and leaders.

A special thanks goes to a long list of people who provided me invaluable support as the project has evolved. Gloria Mims and Virginia Shadron made the archives in Atlanta a pleasant place to work. To the people who have taken the time out of their busy schedules to read the manuscript, my thanks and gratitude. John Dittmer and Ronald Bayor read most if not all of the manuscript draft. My Rutgers colleagues David Oshinsky, David Fogelsong, Jim Livingston, Paul Clemens, David L. Lewis, and Deborah Gray White each lent their time and critiques to parts of the work. David Fogelsong, Paul Clemens, and Jim Livingston read important pieces of the early chapters that guided me in revising the draft. I especially thank David Oshinsky for his friendship. My thanks also to Brian Adkins, John Aveni, William Cobb, Bobby Donaldson, Thomas and Trinidad Edge, Christopher Fisher, Khalil Muhammad, Ann Nicolosi, and the late Ron McGee; you each have seen a lot. To Herbert Shapiro, Donald West, David and Ethel Ford and family, Felton Best, Clarence Taylor, Glennon Graham, Wanda Hendricks, Bruce Glasrud, Allison Dorsey, Lee Formwalt, Joe Trotter, Kenneth Hamilton, Dennis Dickerson, Tom and Helen Davis, Janet Aldridge, Karen Bryant, Mary DeMeo, Dorothy McGrath, Dawn Ruskai, and the basement crowd of Van Dyck Hall, Matt Matsuda, James Masschaele, Allen Howard, and Norman Markowitz, thanks. This does not begin to describe your contributions.

To my new colleagues at the University of North Carolina at Charlotte, thank you for caring, and a very special thanks to my former colleague, Donna Gabaccia. Thanks especially to Julie Basinger and Kelly Hatley for helping me meet the deadlines. To both undergraduate and graduate students and Ronald McNair Scholars at UNCC, thank you for your encouragement. To Jeffrey Leak, Herman Thomas, Robert Smith, and Mario Azevedo, thanks for your counsel. To Danny Smith, Brenda Tindal, Hope Murphy, Eutashia and J. J. Rice, Tiffany Butler, Debbie Kennedy, and Mikal Ison, thanks for listening and sharing.

This project also would not have come to fruition without the patience, guidance, and editing of Stanley Harrold, Randall Miller, and Paula Benkart. To Meredith Morris-Babb and the University Press of Florida staff, thank you for believing in the project and for staying the course.

My family—Mesha, Rahmel, Rosetta, Ra-Heem, J-Lynn, Deborah, Jonelle, Clara, Keith, my late mother Callie, my grandmothers, Mattie and Geneva, cousins Estell and Arletha, Aunt Evelyn, Uncle Gilbert, my father, Toussaint, and his wife, Martha, and Moo-Moo and Kenya—always kept the real world in sight. This book, however, belongs to Nellie Holloway-Mixon. She alone has been through the bad and the good while keeping the world at bay. Thank you, Nellie, for taking the journey.

Introduction

During the summer of 1906, Georgia politician Hoke Smith told his white audience, "We will control the Negro peacefully if we can, but with guns if we must." This statement summed up Smith's persistent reinforcement of the white attitudes behind the Atlanta riot of 1906. His political organ, the *Atlanta Journal,* outlined the sins of African Americans against white Atlanta. Black men grew "more bumptious on the street" and "more impudent in [their] dealings with white men." Was it no wonder, the *Journal* asked, that black men made "no distinction between political and social equality"? As a result, like a "barbarian," the African American man sought to "destroy what he cannot attain," namely, "the fair young girlhood of the South." Political power encouraged his "foul dreams of a mixture of races," so white men had to unite to keep him from exercising that power.[1]

On Saturday, September 22, 1906, several thousand white Atlantans "made war upon the negro population" because they believed that black men had committed "repeated assaults on the white women of Fulton County."[2] White male rioters initially directed their rage against isolated African Americans and black barbershops in the central business district before they stormed streetcars and attacked black passengers, sometimes inflicting fatal injuries. Small black resistance groups shot out streetlights and fired at streetcars.

Early Sunday morning, heavy rain dispersed the rioters. Georgia's militia deployed to prevent black retaliation and to protect property. Racial conflict reignited on Sunday and Monday but shifted to suburban South Atlanta, where deadly confrontations erupted. In response to a white fatality in South Atlanta Monday night, militia units and armed white citizens invaded the black suburb of Brownsville to capture and arrest all the community's black men and boys. The riot ended with at least thirty-two black and three white fatalities, seventy injured (mostly black), and considerable property damage.[3]

The Atlanta riot of 1906 was a critical event in African American and southern history, defining the complex boundaries of class and race consciousness. It embodied most fully and vividly tensions growing since Reconstruction over definitions of black autonomy, now heightened by demands for political and social equality and by city building in the New South.[4]

This book places the Atlanta riot within the larger history of urbanization in the New South. One of the cities that eclipsed the ports of Charleston, New Orleans, and Savannah after the Civil War, Atlanta was not founded until 1847, too late to share fully in the plantation culture of the Old South. Consequently, the fabled paternal relationship between master and slaves that defined the Old South was more readily remade in Atlanta by the impersonal activities of the urbanizing New South. There, an elite intent on development and dominance shaped the city for the forty-five years (1865–1910) that encompassed Reconstruction, Redemption, Populism, Jim Crow disfranchisement, and political violence.[5]

Throughout the New South, as in Atlanta, the quest to reaffirm white male control coincided with the process of city building from 1865 to 1913. In those two simultaneous developments, Civil War era fathers yielded power to the next generation, or "new white men," characterized in this study as the "commercial-civic elite." The self-made leaders of Atlanta from 1874 to 1913, what historian Blaine Brownell calls these "new white men," formed a "quasi-government" of civic leaders who ruled the city both inside and outside municipal government.[6] They also sought, through a variety of mechanisms including violence, to re-create a tractable antebellum African American who deferred to and served the needs of whites.

At least two generations pursued the goal of reconstructing white dominance in Atlanta. They began in 1865 with the returning Confederate veterans who had been members of the city's working classes before the war. Later, the veterans' elite sons were joined by white male migrants to the city, such as Hoke Smith and James R. Gray, who also rose to power and influence. The two native generations and the successful migrants rebuilt Atlanta from its Civil War ashes into the capital of the New South. Amassing considerable wealth from 1865 to 1910, they made the city into a commercial, railroad, and industrial center. At the same time, from federal Reconstruction through the first decade of the twentieth century, Atlanta's commercial-civic elite chafed at "negro domination," meaning only that African American men voted and exercised the privileges of citizenship.

Southern whites characterized their urban centers as vessels of virtue free from northern ills, but in reality they confronted sometimes disorderly efforts to achieve black autonomy and white working-class resistance to factory routines. Because the elite feared that expansion would erode their ability to govern and thus sabotage the city's development, they constantly tried to balance growth and social order by reaffirming white dominance and black deference.[7]

African Americans in Atlanta did not accept the boundaries that white people prescribed for laborers and their social behavior. Although whites hoped such boundaries would restore the predictability and security they assumed had existed before the Civil War,[8] black attempts to construct independent communities and institutions eroded antebellum controls over free and enslaved African Americans. Labor and race relations took on new, interrelated meanings, as blacks sought to regulate their own wages, living conditions, and cultural pursuits and to take advantage of the opportunities that Atlanta provided for creating autonomous black neighborhoods.[9]

As some African Americans rose out of poverty and rural depression to acquire permanent jobs, they were able to become politically active from the 1880s to 1906. The goal of this black "elite" was to participate equally with the white commercial-civic elite in the exercise of power but, at the same time, to carry out the responsibility of uplifting their race by elevating blacks to a property-owning status that produced citizens and city builders. Black achievement never gained the acceptance that the African American elite anticipated from white elite counterparts. Even a small percentage of African Americans who gained federal positions of authority in Atlanta faced the machinations of local white leaders to remove them from office. Blacks with public power undercut the white elite's image of the proper place of African Americans in the New South.[10]

The white commercial-civic elite also opposed the desire of the white lower class to have some control over its work environment and to participate in "unacceptable" forms of recreation. White migrants to Atlanta wanted to maintain the customs and rhythms of work that had evolved over generations in agriculture. Work in a factory, however, undercut the white male overlordship that had sustained traditional values and gender roles on farms and plantations. Instead, industrial employees were told what to do and when to do it day in and day out. When white workers resisted by quitting and seeking new employment, the elite concluded that the labor force had been infected with the ills of crime, instability, and poverty that threatened the modern city.[11]

Class issues and social ostracism did not unite African Americans and working-class whites. Although they utilized similar behaviors to protest industrial discipline, they always were divided by race and economic competition. Streetcars, places of employment, and public spaces were settings for interracial conflict that eroded the commercial-civic elite's vision of a modern stable community attractive to northern investment. On the other hand, that conflict provided the elite some advantages. Violence, white supremacy, and segregation obscured the class and cultural divisions among whites. Calls for white people to defend their homes and communities against black autonomy bridged socioeconomic chasms. In particular, the protection of white womanhood and delineation of the boundaries of social etiquette united white men regardless of social status.[12]

In the 1880s, Henry W. Grady's *Atlanta Constitution* merged the racial issue with those of political reform and home rule, which would end federal enforcement of the Fourteenth and Fifteenth Amendments protecting black voting rights and access to public accommodations. Grady's political protégés, Clark Howell and Hoke Smith, realized this vision with the institutionalization of the white primary in the 1890s and black disfranchisement in 1908. Contending that black attempts to make African Americans contributing members of the South had failed, they guaranteed that blacks and the white southerners could no longer coexist peacefully.[13] In repeatedly arguing that African Americans threatened whites with crime and savagery, white businessmen-politicians created the intellectual foundation for the Atlanta riot of 1906. That riot was more than a spontaneous response to accusations of black male assaults on white women. Rooted in decades of political and journalistic demagoguery, it secured the white elite's vision of Atlanta's development.

This book shows how historical forces converged in Atlanta during the first six years of the twentieth century. It analyzes how black and white people in Atlanta went about constructing a city while they pursued conflicting agendas until violence, race, and class collided in three days of deadly rioting.

This is a three-part study. Part 1 presents the competing visions of Atlanta: the stress on order of the white commercial-civic elite versus the agendas of black and working-class white people. Part 2 establishes the political foundation of the Atlanta riot. Tying the commercial-civic elite to state politics, white supremacy, and black disfranchisement, it discusses the elite's use of gender, race, and class to rationalize the violence against black Atlantans. Part 3 investigates the three days of white rioting and the postriot reconstruction that capped a nearly forty-year effort to reestablish the white elite as Atlanta's sole developer and the city as the capital of the New South.

Part One

Prologue

WHITE ELITE CONTROL, BLACK URBAN MOBILITY, AND WORKING WHITE WOMEN

> I was walking... when I saw a rather good-looking negro come out of a hallway to the sidewalk. He was in a great hurry, and in turning... accidentally brushed my shoulder with his arm. He had not seen me before. When he turned and found it was a white woman he had touched, such a look of abject terror and fear came into his face.... He knew what it meant if I was frightened, called for help and accused him of insulting or attacking me. He stood still... then turned and ran... dodging into the first alley he came to. It shows ... how little it might take to bring punishment upon an innocent man!
>
> *American Magazine,* April 1907

This slight collision, described to journalist Ray Stannard Baker in 1907, was just the sort of incident Atlanta's white newspapers had used during the previous year to spark three days of rioting by white males against African Americans. On Saturday, September 22, 1906, between 5 and 9 p.m., local papers had been distributed to a crowd of rural and urban weekenders patronizing saloons. Extra editions appeared with headlines blaring: "Two Assaults," "Third Assault," and "All Police Called Out." The papers actively encouraged readers to seek the alleged "Negro" assailants of six Atlanta-area white women.[1]

The initial incident occurred Thursday afternoon (map 7.1). A "strange rough-looking Negro" wearing "a soldier's cast-off khaki uniform" knocked at the back door of a green bungalow in Oakland City, a wooded area "a mile beyond the end of the streetcar line." When twenty-five-year-old Knowles

Kimmel answered the door, the stranger asked her a question and then quickly departed.

A few hours later, John Kimmel came home to discover fifty white men in his yard, and "he knew what happened without being told." His wife had become a victim of "prowling idle Negroes." The *Atlanta Constitution, Atlanta Georgian, Atlanta Journal,* and *Atlanta News* described both the assailant and the "attack." According to the papers, Knowles provided "a clear description of the Negro" as small, heavy, and "very black."[2]

The newspapers somehow expanded Knowles's description to include the assailant's age and clothing. Now the story went that she had been working "in the back yard" when she saw the movement of "something yellow" and went to investigate. The *Constitution* reported that the African American met Knowles at the front gate, handed her a note, and then knocked her down before she could read it.

According to the *Georgian,* Kimmel "resisted fiercely and in the fight her clothes were nearly torn off her body." By "scratching and biting" her assailant, she was able to "tear away from his grasp and [flee] into the house, [but] the negro in pursuit ... prevent[ed] her from giving alarm. Reaching the door she slammed it in his face and getting a pistol she shot at him twice out of the window." The *Constitution* reported that Knowles used "her husband's double barreled shotgun." In any case, she "telephoned ... Fullerton's store at Oakland City and Sheriff Ed Ryan was on the scene in five minutes." Dr. W. J. Bell attended to Kimmel's injuries, which "were not serious," even though a "pool of blood was found in a room in the house," and the *Journal* claimed she had "collapsed."[3]

A posse of fifty white men with bloodhounds "so obliterated the criminal's tracks that he could not be traced" in the nearby woods. The mob nearly lynched "a Negro suspect," but as Knowles could not identify him as her assailant, Oakland City citizens were still hoping to catch and lynch "the Black criminal."[4] The *Constitution* reporters followed the posse. At dusk it attempted to kill an African American named Olin who was spirited away to the police station for safekeeping by his employer. By 10 p.m. the mob, expanded to "100 men, armed to the teeth," captured another black man named Troy near Fort McPherson. Although the mob escorted him to the Kimmel's residence for identification, Sheriff Ryan thwarted Troy's lynching by grabbing him and running back to Fort McPherson.[5]

Governor Joseph Terrell ordered three state militia companies from Atlanta to Fort McPherson. Before the militia arrived, Fulton County Sheriff John

Nelms drove to the fort "through the excited crowd" to save Troy. During the night another county patrolman "arrest[ed] James Beatle on suspicion of having committed the crime" against Knowles Kimmel. But an actual assailant was never found.[6]

After the riot, Ray Stannard Baker, a white northern reporter for *American Magazine* and *McClure's Magazine*, interviewed black and white Atlantans concerning "the exact present conditions and relationships of the Negro in American life." John Kimmel told Baker that his wife "had gone away to visit friends" because Oakland City and its "surroundings had become unbearable."

John Kimmel believed he had failed his responsibilities as a white male, because a black male had invaded his household and violated his wife. Kimmel considered "[h]is prospects ... ruined," even though his neighbors encouraged him to stay in Oakland City. The "assault" on his wife so shamed him that he was prepared "to give up his home and lose himself where people did not know his story. He did not believe lynching was the solution. Characterizing himself as "a Christian man," Kimmel said, "I tried to help the Negroes as much as I could. But many of them won't work even when the wages are high: they won't come when they agree to and when they get a few dollars ahead they go down to the saloons in Atlanta." Regarding the pervasive fear of "prowling idle Negroes" who imposed themselves upon defenseless whites, Kimmel said, "The thing has come to me, and it's just about ruined my life."[7]

On Friday, September 21, 1906, the second alleged assault occurred inside Atlanta's city limits (map 7.3). The *Constitution* reported that Luther Frazier, "a sinister looking negro 21 years of age attempted a brutal attack upon Miss Orrie Bryan the pretty 18 year old daughter of Thomas L. Bryan ... while she was in her room at the Bryan home at about 9:30 last night." According to the report, "the boldness of the negro's attack was unprecedented considering the hour ... coming in through the front hall and raising one of the windows to make certain of a speedy escape before advancing on the family." Frazier struck when the "Father Was Not At Home." Although Thomas, a clerk, was not at 232 Courtland Street, his wife and younger children escaped through a door while the "negro armed with a heavy shoe blocked" Orrie's exit. She "lock[ed] herself in a closet, thus frustrating the fiend's purpose." Alerted by the "screams of the frightened women," white male neighbors caught Frazier in the alley behind the house still holding his shoe and "partly disrobed."[8]

The *Constitution's* Sunday morning edition characterized September 22 as the day that the "Culmination of Crime Was Reached in Atlanta." The city's white press blamed the "4 Attempts at Assault in One Day" by black males against white females in metropolitan Atlanta for igniting the Atlanta riot.

The first Saturday "attack" occurred in suburban DeKalb County (map 8.4). According to the *Atlanta News,* a "black brute" wearing blue army pants came to Mrs. Mary "Lizzie" Chaffin's house in Sugar Creek near Flat Shoals and the Soldiers Home. Ordered to leave, he returned "when Mrs. Chaffin was not looking" and "slipped into the barn a short ways from the house with the evident purpose of attacking her as she came to feed the stock." Chaffin "saw the negro in the barn, [and] turned quickly toward the house. She was hardly half way when the negro came hurrying toward her. She screamed and ran into the house, seizing her gun. The negro turned and fled thru the woods back of the barn." The *News* asserted the African American was the same man who had visited Knowles Kimmel.[9]

Saturday's second incident took place in one of Atlanta's racially mixed residential sections (map 7.4). At 6 p.m., Mrs. Frank Arnold, wife of a cabinet-maker-foreman at the Ladder and Specialty Company, was sitting on her porch at 127 Julian when a black man approached and said, "Come with me." Henry Green, a laborer, was later captured by "citizens" near the National Furniture Company at 974 Marietta Street and turned over to Fulton County police officers.[10]

At 8:30 p.m., Martha Holcombe, the elderly wife of a railroad brakeman, "saw a Negro on the side walk" outside her home at 275 Magnolia Street (map 8.2). She screamed, and someone "telephoned the police station," but Mrs. Holcombe herself phoned the police and canceled the false alarm. Nevertheless, the next morning, "in letters five inches high," extra editions of Atlanta's white press described Holcombe's "terrible fright" as Saturday's "Third Assault."[11]

A riotous crowd of white men already was gathering in the central business district at Decatur and Marietta Streets at the time of Mrs. Holcombe's call. The next "attack" came at 9:30 p.m. as the riot erupted downtown. Miss Alma Allen, a phone operator, was washing her hands on a dark porch at 182 Davis Street when someone briefly grabbed her before escaping into the night.[12]

The rioters were given to "much angry shouting about 'vengeance' on the rapist," although none of the six women was raped. A half hour after "a self-appointed leader mounted a dry goods box brandishing a newspaper extra which read..."Third Assault," according to the *Atlanta Journal,* "several thousand people of all classes driven by frenzy because of repeated assaults on women of Fulton County by negroes mobilized at Marietta, Peachtree, Whitehall, and Decatur Street[s]."[13] The Atlanta riot had begun.

Before Knowles Kimmel even picked up the phone to call the sheriff, however, one member of the commercial-civic elite, Judge George Hillyer, had launched a newspaper crusade against black male autonomy. Indeed, the Atlanta press had been proclaiming for a month that black men were out of control. Like Luther Frazier, they allegedly roamed metropolitan Atlanta unchecked, "loafed," and congregated on downtown streets, refusing to work for wages under white people's terms. Black men reportedly frequented dives where images of naked white women decorated the liquor bottles. John Kimmel's "shame" thus meshed with an image of white male helplessness against the urban problem of unrestrained and unemployed black prowlers who threatened white safety and freedom.[14] Atlanta's major white papers and commercial-civic elite demonized urban African Americans in general, but men were seen as especially lawless, morally depraved, and politically corrupt threats to the city's stability.

The inflammatory rhetoric of Judge Hillyer's crusade obscured an important fact. Urban peace was not being threatened by black attempts to rape white women, but the racial status quo was being subverted by black attempts to determine the rules of the workplace. Blacks were seeking to define their working conditions, wages, employers, and hours of work. According to the white newspapers, black workers would quit suddenly and were frequently absent or delinquent from work, but blacks used these tactics to thwart low wages, poor working conditions, and unexpected assignments that extended the workday. The black men on Decatur Street "loafed" because whites would not employ them in positions that provided the consistent wages and long-term employment that enabled blacks to establish stable communities needed for black political participation.

Though seriously restricted in 1905 and 1906, black political power was still partially functional. Black leaders had mobilized black voters in the 1880s and 1890s to defeat prohibition and at least one mayoral candidate. The poll tax and white primary had reduced the number of black (and white) voters by 1906, but whites had not eliminated all black voters. As a result, the commercial-civic elite continued to worry that black leaders might join with the "unpredictable" black working class to contest white supremacy in the twentieth century as they had in the 1890s.

An evolving black urban culture challenged white control of the workplace and of black mobility within the city. Black men and women now lived in their own neighborhoods, rather than in the households of their employers, where whites were in charge around the clock. On Decatur Street and in Atlanta's alleyways, black working people entertained themselves outside the reach of white supervision. The city offered freedom of uncontested movement. Luther Frazier's "alleged" assault on Orrie Bryan and the four Saturday "incidents" that Atlanta's white press blamed for the riot grew out of the free movement that urban life gave not only to black men but also to white women who entered the workplace. It eroded the white male "right" to dominate a household that had once included white women and black slaves. The Atlanta riot followed a distinct convergence of challenges to white male dominance, white supremacy, and the commercial-civic elite's ethos of domination.[15]

1

Atlanta

THE CITY OF PROGRESS

> The first [and] highest duty of Georgians is to protect our
> womanhood from outrage. If this is not done in some effective *way*
> we may be shocked any day by the story of a widespread massacre
> of negroes which will be a stain on our civilization.
>
> Emory Speer, federal judge, 1905

Civic patriotism dominated Atlanta's economic and political life from the 1880s into the 1900s and galvanized the commercial-civic elite. The larger merchants, land speculators, insurance brokers, bankers, and contractors who made up the elite worked cooperatively with attorneys, doctors, clergymen, city officials, and newspaper editors to formulate an urban ethos for Atlanta's evolution into the capital of the New South, a city attractive to capitalists and development.[1]

This chapter examines the attitudes of the white leaders who were critical in sparking the Atlanta riot. From 1865 to 1906, Atlanta's white elite united whites across class lines in order to confront and reduce black autonomy. To those ends, whites pursued home rule as a symbolic final release from the possibility of federal intervention to defend black freedom, and the riot attested to that release from Reconstruction, showing that white men could address black autonomy as they saw fit without federal intrusion. The process itself was not completed, however, until 1908, when white voters approved a law denying African Americans the right to vote. The Atlanta riot clearly indicated that the white elite was about to succeed in its efforts to reaffirm white privilege and supremacy.

The members of the commercial-civic elite shared a set of beliefs about the modern urban community, involving stability and a growth they could control more than social change. Even when they spoke of progress, these men actually hoped to reaffirm the racial, labor, electoral, and gender roles of master and subordinate—white over black, an ethos of domination—they believed existed before the Civil War. Because they somehow seemed to equate social order with white domination, the elite tried to eliminate legitimate working-class endeavors, such as voting and neighborhood development, along with the illicit or disruptive pursuits of crime, drinking, dancing, and loud entertainment.[2]

Atlanta's self-described "best men" from the end of the Civil War to World War I served in municipal government, the state legislature, and the governor's office. They wanted efficient "good government," best achieved by having men like themselves in command of the police department, on water and hospital boards, in newsrooms, and in the chamber of commerce, which made Atlanta the top convention center of the Southeast. The commercial-civic elite consequently became the "quasi-government" of Atlanta.[3]

A new city charter was shepherded through the Georgia legislature by Judge George Hillyer in 1874. It allowed the merchants, financiers, industrialists, newspaper editors, and other professionals to implement electoral reforms that removed municipal government from working-class influence. From 1866 to 1874, African Americans and the white working class had elected their own representatives to the city council, but the commercial-civic elite's reforms reduced black and white labor's input in favor of elite control over the selection of candidates. Yet in 1890 Atlanta's elite still was wrestling with the electoral process to keep the working classes and blacks at bay. At the same time, it wanted to refocus city goals to encourage industrial expansion with the hope of creating "a great South and a great Atlanta."[4]

The elite's city building reshaped Atlanta's preindustrial landscape. Members of the elite themselves retreated to suburban havens away from the daily stresses of commercial life. As they no longer lived where they worked, by 1900 they had developed a streetcar system that served the new suburbs of Inman Park and the West End. At the other end of the line, the central business district, or downtown, also flourished. In 1905 the chamber of commerce sponsored the construction of a "great auditorium" equal to any, including New York City's new hippodrome. The following was completed on the site of the black central business district, which would be relocated out of downtown immediately after the riot and completion of the Candler Building. Paved streets, sewer lines, and streetcar tracks all were added to the downtown infrastructure to the neglect of the working-class and black neighborhoods.[5]

The builders of Atlanta, with few exceptions, were southerners. Civil War veterans James W. English Sr., George Hillyer, and *Atlanta Constitution* owner Evan P. Howell joined post-Reconstruction leader Henry W. Grady in reconstructing Atlanta. Their sons and such protégés as Clark Howell, a national Democratic Party leader, and Hoke Smith, a nationally recognized Progressive reformer, became political leaders of the city, state, and region at the turn of the century. Each generation between the Civil War and the beginning of the twentieth century contained additional self-made men who attained wealth, status, and power that paralleled Atlanta's growth.

The Civil War veterans forsook the plantation and acquired the capital to found factories, railroads, banks, and newspapers. Collectively, they nurtured energetic business values different from those of the older seaports such as Charleston and Savannah, whose elite they outstripped in attracting economic support from northern capitalists. Their "Atlanta Spirit" presented to the outside world a "city of progress," willing to embrace industrial and urban development.[6]

Urban and industrial growth were key components in initiating racial segregation, black disfranchisement, and antiblack violence. Not only in Atlanta but also in the New South cities of Birmingham, Charlotte, and Nashville, members of the commercial-civic elite used the ideals of southern Progressivism to control black autonomy. For African Americans, the "city of progress" and Progressivism meant the very opposite.

The ranks of the southern Progressives included disgruntled Democrats and urban members of the defeated Populist Party. Representing the latter, Aldine Chambers came to Atlanta from rural Georgia in 1896 to study law with attorney James K. Hines, as Populists turned to the city to implement the reform that their party had failed to install during its brief control of the Georgia legislature in the early 1890s. Newspaper owners, clergy, Populists, and the commercial-civic elite all embraced the goal of modernizing the South, independently before 1890, then jointly after the fall of the Populist Party in 1896. At that point, Progressivism offered the modernizers a mutual platform for regulating the populations they believed most troublesome to achieving their aims.[7]

To restore the South to national influence, reformers of all backgrounds sought political control over what they deemed the backward behaviors of the white lower classes and African Americans. Because they also wanted to limit development's excesses, southern Progressives intended to give local and state governments a direct regulatory role in molding social, economic, and political life. They looked to government as the key, but not sole, mechanism to monitor black people and introduced new methods of maintaining health, education, and work routines for the poor. The Progressives shared the belief of their elite component that they alone possessed the education, skills, vision, and right to use government and public policy to produce a New South.[8]

Between 1880 and 1920, southern Progressivism in Atlanta, Birmingham, Charlotte, and Nashville strove to regulate blacks with government-supported segregation and restrictions on their ability to vote. For the working class as a whole, the Progressives hoped to use government to prohibit alcohol consumption and to set boundaries on race relations. In Charlotte, for example, the commercial-civic elite's installation very clearly coincided with the relatively rapid emergence of the textile industry between 1880 and 1900.[9]

Between 1880 and 1920, Atlanta's commercial-civic elite instituted a series of electoral reforms that diminished the ability of the poor and less literate to vote. For example, ballots were no longer color-coded by party and candidate but standardized without these markers of easy recognition by the Australian ballot. After the white primary had effectively limited the electorate to white men, electoral reform culminated in 1908 with black disfranchisement voted in as an amendment to the Georgia constitution.

Progressive reform in New South cities proceeded by starts and stops. Nevertheless, each event such as the rioting in Atlanta seemed to propel the reformers into political dominance. In the end, Atlanta, Charlotte, and the other cities of the New South adopted antiblack policies shaped more by the impersonal forces of urban growth than by the personal paternalism that lingered in Charleston, New Orleans, and Savannah.[10]

To transfer the old South's paternalism to the New South would have required extending the one-on-one relationships between master and slave to employer and employee. Cities with less connection to the plantation past than to the ports preferred to regulate blacks through such urban agencies as the police, municipal inspectors, and city ordinances. Some employers in Atlanta did maintain a close paternal relationship with black employees, but postbellum Atlanta's commercial-civic elite openly discussed the viability of using violence against blacks in the context of urban growth.[11]

Atlanta's early twentieth-century movement to limit black autonomy had antecedents in the policies advocated during Reconstruction by the *Atlanta Constitution* and its most powerful editors. Exploiting a general perception that white privilege was under attack, the *Constitution*'s leadership molded that perception into both a regional mission to reaffirm white dominance and a potential bridge to white national reconciliation via southern home rule. The owners of the *Atlanta Journal* likewise used racist attitudes to build that newspaper's political influence locally and to establish a platform for Progressive reform.

Walter Cooper, newspaper editor and secretary of the Atlanta Chamber of Commerce, described the *Constitution*'s initial years in the early 1870s as a crusade to restore "Constitutional Government" and white supremacy. In 1876 Henry W. Grady joined Captain Evan P. Howell and W. A. Hemphill as co-owners of the newspaper. As editor, Grady utilized the paper to become political boss of Atlanta, to direct Georgia politics, and to secure his claim as national representative of the New South. His skillful use of the press to accrue political power became the model for at least a generation of Atlanta politicians—Judge George Hillyer, Hoke Smith, Clark Howell, James R. Gray, and the family of James W. English Sr.—who influenced race relations in the city. As their hatred of blacks took form in the press, the white primary, and new definitions of crime, each contributed to the impending Atlanta riot. The two major newspapers Grady, Howell, Smith, and Gray controlled, the *Constitution* and the *Atlanta Journal*, provided these elite white "bosses" with the power bases to dominate Atlanta's and Georgia's political and economic structures.[12]

In the late nineteenth century, Henry Grady, an advocate of home rule, white male power, and white supremacy, preached racial peace to convince northern capitalists to invest in the New South. By also hinting that violence against blacks would continue if blacks did not submit to white dominance, however, Grady tried to create white solidarity across class lines. Many postbellum white political leaders demonized blacks regardless of gender or class in order to unify whites. Atlanta politicians Howell, Smith, and Hillyer successfully did so from the 1880s to 1908, but Grady provided the earliest model.

Grady sounded the call for home rule, meaning an end to the federal defense of black citizenship and voting rights protected by the Fourteenth and Fifteenth Amendments. In this way, he built his New South creed for Atlanta, and the region, on a foundation of antiblack proposals. Although Grady's reign as boss occurred after federal Reconstruction ended in Georgia in 1872, he still espoused white political, social, and economic dominance over the New South.[13]

To promote the New South, Grady took his well-honed communication skills to address northeastern capitalists. The South that Grady described in 1886 at New York City's New England Club had overcome the ruin of war and the fires of General Sherman's armies. Atlantans had rebuilt their city on the Yankee model, and the entire region was willing to declare "slavery and secession ... dead."

Now the South stood ready to reclaim its antebellum position as a full-fledged participant in national policy making. Grady told the capitalists that black and white southerners were "indissoluby [sic] connected" by their mutual history in the region. Because limited "liberty and [federally supported black] enfranchisement is as far as law can carry the Negro," southern whites had to set the parameters of race relations.[14] According to Grady, citizenship belonged only to a reconciled brotherhood of white southerners and northerners, for it included the right to vote and so to rule the South and the nation. Whites had to participate in a racial "revolution that shall save liberty and law and religion" and create an overwhelming "Anglo-Saxon current" strong enough to counter the dangers of black autonomy and intrusion, Grady cleverly told northeasterners who were experiencing an influx of non-Anglo-Saxon immigration.[15] Yet the federal government had saddled the South with black voters, "a problem without precedent or parallel."[16]

Having declared slavery dead, Grady could not resist waxing nostalgic about the plantation. Though a symbol of slavery and underdevelopment, it represented white male freedom and local control over political decisions. The point he wanted to make was that now the independence of the household was endangered by anti-local forces such as antisouthern corporations that used their influence to prevent local white men from dealing with railroad freight rates and political corruption, two key issues in pre-riot politics. In manipulating the differences between the races and classes, outside corporate power in the South had corrupted rule by "the people" with the demand that southern "ballot boxes shall be hedged ... by ... [federal] bayonets."[17]

Grady wanted a world where whites maintained friendships with African Americans who were tied "to the soil" as the white-supervised agricultural labor force.[18] He lauded the emergence of an African American professional class, perhaps just because black professionals appeared to have a vested interest in segregation as the source of their clientele. In the end, however, Grady believed the plantation was the "ideal" household, led by a white man who relied on the work of dependents whom he controlled and represented in public on political questions.[19]

Although Atlanta's growth had been a blessing for Henry W. Grady and the rest of the commercial-civic elite, it had undermined white male liberties and traditions of popular government. Population growth brought in "strangers" who lived beyond the control of the commercial-civic elite. Control was key. In Grady's vision, Atlanta was a place where capitalism was nurtured and welcomed if southerners controlled it. Above all, he endorsed segregation, as the policy Atlanta's commercial-civic elite would use to maintain control of their city and leadership of their region in the twentieth century.[20]

Grady the political boss was mentor to Hoke Smith and Captain Howell's son, Clark. In the 1880s, he taught them how to construct a political machine within the offices of a newspaper. Having graduated, like Grady, from the University of Georgia, Clark Howell had apprenticed with newspapers in New York City and Philadelphia before joining the *Constitution*'s staff as Grady's assistant in 1884. He was elected to the Georgia legislature in 1887 and reelected in 1890, becoming Speaker of the Georgia House of Representatives that passed Georgia's first segregation statute regulating transportation in 1890. Howell still was speaker in 1900–1901 when he purchased the *Constitution* at age thirty-seven. He served for fourteen years (1892–1906) on the Democratic National Committee. Locally, Howell controlled county officials, judges, oil and fertilizer inspectors, and a network of newspaper editors.[21]

Hoke Smith was the first of the *Atlanta Journal*'s two owner-editor-lawyers. Born in 1855 in North Carolina, he dropped out of the University of North Carolina at the age of thirteen when Radical Reconstruction opened the doors to black students.[22] In 1872 the Smith family moved to Atlanta, and a year later eighteen-year-old Hoke joined the Atlanta bar. For the next twenty years his practice in railroad liability law struggled until he won two murder cases. Then as his fellow Atlantan Woodrow Wilson put it, Smith began "representing anybody, and everybody that had a grievance against any railroad." Meanwhile, Smith's political career had taken off more quickly, and by 1876 he had become a political fixture in the state. George Hillyer later recalled Smith as one of the individuals in Atlanta who had delivered "our people from carpetbag rule," although he did not move to Atlanta until 1872, the year Reconstruction ended in Georgia.[23]

In the 1880s Smith socialized with both the noted antiblack Georgia politician Benjamin Hill and *Constitution* editor Grady. Smith and Clark Howell each envisioned himself as Grady's political successor, and they worked cooperatively with Grady to secure Democratic dominance over Georgia and their own influence in the national Democratic Party. But Smith became disillusioned with Grady and Howell before Grady's death in 1889. He purchased his own paper, the *Atlanta Journal*, in 1887.

In 1892 a Democrat won the White House, and Hoke Smith was appointed secretary of the interior in the first Grover Cleveland administration. Smith thus became the "chief administration spokesman in Georgia," meaning he had charge of Georgia's federal patronage, and he catapulted over the Howells as political boss of Georgia. Cleveland's opposition to the free coinage of silver, however, made Smith unpopular among Georgia farmers. To counteract the taint, Smith focused on local affairs: leadership of the local board of education, shaping state education policy, and investment in a streetcar company and local real estate along with his newspaper.

The *Journal* had been founded in 1883 to report on local affairs, and it merged its goals with Atlanta's development as a modern urban center. As the contemporary historian of Fulton County, Walter Cooper, put it, the *Journal* "launched many enterprises" and fought battles for the city. Smith had learned from Grady that in Georgia the key to power was ownership of a newspaper,[24] so in 1887 Smith had led a group of nine men who purchased the *Journal*. For the next thirteen years he placed the *Journal* in the limelight of city building, promoting an urban agenda of good roads and other infrastructure improvements, tariff reform, anticorporate abuse, and opposition to lynching, which he believed eroded both established authority and Atlanta's potential to attract northern capital investment.[25]

Smith embraced racial paternalism in the hope that blacks would continue to hoe cotton. At first, he believed that trained black laborers had a right to the ballot if guided by "the more intelligent whites." Smith's ethos of paternalism and racial moderation lasted only until 1905. Thereafter, Atlanta's African Methodist Episcopal bishop Henry McNeal Turner observed, political power transformed Smith from a man "generous in disposition liberal in everything involving human rights regardless [of] race, color, or previous condition" into a race baiter.[26]

When Smith returned from Washington to Atlanta in 1896, he committed his energies to civic reform, the law, business ventures, and the rivalry between his *Journal* and the *Constitution*. He changed his paper's reporting style to sensationalism in 1898–99 after finding it useful during the Spanish-American War. The *Atlanta News* and *Atlanta Georgian*, founded in the early years of the twentieth century, drew their staffs from the sensationalized *Journal*, where Walter Cooper, Charles Daniel, and John Temple Graves had learned that exaggeration, especially of racial issues, increased circulation. Daniel's *News* led the drive for violence against blacks on the eve of the riot, while Graves's *Georgian* demanded subservient deference from blacks before and after the deadly violence. In 1900 Smith sold the *Journal* to a syndicate headed by James R. Gray, who espoused the same sort of sensationalism to boost circulation.[27]

Gray learned newspaper editing and constructed a political machine within five years. He also revived Hoke Smith's political career as a reformer in 1905 and 1906. A native Georgian born in 1859, Gray started his successful law practice in Atlanta in 1879, but the *Journal* provided him with influence nearly equal to that of Clark Howell and the *Constitution*. It was Gray's *Journal* that serialized Thomas Dixon's antiblack novel *The Clansman* in 1905.[28]

The capital development activities of the English family made it a key political force behind the scenes in contrast to Howell and Smith's public efforts. Confederate officer James Warren English Sr. and his sons, James Jr. and Harry L., ascended to economic and political dominance as capitalists in Georgia's coal and mineral development and owners of the Chattahoochee Brick Company. Their concerns used and abused black convict lease labor; the brick company alone "employed more than 1,000 state convicts in saw mills, brick yards, coal mines and turpentine farms." The profits from English companies in convict leasing fees brought more than $200,000 per annum to state government coffers. In other words, the English family built its fortune on the backs of the unfree black laborers of the industrial New South.[29]

Captain English established his own political machine before his sons reached maturity. In 1881 Atlanta elected him mayor, and at the end of his term in 1883 he was appointed police commissioner, a capacity in which he served until 1905. Because police officers monitored and manipulated voting in working-class districts, English and merchant William Brotherton, his fellow commissioner but political rival, were able to influence election outcomes, even at the state level. Through the mutual reinforcement of his entrepreneurial and political activities, English elevated himself from the orphan of plantation parents and migrant work to a leader of Atlanta's commercial-civic elite rivaling the newspaper bosses.[30]

Captain English's sons were less powerful than their father but took the family into the influential realm of newspaper ownership. James joined his father on the directorate of the Fourth National Bank, presided over the Lookout Mountain Coal and Coke Company and the Central Mining Company, and served as a trustee of the municipally owned Henry W. Grady Hospital. In 1902 Governor Joseph Terrell appointed him "chief of staff," a position he held during the 1906 riot. In summer 1906 James Jr. became president of the board of directors of the *Atlanta News,* and Harry became a board member; together they exercised financial control over one of the primary newspapers responsible for the antiblack attitudes behind the Atlanta riot.[31]

Judge George Hillyer was another post–Civil War Atlantan who combined capitalism with politics. A contemporary of Henry W. Grady, he pursued his legal, civic, and political careers for over seven decades, from 1855 to 1927. Hillyer, who had actively participated in the state and national Democratic parties before the Civil War, resigned from the Confederate Army of Northern Virginia in 1863 to become auditor of Georgia's Western and Atlantic Railroad. In 1866 he helped organize one of four building and loan associations that capitalized Atlanta's postwar development, and remained involved with railroad matters until his election to the Georgia Senate in 1870. His four-year senate career was capped in 1874 by approval of Atlanta's new city charter, which reduced worker participation in city governance and gave the business elite greater power and control. Elected mayor in 1884, Hillyer helped make Grady a national spokesman for the New South. He then headed the water commission until the first decade of the twentieth century.[32]

Although Hillyer served as a trustee of Spelman Seminary and Atlanta University, two black colleges, he was best known for his concern that "idle" African Americans were a threat to white women. He wanted to strengthen the authority of juries over judges who allowed legal technicalities to protect criminals—particularly black criminals. In 1906 Hillyer's slogan of "immediate justice" for black men marked the farthest extreme of the commercial-civic elite's forty-one-year struggle to reaffirm white supremacy.[33]

Despite successfully obtaining a new city charter in 1874, Atlanta's commercial-civic elite spent the 1880s and 1890s experimenting with electoral reforms aimed at further restricting black and white working-class voters. Segregation, prohibition, and antiblack violence, however, were probably more effective in fragmenting black and white labor's political influence in the 1890s and the first decade of the twentieth century.[34] Beginning in the 1880s, members of the commercial-civic elite embraced a vision in which the "famous Atlanta Spirit was in flower . . . and any worthy cause or progressive idea drew immediate support and financial backing from civic leaders."[35] But in the late 1880s, prohibition was not such a cause.

Initially, while whites on both sides of the prohibition issue courted black votes, African Americans had seized the opportunity to fight for economic and political roles in Atlanta's development. Black laundresses went on strike for better wage rates and working conditions for themselves and created a union in 1881. They also wanted to determine where they lived and how they spent their leisure time. At the other end of the black social spectrum, men of an emerging elite, such as Henry A. Rucker, C. C. Wimbush, and Jackson McHenry, had wrested control of the Republican Party from white leaders and old-line African Americans, such as ex-slave Aaron Bradley and Henry M. Turner, in 1880.

Backed by a Republican electorate that was 75 percent black, Republican leaders held sway from 1880 to 1882, but white Republicans refused to work under the young, educated black leadership. In 1882 President Chester Arthur sided with the white faction as part of an early "southern strategy" for winning white voters to the Republican Party. In exchange for relinquishing control, the young black faction was promised patronage positions at the state and national levels. Afterward, during the 1880s and 1890s, Atlanta's young black elite unsuccessfully worked for neighborhood improvements, better education facilities, employment on the police and fire departments, and improved sanitation.[36]

As long as African Americans held the "balance of power" between the contending white camps on prohibition, black voting increased from a low of 29 percent in 1884, under the poll tax, to nearly 50 percent in 1888 and 1891. After prohibition failed in both 1888 and 1891, Atlanta's white organized labor and reform Democrats in 1892 implemented a white primary, which reduced the number of black voters without totally eliminating them from the electorate.

Georgia's Democratic Party expanded the scope of the white primary statewide in 1897. By this time the state's Republicans of both races still competed for federal patronage, but did not even bother naming candidates to compete against the Democrats. The few black Georgians who remained active in the Republican Party statewide helped shape the national Republican Party as convention delegates nominating presidential candidates.

For their role in securing the party's 1896 presidential nomination for William McKinley, black Georgians received such federal appointments as collector of internal revenue for Georgia and collector for the Port of Savannah along with an income and autonomy that threatened white dominance. Indeed, whenever they challenged whites within their narrow realm of Georgia's Democratically controlled political world, black Republicans reminded white observers that African Americans had minds of their own even in the face of white "authority."[37]

Reminders of black independence were particularly unsettling to whites who witnessed how urbanization enabled African Americans to move freely about the city. In particular, white suburbanites feared that isolation made them vulnerable to the unregulated black men who traveled about metropolitan Atlanta. As a result, reformers proposed annexation not only to dilute the power of black voting blocs inside the city but also to curtail black mobility.

Arthur Inman, the grandson of Samuel Inman, the "largest cotton dealer in the world," was one of the members of the commercial-civic elite who feared the effects of industrialization and urbanization would lead to an "Armageddon between the white and colored races."[38] To forestall the cataclysm, Hoke Smith, Judge George Hillyer, and James R. Gray embraced Progressivism in a fight against nonsouthern corporate influence over public policy. According to Smith and Gray, for instance, railroads cultivated and utilized the black vote in order to thwart reform. With this mind-set, the new Progressives supported extending the Jim Crow segregation initiated in 1890 by a Populist-controlled Georgia legislature under Speaker Clark Howell. The reformist Georgia Child Labor Committee joined the *Atlanta Journal* in concluding that Hoke Smith was the man to lead the state at a time when "a political revolution" (i.e., black disfranchisement) was required to give Progressives electoral control.[39]

While embracing Speaker Howell's segregation, the Progressives saw Clark Howell as the chief defender of machine politics and main opponent of the white primary. The Howell machine also opposed public ownership of utilities and mass transit, but the conflict between the Howell and Smith factions centered on supporters' annexation of suburban communities such as Copenhill and Oakland City and on the power of municipal boards, including the police commission.[40]

In 1901, George Hillyer and Hoke Smith were appointed to a citizens committee to revise the city's charter, reprising the effort Hillyer led twenty-seven years earlier that undercut black and working-class political influence in city government. Now electoral reform was aimed to offer the less densely populated white sections in rapidly growing black wards a weighted advantage in selecting the ward representatives who nominated candidates for public office. The redistribution plan also addressed elite out-migration to suburban areas by proposing annexation. Although the committee abandoned annexation after debate revealed the fissures among the commercial-civic elite,[41] the controversy had stressed how vulnerable suburbs were to black "crime." For example, Hoke Smith attempted to make a case for annexation out of the "Pittsburg riot" on May 16–17, 1902. There African American Will Richardson killed several Atlanta police officers and white citizens before local whites and police cornered Richardson and burned him to death in a neighborhood house. Smith argued, "Suppose the city limits of Atlanta had extended over this territory. There is no question that the police would long ago have learned of the Will Richardson arsenal, and lives lost . . . would have all been obviated." Subsequently, each community proposed for annexation was the site of an alleged black "assault" upon a white female or the location of white rioting against African Americans.[42]

While the conflicts over political reform raged between Clark Howell and Hoke Smith and their respective newspapers, the *Constitution* and the *Journal*,[43] in 1904 Howell was at the peak of his power. After he secured the nomination of Governor Joseph M. Terrell for a second term, Howell declared that Georgia did not need new laws to end black voting because the white primary was serving that purpose and more restrictions invited federal intervention under the Fourteenth and Fifteenth Amendments. Hoke Smith countered that the threat of federal intervention no longer mattered, as northerners and southerners agreed that electoral reform removed unqualified voters, a race-neutral act.[44] Indeed, federal power already had endorsed Mississippi's 1890 disfranchisement statute, and Georgia's primary for whites only was in place statewide in 1902.

Although the commercial-civic elite's hold on Atlanta was neither monolithic nor always certain,[45] it enabled members of that elite to spend over twenty years deconstructing Reconstruction. They dismantled white working-class political power first, then took on black autonomy. Early twentieth-century Progressive "ballot" reform provided the mechanisms to reaffirm white supremacy without federal intrusion. The Democratic primary in 1897 ended statewide political competition from both blacks and the Populist Party, the foundation for racial segregation in 1890. For all practical purposes, the Republican Party removed itself from the fray as white Republicans vainly sought white votes by trying unsuccessfully to separate themselves from black political power.

With partial dominance over public policy institutionalized in the white primary, by 1906 Atlanta's commercial-civic elite finally felt free to restrict black autonomy further by completely removing African Americans from the electorate. Ironically, however, Henry W. Grady's vision of white male liberty would have to be realized by "revolutionary" violence, even with black disfranchisement clearly in sight. The white elite's quest to control an orderly, progressive society was derailed by working classes and black elite who aspired to be city builders, too.

2

"If Folks Don't Treat Me Right"

ATLANTA'S WHITE WORKING CLASSES

> It is [a] fight for the conquest of the state by the people.
> It is not surprising that the people of Georgia are revolting.
>
> Hoke Smith, campaign speech, June 29, 1905

On September 22, 1906, white Atlantans initiated a brief, violent "revolution" of "the people" that climaxed more than forty years of adjustments to social change. For three days, white males of "all classes . . . made war upon the negro population,"[1] fighting to restore their rural privileges of household, community, and race in the New South's urban industrial order. After four decades, they no longer were willing to compete with African Americans for political power, public space, or jobs in a capitalist-controlled workplace that undercut the privileges of whiteness. They focused on the well-circulated message that the free movement of black men across metropolitan Atlanta had destroyed the white man's role as protector of his own home.[2]

This chapter examines the white men who participated in the Atlanta riot. Skilled and unskilled workers sought to carve out an independent working-class status in Atlanta, using "whiteness" to protect their place in the new industrial hierarchy. In other words, white men wanted to regain the independence that race had secured for them as heads of self-sustaining rural households before the agricultural marketplace had driven them to town in the 1880s and 1890s.[3]

During the first decade of the twentieth century, Atlanta was a city of strangers, many of them disappointed. Rural migrants moved to the city with rural work habits that challenged factory schedules and work rules.[4] After 75 percent of the white tenant farmers and 85 percent of the white farm laborers of Cobb County dispersed to Atlanta and other cotton-mill sites between 1880 and 1900, they failed to gain the opportunities, connections, or stability they had envisioned when giving up the autonomy that yeoman farming was supposed to provide. Few attained job security that lasted ten years or more. Many either moved from job to job or left Atlanta to pursue the elusive financial promises of the New South elsewhere.[5]

Members of the commercial-civic elite had to notice that Atlanta had "more country people and more negroes than businessmen and well dressed ladies." In 1906, 150,000 people lived within the city limits, most of them relatively new arrivals. African Americans had tripled in number from 16,300 in 1880 to 51,900 in 1910, and the white populace had grown almost 500 percent, rising from 21,000 in 1880 to 102,900 in 1910.[6]

In the age of the streetcar, transportation rearranged class relations in the American city, and Atlanta was no exception. Laborers once had lived on the city's periphery and walked to work, while the business elite resided close to their downtown enterprises. As the elite moved to the suburbs opened by streetcar access, they rebuilt downtown with infrastructure improvements and commercial development that prevented workers from obtaining housing there.[7]

Whites from mountainous north Georgia and black migrants were relegated to the still unimproved sections of Atlanta that had primitive or decrepit sewers, water systems, and housing stock. The young families with numerous children overwhelmed the schools and social systems. Nevertheless, white and black workers flocked to these enclaves in Atlanta as their quest for self-determination, reinforced by their physical and social isolation, countered the commercial-civic elite's desire to regulate them.[8]

Despite their communal independence, white working-class men in Atlanta were not economically or politically secure. During the last three decades of the nineteenth century, industrialization, urbanization, and segregation forced them to seek political alliances, sometimes with blacks and at other times with members of the white commercial-civic elite. White reformers, however, made the racial—as opposed to class—alignment prevalent at the beginning of the twentieth century. The resulting white partnership was formulated on the premise that white workers' rights were being eroded by corporate abuse and black equality. Through temporary and unstable coalitions to reaffirm whiteness, reformers and organized labor promoted working-class political involvement to restore white privileges in politics, the workplace, and the home.

Politically, black and white Atlantans began competing in 1868, when African Americans voted for the first time in Georgia. Voting also conferred the right to hold elective office and make public policy, but whites refused to recognize African Americans as citizens or as rightful participants in the political process. Consequently, political violence plagued Georgia's Reconstruction. Although even federal troops failed to constrain white violence against black voters, whites searched for "legal" ways to narrow the electorate. In 1868 Atlanta's city attorney argued successfully at the eleventh hour that the city's charter made no acknowledgment of black voting. The next year, city council implemented a two dollar poll tax, but Republican governor Rufus Bullock and Radical Republicans in the 1870 state legislature circumvented it with ward-based elections.[9]

The ward system gave Atlanta's black and white workers their best avenue to political influence. In 1870, black Third and Fourth Ward voters elected tailor William Finch and carpenter George Graham to the city council.[10] Meanwhile, the Republican Party continued a policy begun in 1868 to attract white workers. In 1870, the Republicans placed a white railroad engineer and conductor on their slate, and victorious African American William Finch promoted improvements to the working-class Third Ward such as better sanitation, public education, and police reform, on which both races agreed.[11]

The Republicans' success lasted only a year. In 1871, the Republican governor resigned, black Republicans lost their leadership of the legislature and the Atlanta City Council, and Democrats took control of state and city politics. The Democrats' violent and racially divisive tactics and the Republicans' conflicts over patronage, political offices, and dominance within the party subverted Republican unity throughout the rest of the nineteenth century.[12]

Specifically, to neutralize the ward system that had unified working-class voters of both races, Atlanta's commercial-civic elite initiated citywide elections in 1871. Although the elite appealed to white solidarity, their real aim was to diminish popular influence in city governance by terminating partisan politics and de-politicizing elections. The citywide elections were the first step, removing blacks and labor from public office, though not yet eliminating blacks from the electorate.[13]

The white Democratic general primary installed in 1871 and certified in 1874 was the work of the Committee of Forty-nine on which George Hillyer and John L. Hopkins served from 1873 to 1874. The same committee proposed a new charter for Atlanta that restricted the city council's expenditures and, following a national urban trend begun thirty years earlier, created the board of police commissioners. Meant to remove the police from political influence, the board subjected Atlanta's force to twenty-two years (1883–1905) of political manipulation by the commercial-civic elite as commissioners James W. English Sr. and William Brotherton led opposing factions that used police officers to influence elections. Because the 1874 charter was also designed to reduce city services to "less prosperous citizens," voters never ratified it. Instead, Hillyer and Hopkins used Democratic control of the legislature to certify the charter and implement the white Democratic general primary in the mid-1870s.[14]

Besides reducing the popular electorate in the 1870s, "reform" curtailed partisan politics, continued the assault on the Republican Party, and minimized black political power in Atlanta. Nevertheless, Henry W. Grady's *Atlanta Constitution* noted several times between 1879 and 1884 that the electoral system was still "free wheeling" and too often rewarded the lower classes and political independents at the expense of Atlanta's progressive elements. The *Constitution* wanted the "best class" to have no less than total control over municipal governance.[15]

As the commercial-civic elite pursued Grady's demand, the mid-1880s ushered in a clash among the elite reformers, African Americans, and white working people that set up divisions critical to the Atlanta riot. Three major events destroyed what remained of black and white working-class political collaboration. The 1884 creation of a city executive committee gave the elite greater control over the selection of municipal leaders. Reformers then sought more electoral changes to reinforce their regulation of city governance. Finally, prohibition divided all political participants along lines of class and culture.

In 1884, 100 members of the white elite met to "reform" Atlanta's political structure once again. To "prevent rings and cliques from taking the city's affairs into their own hands," Atlanta's business and professional men constructed the city executive committee to nominate candidates for public office. As John Hopkins noted eight years later, Atlanta's mayoralty was "a question not of politics but of business." The committee wanted to "avoid the misfortune which a scramble at the ballot box might engender" and to "harmonize conflicting elements."

The city executive committee that the 100 reformers created unintentionally reopened the door to black and white working-class political participation by requiring election of ward representatives to the committee. Those delegates and the "representative citizens" appointed by the committee chairmen were to decide upon one "slate" or "ticket" for public office in a mass meeting. As the process unfolded, however, white working men took the opportunity to construct their own ticket. The resulting "People's Ticket" was led by mayoral candidate Reuben Arnold, a lawyer, against the "Citizens' Ticket" headed by Hillyer. Ominously for Atlanta's future, Hillyer was elected mayor because black voters supported his ticket against the white working-class slate.[16]

Prohibition likewise began to increase the importance of the African American vote in 1884. Some members of the black elite, particularly the clergy and skilled workers, supported prohibition in order to "save" the moral fabric of the black community and prove that blacks, especially the elite, were worthy of citizenship. Black antiprohibitionists wanted to protect working people's recreational rights as well as the right of African Americans to equal treatment before the law. Many of them realized that the liquor trade sustained such black enterprises as saloons, lunchrooms, restaurants, and dives.[17]

From 1886 through 1888, the integrated Knights of Labor and black antiprohibitionists tried to hold the black and white working classes together. Nevertheless, with two white workingmen on the People's Ticket, and no African Americans on any slate, black voters again aligned with the Citizens' Ticket to defeat the People's slate. In 1887, printer James G. Woodward was elected to city council, but the black antiprohibitionists supported the Citizens' Ticket. The following year, although nineteen African Americans served on the nominating committee, white workers refused to place a black man on the People's Ticket. Mayoral candidate Walter Brown "proposed a Negro fire department, the erection of different schools for both races, and just treatment of all citizens," but threatened to reinstall the 1871 white primary when blacks still favored the Citizens' Ticket.[18]

White working-class opposition to black political participation increased between 1888 and 1892. In 1889, white labor joined the white elite and even Republicans in a victorious joint effort to quiet political conflict and limit black influence. Three white workers were placed on the 1889 Citizens' Ticket, and printer James G. Woodward was elected alderman.[19]

In mid-1892 Woodward announced his candidacy for mayor. Days earlier, he had stated, "I voice nine-tenths of the people of Atlanta when I say that a primary is the proper way to select the mayor and council this fall.... I can see no necessity for a different mode of nomination" such as "a mass meeting or a committee of one hundred." On the "Ticket of Industrial Legislative Council" on September 4, 1892, Woodward "enter[ed] the race for mayor," although it was the committee of 100 that decided when, how, and why an election occurred.

On October 18, 1892, the *Atlanta Constitution* reported that Woodward had "announced himself for a white primary."[20] That same day, in room 104 of the Kimball House Hotel, Chairman Hopkins convened the "100 . . . white and colored [citizens] from different wards" to "discuss matters which probably ought not to have publicity" and "to use our private knowledge for the public good." The agenda centered on white labor's demand for a new white primary. M. T. Evans, representing "twenty-one" unnamed white labor organizations, argued for such a primary on "the same day as the presidential election" with the polling places open 7 a.m. to 7 p.m. for white workingmen only. Dave M. Vining, a former city councilman, also produced "a paper" with "723 names asking for a white primary."[21]

The city executive committee was split over the issue. J. Tyler Cooper opposed the white primary, but Fourth Ward member T. W. Latham argued against disfranchising African Americans. Because black Republican Jackson McHenry and others "had helped to make the executive committee" viable a year earlier, Cooper "did not see how [blacks] could be answered when they asked why they were not permitted to vote in the primary." Colonel W. S. Thompson countered that black executive committee supporters "were brought into the citizens' movement last year to be used" to resolve the antiprohibitionist and prohibitionist divisions. But "[i]f we let the negroes know that we are afraid of them we will have more of them than ever by postponing this action. This is a white man's country." The motion to hold a white primary passed with only four dissenting votes. That primary placed the elite Citizens' Ticket in command of municipal government.[22]

The coalition between white labor and the reforming elite did not last beyond the election of November 14, 1892, but the city executive committee's exclusion of black voters proceeded from 1893 until 1897. In 1895, in order to keep out black candidates, the committee decided that no nominations were needed for public office. The 1896 election restored the white primary just as the Hoke Smith and Clark Howell factions vied over transit franchises, public ownership of utilities, and control of the police commissioners.

In 1897, the primary was introduced by the Democratic Party as a statewide electoral reform, allowing the elite to train its sights on the white working class. The Australian ballot followed in 1898. In 1902, the primary was exclusively for whites. By 1903, polling places had been reduced to one per ward, and elections were scheduled during working hours. With these "reforms" and old cumulative poll taxes, dating back to their initial use twenty-six years earlier, the commercial-civic elite removed white workingmen from the electorate almost as thoroughly as they had eliminated black voters.[23]

Disfranchisement was a second major loss of autonomy for the displaced yeoman farmer, for low wages, long hours, and dangerous machinery already had put management in control of the rhythms and nature of his labor. Managers, who answered to either the local commercial-civic elite or some distant corporate board, regulated hiring, firing, and the lines of authority in the workplace. For the time being, the realm of leisure remained outside the control of the elite, who increasingly defined activities there as criminal, disruptive, and threatening to progress. Like the worker's household, it was under attack.

In the Decatur Street entertainment zone, workers of all races escaped employer supervision. Twice, citing the destabilizing effects of raucous behavior, reformers closed the saloons in the 1880s and the middle years of the twentieth century's first decade. White laborers assumed, a social worker stated, that custom and "inheritance" entitled them to take "a day or so of leisure." The social worker continued that the "right" appeared to be connected to the workers' sense of fairness. As one of them informed an *Atlanta Constitution* reporter in 1899, "If folks don't treat me right, I light out."[24]

Mistreatment of the workforce, especially payment of low industrial wages, had multiple repercussions. Female members of the household often had to seek work to ensure family survival, changing their socioeconomic positions relative to their fathers, brothers, and husbands. No longer wholly dependent on their head of household, during work hours they were under the authority of other men as well as more visible—and vulnerable—in the public realm of urban life. Worse yet, the factories exploited the male worker's dependents in ways that elevated them closer to his own reduced status. In Atlanta, Jacob Elsas, an immigrant, Union veteran, and founder of the Fulton Bag and Cotton textile mill in 1875, was hiring white women and children at relatively high wages, indirectly undermining the workingman's primacy within his own household.[25]

Besides manipulating gender roles, employers took advantage of racial antagonisms to control the workforce. Large and small enterprises, ranging from the Western and Atlantic Railroad to Elsas's fledgling Fulton Bag, played black workers against white workers, threatening to replace whites with blacks whenever the owners wished to cut wages or prevent unionization. At other times, the industrialists were willing to reinforce white supremacy to keep labor working within the parameters of industrial routines. Craft positions were for whites only, and black workers also were excluded from the main sectors of industrial production.[26]

Between 1880 and 1920, Atlanta's white laborers closed all types of skilled and semiskilled employment to black workers. At first, in highly public venues, such as on municipal projects, work was racially integrated, while indoor production lines were segregated. At the turn of the century, however, Atlanta's white press called for greater employment of white workers and the banishment of black workers to agricultural and domestic labor. In this way, the newspapers championed white labor's cause, urging local police to utilize state vagrancy laws to force blacks to work in areas that did not compete with white labor. The *Constitution* proposed that arrested "Negroes should be made to work six days a week!"[27]

Jacob Elsas supported segregation and complied with employee demands for racial separation in the workplace until 1897. Then, for business reasons, he hired twenty-five black women to fill production line positions traditionally reserved for white women. The resulting strike was a turning point in local labor–management relations.[28]

Atlanta's white men made the strike a question of who would protect white women from black workers and corporate power. The male workers who walked out in support of the women did not frame the strike as an economic challenge, although the women strikers did. Rather, Fulton Bag workingmen claimed management would "degrade manhood, prostitute womanhood and debauch childhood" by making black women equal to white women.[29]

Atlanta Journal owner Hoke Smith returned from his tenure as secretary of the interior in time to negotiate a settlement removing the black women from Fulton Bag. Smith's successful legal career against the railroads served him in good stead, as his own paper portrayed him as "in a position to act as mediator without prejudice to their [workers'] claims or their cause."[30] Over the next eight years, leading up to the Atlanta riot, organized labor and Hoke Smith found they had many more views and interests in common. The *Journal of Labor,* the organ of Atlanta's American Federation of Labor, and Smith's *Atlanta Journal* agreed on the need for municipal ownership of utilities and streetcars for an end to leased convict labor and for expansion of Fulton County's police departments to counter black crime. Independently the labor journal also advocated the importation of selected European immigrants, arguing that white worker reliability depended upon a fair livable wage and high-quality white colleagues. True, unlike the immigrants, the black worker already was entrenched in the southern economy, but "we can't control him and make him work."[31]

Atlanta's white workingmen and their dependents reported a series of crimes and other incidents involving black men in 1905 and 1906. Ten days after a black man allegedly fired a gunshot into a white home in suburban Kirkwood, twelve-year-old Alicia Clark of Oakland City claimed that a black man named Jerry Winn chased her in the woods on November 21, 1905. Clark was the daughter of a stockman in a cotton mill. Other reports involved robberies by "negro highwaymen." On December 5, 1905, on Atlanta's Decatur Street, intoxicated African American Will Barefield told the arresting police officer that he would whip him the same way Will Richardson had in 1902 during Atlanta's "Pittsburg riot." Barefield apologized later to Recorder Nash R. Broyles, who fined him $10.75.[32] In July 1906, white trainmen, silhouetted against the night by their lanterns, were fired on by "twenty" black men who were "drunk." Twice in the summer of 1906, the white press depicted collisions between buggies driven by white ladies and delivery wagons driven by black men as deliberate assaults on the part of the black drivers.[33]

In 1905 and 1906, as the reported assaults mounted, streetcars became the site and symbol of black challenges to white dominance. White males were repeatedly reminded that they could not defend white women on streetcars where blacks jostled for space. Indeed, on September 22, 1906, white men started the riot by attacking Atlanta's streetcars.

As early as 1890, the Georgia General Assembly had passed Jim Crow legislation to segregate passenger railroad travel and urban public transit. In municipalities, including Atlanta, streetcar conductors tried to divide passengers by race within the same car, but blacks successfully challenged streetcar segregation with boycotts. In 1896, blacks even took Atlanta's streetcar conductors and motormen to court, where Judge Andy Calhoun upheld the obligation of motormen and conductors to eject black passengers who violated segregation laws, citing the Supreme Court ruling of May 18, 1896, in *Plessy v. Ferguson*.[34]

In 1900, the Atlanta City Council sought to reinforce streetcar segregation with a sign: "White People Will Seat from Front of Car toward the Back." But the demarcation of front and back was never clearly defined by transit employees.[35] Unionized white conductors and motormen with rural roots dominated the transit system. They encountered the most public examples of black autonomy each time a black person paid a fare and claimed the right to ride freely across the metropolitan terrain. At the same time, in the white public's mind, the motormen and conductors themselves represented the interests of a transit company that tolerated, if not encouraged, black ridership out of corporate greed. White Atlantans wanted "whites only" streetcars to protect white women from advances or contact by black men. Seated in the back of the same vehicle, African Americans could stare right at the women in front of them. Ray Stannard Baker noted that on the streetcars transit employees worked where "the races came together physically" in public "each paying for the right to ride," but he could have added that it was where the sexes came into proximity as well.[36]

Jim Crow segregation had not diminished black self-assertion to the degree that whites had intended. Although blacks in protest used streetcars "as little as possible," some persisted in challenging the Jim Crow laws.[37] Whites and white newspapers consequently viewed the trolleys with suspicion, if not alarm.

On July 16, 1905, the *Atlanta Constitution* and white participants reported a streetcar incident to the police as "a riot." At 6:30 p.m., William M. Brantley, son of a prominent local physician, alleged he "was cut" in an altercation with five "intoxicated" blacks. The conductor claimed Brantley and his brothers-in-law, J. H. Bullard and J. M. Graham, initiated the conflict "by speaking to a negro." According to the *Constitution,* however, "the row grew out of negroes being crowded together on the car."[38]

One "EKF," in a letter to the *Constitution* entitled "Separate Cars for Negroes," called on the city council and newly franchised Georgia Railway and Electric Company to implement the 1890 Separate Car Law. Otherwise, EKF advocated replacing it with State Senator H. B. Strange's new streetcar segregation bill to overcome corporate devotion to "dollars and cents." The writer also condemned white men for compelling "ladies and children, mothers, [and] wives ... to ride ... [Atlanta's streetcars] with a motley gang of negroes reeking with the most sickening odors."[39]

Streetcar combat continued. In November 1905, Fair Street trolley conductor J. Cleveland emptied his pistol in a gun battle with a black customer he attempted to put off his streetcar. Eight months later, Hunter Street conductor E. M. Rosler verbally clashed with black mail carrier J. T. Feagan and knocked him off the streetcar. The police arrested both men.[40]

That same month, Sidney Barnes, a twenty-two-year-old African American, narrowly escaped a midnight lynching at the corner of Edgewood and Butler Streets. Barnes was accused of saying, "Hello, Honey," when the sixteen-year-old daughter of bailiff John Miller disembarked from the streetcar. It was John Miller who persuaded a mob to allow the police to arrest Barnes. He had not thought it unsafe for his daughter to travel across the city without male escort to see a female friend late at night. Public spaces, whites believed, belonged to them alone.[41]

In 1906, the *Journal of Labor* called for municipal ownership of streetcars and all utilities on August 31, September 14, and shortly after the riot on October 5. Because nickel fares sucked "the blood" out of low-paid workers, the *Journal of Labor* called for a two-cent reduction so that they could afford to ride the cars as elite African Americans did.[42]

Reformer Hoke Smith, a friend of labor since 1897, complained that corporate power had refused to constrain black streetcar equality with "separate cars." After sixteen years, the white primary and segregated streetcar laws had proven ineffective, as whites seemed powerless to restrain corporate and black influence in a growing city.

In November and December 1905, Smith's *Atlanta Journal* began sounding a call for black disfranchisement to benefit white workers and, in the words of Georgia congressman Thomas W. Hardwick, make the black worker "a more useful laborer."[43] The crusade culminated nine months later with Hoke Smith's victory in the white primary for governor on August 22.[44]

In early September 1906, Fulton County hired new officers from the working classes for the county police force, giving suburban Atlanta what the *Journal* called "a system of control for negroes [similar to] the days of slavery" when the patrol system would have been the "final solution of that problem" if the Civil War Amendments had not "interfered with . . . [the] plan of control." White workers knew, Smith's paper asserted, that "the negro population has manifested a tendency to criminality" wherever it lived in significant concentrations. A month after the primary, on September 22, 1906, white workingmen attacked blacks on the streetcars. Violence in Atlanta's mobile public venues thus followed the vote, as whites lashed out against "the repulsive negroes who gloat."[45]

3

African Americans in Atlanta

> The fact that we are, as a people, laborers and not, capitalists, makes us . . . under obligation to the capitalists, who in our case, are white.
>
> John Hope, incoming president, Atlanta Baptist College
> (now Morehouse College), 1905

African Americans in Atlanta sought independently and collectively to create and live in an environment they controlled. From Reconstruction to the riot of 1906, working-class blacks patronized dives, restaurants, and saloons around Decatur and Peters Streets, spending their free time and discretionary income outside white elite supervision. In addition, black laborers refused low wages and persisted in moving at will throughout metropolitan Atlanta. African Americans regardless of class, but mainly the working classes, challenged Atlanta's social boundaries by exercising their autonomy whenever and wherever they could.

Members of the black elite intended to prove that they had earned the right to be equal partners with white Atlanta's commercial-civic elite. Their business enterprises catered to a white elite clientele, and they established political alliances with white leaders. Through stable employment this small group had risen out of their working-class origins among the former slaves and free blacks who flocked to Atlanta. New black institutions of higher education—Atlanta, Clark, Spelman, Morris Brown, and later Atlanta Baptist (Morehouse)—founded immediately after the Civil War made the city particularly attractive to ambitious newcomers. They, in turn, helped build the cohesive African American neighborhoods in the Third and Fourth Wards: Summerhill, Pittsburg, Mechanicsville, and Beaverslide.

As part of the migration, Betsey Rucker, a slave who was freed at the death of her master in 1855, settled her family permanently in Atlanta in 1866. Her son Henry was enrolled in Storr's School, one of the first American Missionary Association institutions in the South. Because his father was an invalid, Henry worked as a train porter and a barber, eventually serving white clients, while attending Storr's night school. The Rucker family purchased a house in the 1870s, and after studying at Atlanta University for two years, Henry A. Rucker became a prominent entrepreneur in the ranks of Atlanta's fledgling black elite.[1]

Graduation of the first generation of college-trained blacks in the 1880s accentuated a class and cultural divide among urban blacks in the South. Higher education transformed students such as John Wesley Dobbs, who migrated to Atlanta to attend Atlanta Baptist College in 1897, into elite people who opposed working-class recreation in dance halls and saloons. Receiving his degree in 1903, Dobbs passed the federal examination to become a mail clerk,[2] a position that entitled him to carry a firearm. Federal employment both attested to black reliability and character and offered a permanence that enabled Dobbs and others to become homeowners.

Rucker also worked for the federal government in the 1880s and 1890s while maintaining his barbershop. A series of jobs in the Atlanta office of the Internal Revenue Service prepared him for appointment as collector of internal revenue for Georgia. Rucker supervised white employees, regulated taxation for both races, and exercised some control over Georgia Republican Party patronage. That patronage and political contacts with national Republican boss Marcus A. Hanna as well as Presidents William McKinley, Theodore Roosevelt, and William Howard Taft gave Rucker the economic flexibility to help create the Color[ed] Business League and erect the Rucker Building. A multipurpose structure in the new black central business district on Auburn Avenue, the Rucker Building was home to a mortuary, lodge hall, and recreation room for black Masons.[3] Other African Americans became property owners, but even the majority who rented patronized the emerging black-owned grocery stores, drugstore, barbershops, and dry cleaning businesses.[4]

At the beginning of the twentieth century, the black elite's access to white clients was ending. Passing of members of the old white elite ended the old paternalistic one-on-one relationships. Their younger white successors proved much less committed to utilizing black businesses, such as barbershops and caters. Elite African Americans realized that their livelihood required serving a black working-class clientele.

Successful capitalists were the leaders of black Atlanta. Alonzo Herndon's barbershops on Decatur Street retained their white customers during the early twentieth century, but in 1905 Herndon used their profits to found the Atlanta Life Insurance Company, geared to the needs of blacks. Benjamin Davis's *Atlanta Independent,* considered to be the voice of black Atlanta, competed with J. Max Barber's weekly, *Voice of the Negro,* for patrons and influence among both blacks and whites. Herndon, Davis, and Barber all felt a responsibility to advance their race while cooperating with the white elite, their class partners. At the same time, the African American elite resisted the white tendency to hold the elite responsible for the actions of the black population in general.[5]

The black elite was, however, willing to share responsibility with the white elite for supervising the working classes. Their ranks included John Hope, W.E.B. Du Bois, and Rev. Henry H. Proctor, all of whom had migrated to Atlanta pursuing jobs. Educated at white or black colleges, they had graduated with a sense of obligation to lead blacks out of the wilderness of "ignorance" into a new life of culture, decision making, property ownership, respectability, and full citizenship.[6] Doing so entailed removing the impediments to black advancement and demanding full citizenship, full employment, voting rights, and legal protection in the courts against white lower-class violence.[7]

The black elite carried out an all-encompassing racial improvement campaign to make blacks respectable in white eyes. In contrast, white leaders expected the black elite to establish clear demarcations among blacks, in order to guarantee a reliable, compliant black workforce. Whites also expected the black elite to submit to segregation and, by this example, to convince all blacks to accept life in Atlanta as whites defined it for everyone.[8]

The black elite's position was illustrated by the Negro Young People's Christian Education Congress, which met in Atlanta in 1902. Organizers Irvine Garland Penn and John Wesley Edward Bowen of Atlanta's Gammon Theological Seminary wanted it to provide "an object lesson of the bright side of the race to the brother in white." The conference would show "that there are two distinct classes of Negroes," the educated and Christian deserving white respect and the lower classes in need of uplift. Members of Atlanta's white commercial-civic elite commented positively about the Congress and its participants. One characterized the meeting as "an exhibition of right thinking and the correct putting of things," the African Americans' first step toward development.[9]

Four years later, reformer-publisher Hoke Smith drowned out any positive comments about the black elite. He maintained that "the wise course is to plant ourselves squarely upon the proposition in Georgia that the Negro is in no respect the equal of the white man." For that reason, "[t]he uneducated Negro is a good Negro; he is contented to occupy the natural status of his race, the position of inferiority." Accordingly, "[t]he educated and intelligent Negro, who wants to vote, is a disturbing and threatening influence. We don't want him down here; let him go North."[10]

While Smith extolled the goodness of the "uneducated Negro," working-class blacks continued to demonstrate discontent with their "position of inferiority" as they had since the end of the Civil War. Besides regularly registering their protest against the tide of Jim Crow segregation in daily encounters with white workers, police, and employers, they quit jobs, worked irregularly, organized to control wages and the work environment, competed for space on streetcars, and carried on a recreational life in parts of the city that were relatively free from white supervision.[11]

At the outbreak of the Civil War, only 25 blacks lived as free people in Atlanta while over 1,900 slaves resided there serving a white population of 7,615. Between 1865 and the 1870s, the African American population increased by nearly 10,000, and between 1880 and 1900, 26,000 more African Americans migrated to Atlanta, creating by 1900 a black population of 35,727, the majority of whom lived in the First and Fourth Wards. In the following decades, the number of black Atlantans increased by another 16,000 to 51,902.

The fifty-five years of post–Civil War migration expanded the traditional black sections of Atlanta's west side, located between downtown and Atlanta University. W.E.B. Du Bois, an Atlanta University professor from 1898 to 1910, described the city's black residential patterns as "a great dumbbell [stretched] across the city [with] one great center in the east and a smaller one in the west connected by a narrow belt." Both internal factors within the black community and external white forces outside it had combined to determine those patterns.[12]

African Americans initially settled in areas offering the least white resistance. They took the low-lying regions; whites took the high ground. The central city became a primary district of black residency, in unimproved downtown alleys. In 1908 Du Bois described Atlanta's alley dwellings, particularly the one-room cabin that accounted for 20 percent of black residences. It was "a cheerless box set directly on the ground without cellar or foundation." Also without a ceiling, plaster, windows, or paint, it regularly accommodated six or more people.

Another 45 percent of black Atlanta lived in "shotgun houses," simple wooden shacks of two or three rooms that shared the alleys with the one-room cabins. Denied running water, sewers, and inside toilet facilities, residents of the alleys had to utilize communal outhouses and wells in these "poorly drained hollows." Little wonder, then, that so many resorted to nightspots for light, portable drink, or just some space to exercise their own individual autonomy.

Unrelieved overcrowding led to brawls and street fights. The alley was one of many public areas, including side streets, rail depots, front porches, and lunch carts, where black workers met for loud discourse, alcohol consumption, and recreation. Whether bellicose or festive, the sounds of street life and large crowds brought the police, who routinely arrested black alley residents for disorderly conduct and other disturbances of the public peace.[13]

Conditions in the black neighborhoods especially mocked one of the leaders of the commercial-civic elite, water systems expert Judge George Hillyer, who promoted the city's advances in hydro-technology. Black mortality in 1900 (19.5/1,000 deaths) exceeded white rates (11.5/1,000) by 69 percent. Forty-five percent of the 431 African American babies born that year died before their first birthday. Until 1910, when the white elite became concerned primarily about the health of their own domestic servants, African Americans in the alleys used polluted wells and privies while downtown businesses on the main streets enjoyed modern facilities.

The 1890s were, in several senses of the term, a watershed, dividing black and white people into distinct enclaves. Jim Crow segregation, restrictive covenants, and Ku Klux Klan–type terrorism confined blacks to Atlanta's underdeveloped areas. As a result, Atlanta became Georgia's most segregated city and joined Charlotte, North Carolina, in systematically restricting black residency in the 1890s.[14] At the same time, Atlanta used the area between Beckwith and Fair Streets, where poor blacks lived in shanties, to dump its trash. Atlanta's primary slum, Vine City (also called Mechanicsville), east of Atlanta University, had hovels and trash dumps, too.[15]

The intersection of Decatur and Marietta Streets, later a focal point of the Atlanta riot, was once the site of the black central business district where commerce, entertainment, and crime coexisted. After the black presence on Decatur Street began near the Kimball House Hotel in the late 1860s, dance halls, saloons, and other "dens of iniquity" operated beside respectable establishments. At Decatur's intersection with Collins and Butler streets, black owners operated white and black brothels.[16]

Decatur Street was best known for its dance halls and dives (night clubs for dancing also called "Jook joints"). Where African Americans in these establishments shared old and new cultural forms, the blues and ragtime music and dance routines, such as the cake walk, violated elite definitions of polite decorum and intimately integrated the sexes. The dives were located in basements, storefronts, saloons, or assorted rooms along Decatur, Peters, and Harris streets. Their atmosphere combined music, dancing, dim light, thick smoke, sweat, bootleg liquor, and bodies in close proximity. Using their leisure time as an opportunity for personal rejuvenation, blacks patronized the dives to resist white efforts to regulate their bodies, labor, and place in Atlanta.[17]

Although white newspapers preferred to write about the dives, the African American working class created other independent institutions, including churches and benevolent societies, between the 1860s and the 1890s. Condemned as a waste of resources by W.E.B. Du Bois and Rev. H. H. Proctor, the benevolent societies actually met the needs of orphans, widows, and the very poor. Nonrecreational businesses, such as lunch carts, barbershops, and home laundries operated by black women, were also crucial in defining black autonomy.[18]

Pittsburg, the black neighborhood that developed around Atlanta's railroads, was home to African American railway workers, domestics, skilled laborers, plasterers, and cement finishers. Among its institutions were churches, upholstery shops, and poolrooms. But the area known as "Tin Can Alley" was where the city dumped its rusting scrap and trash. The community established its own school on land donated by residents and a wealthy black real estate dealer. Classes met in a shed held together by an assortment of leftover materials.

Other black communities across Atlanta were a mix of poverty and some prosperity. In the Fourth Ward, tightly packed one-story wooden homes made up "Darktown," where a black mail carrier who owned a home with a fenced yard was one of the more prosperous residents. Also the site of "Produce Row," the heart of the regional wholesale food market, Darktown was traversed by Auburn Avenue, to which black businesses relocated after the riot.

Summerhill evolved into a neighborhood of small property owners but without the electric lights, sewerage, water supply, paved streets, or trash removal that respectable white neighborhoods enjoyed. Despite the absence of these vital services, African Americans since 1865 had constructed neighborhoods beyond the personal white control that characterized antebellum slavery.

There, in the Third and Fourth Wards, they voted their (and their community's) own interests between 1866 and 1897.[19]

Not only the politician-controlled newspapers but even elite white clergy blamed the riot of 1906 on the black refusal to defer to white dominance. The working classes, in particular, seemed to have lost their "respect for the white man." Pastor James Lee of Atlanta's Trinity Methodist Church "never heard of a negro before the war offering even an insult of those over him." White churchmen concentrated their attention on Decatur Street, as did the press.

Working-class whites patronized Decatur Street dives, restaurants, and saloons, but white religious leaders blamed the black dives and dance halls for the violence that erupted against blacks in 1906. Such places allegedly bred alcoholism, the use of morphine and cocaine, and crime as well as diseases that cooks, personal nurses, day-care servants, and household workers brought into white homes. Temple Baptist Church's Rev. A. C. Ward argued that the black worker was no longer wanted "in our homes, our schools, nor anywhere else that brings us in direct contact with him."[20]

Atlantans turned to two institutions, the church and the jail, to regain some control over the impersonal urban environment. The white ministers and the *Atlanta Constitution* agreed that antebellum Christianity had been a key slave control mechanism. They proposed that new application of Christianity could help re-create the black worker who was "useful ... in the fields" and capable of processing "iron in the shops."[21] Meanwhile, journalist Ray Stannard Baker noted, Atlanta had "the largest number of arrests, considering the population, of any important city in the United States." In 1906 alone, blacks constituted 62 percent of all those arrested (13,511 of 21,702) in the city, but made up only about 30 percent of the population. African Americans of both sexes between the ages of twelve and thirty were arrested at the most disproportionate rate of all.[22]

Institutional control may have owed its appeal to an obvious breakdown of whatever personal bonds had existed between whites and their household servants. White homes were said to be "collapsing" because of "Ethiopian ignorance and uncertainty." A particular problem was "the cook and her ways."[23] Domestic servants now joined other black workers who used quitting without notice to resist low wages.[24] In late 1904, the frustrated commercial-civic elite of Atlanta's West End even sought a municipal ordinance requiring domestic workers to live on their employer's premises. Because proponents could not agree on whether the employer or local and state governments should be in charge of enforcing compliance, failure of the proposal left the servants in control of their own personal time and their ability to disappear from the job site as a form of protest.[25]

Between 1900 and 1910, up to 13,000 black women in Atlanta worked as laundresses and domestic servants. These respective labor categories ranked second and third in the city behind transportation in total employment, which was dominated by white men. While the ranks of the servants grew from 4,261 in 1900 to 5,687 in 1910, those of the laundresses increased from 4,817 to 7,430. Laundry work was preferable to service because laundry could be done at home with minimal white supervision if the home had water. The elites of both races, however, thought it appealed to the "shiftless."[26]

In any event, by the early twentieth century the opportunities for African Americans in housekeeping and laundry service were on the wane. The attempt to govern servants' living arrangements was a minor skirmish compared to the battles for prohibition and entirely separate streetcars, but it encouraged the thwarted elite to think about eliminating black workers, even from the sort of jobs they had performed under slavery. When Hoke Smith's Piedmont Hotel opened in 1903, it launched a two-decade process of turning black jobs over to the white working classes, employing only white chambermaids and bellhops.[27] In support, the *Atlanta Constitution* railed against the "negro labor trust." The *Constitution* explained that "the willingness of the southern negro to work is fast dying out" because "the negro generally prefer[s] to lie around idle and beg or steal for a living" with "loafing, semi-criminal, cocaine crazed creatures . . . multiplying at an alarming rate." The resulting loss of agricultural skills made African Americans expendable on the land.[28] According to the *Constitution*, Italian immigrants were more suited to cotton culture than blacks, for Italians "learn[ed] modern scientific methods of agriculture" and were "reliable," apolitical manual laborers.[29] After less than a decade, Atlanta's commercial-civic elite was studiously ignoring Booker T. Washington's celebrated address to the city's Cotton States Exposition on the role of black labor in the New South.[30]

Washington's speech had been rejected almost immediately by some of Atlanta's black elite. According to educator John Hope, "equality" was the ultimate objective of black American citizens across the social spectrum.[31] Hope personally participated in the struggle by local African Americans to attain political equality.[32] By the 1880s and 1890s, black civic leaders Henry A. Rucker, Nick Holmes, F. M. Crumbley, and Jackson McHenry served on such politically significant citizens groups as the "Committee of Seventy" and on the city executive committee of the "Committee of One Hundred." They used their positions to demand infrastructure improvements in black neighborhoods, and tried unsuccessfully to reduce employment discrimination in Atlanta's courthouse, public schools, and safety services. In the 1890s they went so far as to propose an all-black mayoral and city council slate.[33] Jacob McKinley, a grocer and contractor, headed the ticket as candidate for mayor. Fellow grocers Willis Murphy and I. P. Moyer as well as Charles McHenry and H. H. Crumbly campaigned for alderman or city councilman, while L. L. Lee, R. L. Lovinggood, J. W. Palmer, and J. D. Render rounded out the black city council candidates. The campaign was carried on in secret in order to seize the government before whites realized black ambitions.

Whites uncovered the black leadership's plan and, led by W. A. Hemphill, a controlling partner of the *Atlanta Constitution,* counteracted it with the "People's Ticket" in 1890. Winning by 1,773 votes, the Hemphill Democrats had reminded white voters that an all-black government meant the return of Reconstruction and "negro domination." The "black grocers" obtained most of their support from the Fourth Ward's growing black constituency.[34]

Six years later, Henry A. Rucker led Georgia's delegation in making William McKinley the Republican presidential nominee. His efforts failed to advance political equality for blacks. Instead, the national Republican victory demonstrated that a new coalition of businessmen and voters in the western states was more effective than the party's traditional commitment to black patronage. Populism failed in the same election, crushed, many southern Populists believed, by Democratic manipulation of black voters. Blacks in Atlanta no longer had any real political allies, and their powerlessness made them susceptible to white violence.[35]

Atlanta's black elite experienced a brief respite from growing criticism when professors at Gammon Theological Seminary organized the Negro Young People's Christian Education Congress in 1902. Founders Irvine Penn and John W. E. Bowen wanted the meeting to showcase the reasons why the African American elite "should be treated . . . without respect to race." The organizers and panelists alike stressed "conservatism" instead of the "incendiarism and radicalism" associated with black political activism.[36] In the published proceedings, Governor Asa D. Candler, an advocate of disfranchisement, complimented the congress for not including the "radical" and "un-Christian" discussion of voting rights on its agenda.

By 1902, black ministers and theologians were shifting their focus from politics to education. The governor's brother, the Rev. Bishop Warren Candler of the Methodist Episcopal Church South, asserted that the convention of conservative Christians could not fail to generate "good results among right-minded people of both races."[37] The white Protestant Episcopal bishop of Georgia, the Rt. Rev. C. K. Nelson, D.D., described the congress as "the correct putting of things" within an established racial hierarchy. Sober, temperate black Christians had taken the "High Ground" in criticizing black customs rather than selfishly demanding all the rights and privileges due a citizen. The convention's message deserved to be rewarded with significant financial support for black education and religion.[38]

The congress itself, not any individuals, delivered the black reply to white prelates. It was an opportunity to showcase—not merely demand—black citizenship after slavery. African Americans already were striving to be productive contributors and members of a modern civilization. Right thinking thus was an avenue for black self-affirmation.[39]

The Reverend Henry Hugh Proctor, a graduate of Fisk University and Yale Divinity School, exemplified the right thinkers. As pastor of Atlanta's First Congregational Church for twenty-five years, Proctor joined the white commercial-civic elite in boosting the "Atlanta Spirit," romanticizing Atlanta as "a goddess" who united the financial power of the Northeast with the raw material production of the South.[40] A mecca for African Americans, according to Proctor, Atlanta led "all nations" with black colleges "like bonfires of living light." Proctor also thought the religious fervor of southerners, regardless of race, could overwhelm the blood lust of racist and hotheaded young whites. White people were "the very backbone of American orthodoxy"; African Americans were "the most religious people in the world."[41]

Taking his first pastoral assignment in 1894, Proctor built a congregation from a scant 100 to over 1,000 souls. He envisioned the church as an instrument of community service that ministered to the needs for housing, employment, education, and health while nurturing black self-help.[42]

Other new leaders of Atlanta's black spiritual community, including John Bowen of Gammon Seminary, focused on education. Under John Hope's presidency, Atlanta Baptist College was another of the schools that trained ministers to become community leaders and reformers shepherding blacks into respectability.[43]

Beginning in 1902, Proctor mobilized opposition to black dance halls. On July 6, 1903, along with twenty-four other black ministers and several white pastors, he prevented the relicensing of the "cesspools of vice" that had spawned "a carnival of crime among the lower element of the colored race" across Atlanta. Specifically, Proctor wanted to prevent the sort of bloodshed that had taken place between the races in New York City in 1900.[44]

In 1905, Clark Howell of the *Atlanta Constitution* praised Proctor for his sensible recommendations and argued that closing the dance halls would permit African Americans to concentrate on their assigned jobs and avoid the criminal activities and midnight orgies that dance halls were assumed to nurture. Proctor, however, had a more progressive vision of the black future that Howell did not mention. He foresaw that "respectable" African Americans could become property owners and so gain power and influence in urban development and public policy making.[45] In fact, property ownership was the endpoint of "right thinking," which included the right to decide what was important for the development of black Atlanta.

In 1905 Proctor and Du Bois served on a biracial committee with members of Atlanta's commercial-civic elite. African Americans had donated the land, and philanthropist Andrew Carnegie had provided the funding to build a public library for African Americans. When Du Bois and Proctor demanded that at least one member of the black elite be appointed to serve on the library's board of trustees, the *Constitution* condemned them as "impudent." As recent immigrants, Proctor and Du Bois were "aliens" corrupting "right thinking" blacks "who have lived in Atlanta and Georgia practically all their lives." Du Bois and Proctor persisted. Although the library promised to create "law-abiding and self-respecting" black citizens, the white elite viewed its board of directors as an instrument to reaffirm black subservience.[46]

Atlanta's white press complimented Proctor only when he condemned institutions such as dance halls and gambling dens.[47] Nevertheless, the black elite's own agenda for uplift contradicted the white elite's one-sided emphasis on control. Proctor refused to endorse any constraints upon black self-affirmation and constructive citizenship.[48] To this end, he and his colleagues in the black elite challenged the white newspapers' preoccupation with black working-class crime. In 1904, Atlanta University hosted a conference originally intended as a national survey of black crime. Edited by Du Bois, but compiled by Proctor and Monroe N. Work of Savannah, the conference report concluded that the "amount of crime among Negroes in this state is very great" because emancipated blacks had "not yet learned to be law-abiding citizens and steady workers." At the same time, the report portrayed African Americans as city builders who constructed churches, businesses, benevolent societies, and literary circles in

Atlanta. But failures of some blacks to embrace self-respect, thrift, property ownership, and freedom "are not racial traits."[49]

On the contrary, the "historic cause" of black crime, according to the report, was "slavery... and its great evil... low sexual morals." Historic circumstances, not inherent biological faults, prevented black advancement. Black crime was increasing because of peonage, convict leasing, the white primary, and illiteracy. Yet it was not growing as rapidly as whites feared, for exaggerated claims of "rape" and "assault" elevated black crime statistics, as did the double standard of justice that pervaded Georgia. For proof that "serious Negro crime" was decreasing in Atlanta and Savannah, Proctor and Work cited Atlanta's own 1904 annual report, which showed "just one man ... was arrested for [the] unspeakable crime," a white man who raped a black woman.[50]

In 1905, John Hope joined Du Bois as a charter member of the Niagara Movement for black self-determination and public promotion of black political rights. In Atlanta, Hope pressed for the right to vote because powerlessness allowed mobs, police officers, and judges to violate black freedom. Jim Crow reigned in 1906, but Hope continued to vote because blacks needed to "stand forth as men ... willing to do all within our power to be full-fledged citizens." Since his own childhood, the opposition to Republicans had become opposition to African Americans. In 1905, Hope observed, "It is not a party line [any more], but a race line."[51]

Part Two

4

"Sowing Dragon's Teeth"

WATSON, HARDWICK, AND PROGRESSIVE REFORM, 1904–1906

> For more than a generation "the nigger" has been the stock-in-trade of the Democratic Party in the South.
>
> Thomas E. Watson, 1905 editorial

Thomas E. Watson and Thomas W. Hardwick spent a decade promoting the antiblack attitudes behind the Atlanta riot. Not Atlantans, they did not take an active role in the riot itself. Rather, as leaders of the state Democratic Party, they used antiblack rhetoric as the principal means of uniting a politically fragmented white population.[1] To gain control of the party, they organized political support around black disfranchisement and other antiblack policies promoted as "reform" or as a "revolution of the people" against corporate control of state government.

In 1905, the *Atlanta Journal*'s Hoke Smith and James R. Gray adopted Watson and Hardwick's antiblack platform in order to unseat Democratic Party boss and *Atlanta Constitution* owner Clark Howell. That platform promised to generate the mass appeal needed to place Smith and Gray in power. An urban-based Progressivism aimed at regulating corporate power and influence over local government then would provide Smith with national recognition as a Progressive reformer and give Gray a local agenda for leading Atlanta's development as a modern metropolis. While Watson promoted Smith nationally as a champion of Progressivism in *Tom Watson's Magazine* in 1905–6, Watson and Hardwick's disfranchisement movement enabled Smith and Gray to overcome the "boss politics" and corporate control of Georgia's Democratic Party by rallying the white masses.

First, however, a yearlong process was required to heal the political wounds that had separated the Populist Watson of the 1880s and 1890s from the Democrats Hardwick, Smith, and Gray. That same process united an older generation of politicians, Watson and Smith, with the new generation of Hardwick and Gray in the endeavor to manipulate the white electorate.

Dubbing themselves "reformers," Watson and Hardwick developed black disfranchisement as a pivotal issue in Georgia politics and thereby secured the governorship and domination over the Democratic Party. The 1906 gubernatorial primary offered them the chance to change Georgia's political structure and gave Gray and Smith the opportunity to remove Clark Howell as boss.

Each of the four politically ambitious men pursued the pathways to power that might have made him "boss" of Georgia politics. Urban leader Hoke Smith was emerging from a self-imposed political exile in the mid-1890s. Less than a decade later, Gray discovered the power of the press in politics and urban development. Watson rallied the remnants of Populism to join the Democratic Party in order to transform it from within and gain a more secure way of controlling electoral politics. From 1906 to 1920, Smith and Watson competed for control of the party. In 1905, Gray and Hardwick accepted the roles of public mouthpiece and campaign manager, but while Gray continued to use the *Atlanta Journal* as his primary source of power, Hardwick became first congressman, then senator in 1914 with Smith's support, and governor in 1920 with the help of Watson.[2]

In March, April, October, and November 1906, Watson defined the "people's revolution" as a "great revolt" against black autonomy. As examples of the black elite's violation of established racial boundaries, he cited African Methodist Episcopal bishop Henry McNeal Turner's antilynching protests and charges that the American flag was "a dirty contemptible rag." According to Watson, Turner had claimed that black southerners had attained progress, prosperity, and knowledge "more rapidly than the whites of Russia, of Hungary, of Italy, and of Spain!" Watson charged that Turner's claim showed that blacks were "ungrateful," failing to acknowledge that the white man opened "the door of opportunity to the black [man] and gave him a chance in every field of human endeavor." Since the Civil War, whites had given blacks all the tools to acquire homes, banks, colleges, manufacturing, newspapers, magazines, and modernized farms. Turner's sons received federal appointments from Hoke Smith in the 1890s. In Watson's estimation, they had "ungratefully" abused white charity.[3]

Watson asserted that black preachers and teachers also misused the "white man's money." In Baltimore, Chicago, New York City, and Washington, D.C., black federal officeholders held "white women in a state of slavery" and used their political power "to *minister to their lusts.*" Consequently, Watson carried on, it was "utterly [impossible] to free these white slaves from the bestial degradation in which they are held by their black masters." Yet that effort had to be undertaken. "Whites made this Republic ... and if it is to be kept up to its high standard of civilization the whites must boss the job."⁴

According to Watson, the Atlanta riot occurred because "Northern editors, preachers and book writers ... denounce[d] the South for ... lynching ... negroes" without seeing "the matter from the point of view of the father, the brother, and the husband" of the "southern white woman who is the [real] victim." In 1906, "every community in the South [was] standing with its hand close to its weapons." These white people, Watson noted, universally realized "that a great change was taking place" in the attitudes of blacks toward whites. In taking stands "for absolute equality in all things, civil, political, and social," both elite and working-class blacks were "sowing dragon's teeth which will spring up armed [white] men."⁵

Watson also claimed that before the riot, a northern white man, Leonard Brown, had circulated a document "filling the negro with a blind raging hatred of Southern whites." Black newspaper editors T. Thomas Fortune of the *New York Age* and Atlantan J. Max Barber of the *Voice of the Negro* also allegedly promoted antiwhite attitudes before and after the riot.⁶

The final cause Watson gave for the riot was the failure of white people to present a unified face to blacks. African Americans, on the other hand, were finding ways to act in a centralized manner through "negro secret societies," evidently meaning the charitable and benevolent organizations. Should whites fail to meet this challenge of unity, "the Booker T. Washingtons" among blacks will "practice social equality." It even was possible "that the negroes of Atlanta will kill the whites in retaliation for the whites killing the blacks," Watson warned, for an organized black population would enjoy "the immense advantage which a disciplined army has over a mob." Whites faced a black "revolution" in 1906 exactly like the Haitian Revolution of 116 years earlier where "the black man ruled the white."⁷

Watson captured the Democratic Party in 1906, reversing his failure in 1896 to institutionalize a political agenda under Populism. Over the intervening ten years, his vision of a biracial farmers' coalition governed by white decision making had been replaced by the reality of an all-white group of reformers dissatisfied with a corporate- and boss-controlled Democratic Party.

Thomas Edward Watson was born in 1856 on the family plantation near Thomson, Georgia, shortly before the Civil War and Reconstruction destroyed the family's agricultural prominence. Watson restored his family's position and plantation through the lucrative practice of criminal law in Screven County. Intending to improve the South's economy and polity as well, Watson embarked upon his career as a self-styled reformer in the 1880s. His goals were to help farmers adapt to "an age of progress" and to "win back the empire" for agriculture by merging farming with industry.[8]

Supported by some African Americans, Watson was elected to the Georgia legislature in 1882. He had promised to push the legislature to reestablish free public schools for African Americans and reform convict leasing. Watson succeeded only in having the convict lease system investigated. When he later embraced Populism and used it to get elected to the House of Representatives in 1890 and 1892, Watson encouraged blacks to support the Farmers' Alliance but assured whites that he did not endorse social equality between the races, only the need for farmers to close ranks against corporate capitalism. At Watson's political rallies, blacks appeared on the same platform with him, signifying his compassion for black agriculturalists and one of the few circumstances in which he gave black political goals any consideration.[9]

In the early 1890s, the Populists dominated Georgia's state government and passed Georgia's first Jim Crow laws segregating public transportation. The Democrats, in response, targeted and defeated Watson's attempts to retain his seat in Congress. Watson, however, blamed black corruption for the Democrats' success in preventing white farmers from reforming the South.

After the collapse of Populism in 1896, Watson set out to transform "the hidebound rock ribbed Bourbon South" with his own answer to "the Negro question." For Watson, African Americans were pawns manipulated by Democrats, Republicans, Populists, and independents against various white political opponents.[10] Although historians have identified the 1904 presidential campaign as the moment when Watson publicly committed to disfranchisement, a private letter Watson wrote in 1902 to political independent, feminist, and racist commentator Rebecca L. Felton establishes the earlier landmark transformation in Watson's personal beliefs. In a passionate and angry, but friendly, correspondence with Felton, Watson outlined his thoughts on politics and the black and white lower classes. He questioned whether the ignorant and easily manipulated lower classes were the "real evil." "At the other end of the line," for example, could be found the "rich, educated white who debauches [the] poor white &

nigger—isn't he the really dangerous man?" Wall Street, the cities, and banks were parasites feeding upon the "real" producers, the farmers. To circumvent—rather than directly confront—these "evil" powers, Watson proposed not just terminating black access to political influence but also disfranchising "white trash."[11]

With the political defeat of 1896 and the Populist disintegration that followed, Watson had withdrawn from politics, and four years later he declared himself politically dead. Nevertheless, he returned to public life in September 1904 as a reformer. Typically, for a reformer in the Progressive Era, he turned on the victims of electoral fraud. He assumed that African Americans and working-class whites were inferior, unable to resist the resources of the wealthy. Although Watson espoused the reformers' notion that only the qualified and educated southerners should vote, he maintained a general commitment to farmers and sought to make the remaining fragment of Populism the "balance of power" in Georgia.[12]

In 1904, Watson planned to prevent the Democratic Party from using "the negro to beat us" in the way that party heads had undercut the white primary of the 1890s to impose the dictatorship of the "solid South." Watson offered his name, Populist support, and his public endorsement of disfranchisement to any candidate who would confront the Democratic machine and "perpetuate white supremacy in Georgia." Watson hoped to join forces with political independents and disaffected Democrats who wanted to reform their party. In August 1904, Atlanta attorney Hooper Alexander advised Watson that "Georgia needs you" to overthrow "machine politics" to install "a progressive and virile democracy." The Populists now could "turn the wavering balance" by joining Democrats sympathetic to "the new ideas" percolating within the "white party of Georgia."[13]

Watson at last saw a real chance to change Georgia's political structure. By returning to "Jeffersonian Democracy," which was an exercise "in the principles of [southern white] popular self-government," whites would control corporations and own public utilities. Opponents, he warned, would find reformers "as white as you are" who "love our wives and daughters as dearly as" the Democrats who fought "negro domination." What was needed was to put "into law the exclusive rights of the white man to govern this state."[14]

Throughout the South, Progressive reform appealed to disenchanted members of the commercial-civic elite. Ministers, lawyers, editors, businessmen, young politicians, railroad commission experts, and agricultural scientists were the nucleus of southern reform. They pursued order and racial solidarity as the foundation for a stable white community. To attain those ends, Progressives wanted to utilize the power of state and local government to purify institutions and public morals. They did not intend to replace the white employer's person-to-person supervision of black employees, but they did mean to set social boundaries with governmental regulations. As a result, city ordinances, licensing, and police raids extended the arm of the municipal or state agency into race relations. Similarly, antitrust legislation, railroad regulation, and restricted suffrage all reaffirmed virtue and gave southern reformers absolute control over the New South.[15]

Reformers invoked whiteness to overcome the divides of class, labor, politics, and culture. Members of the reforming commercial-civic elite, however, set the reform agenda, believing that their class alone possessed the education and qualifications to do so. They favored businesslike efficiency, a "responsible electorate," and "good government" to reduce the influence of corporations, political machines, and black voters.[16] As Thomas W. Hardwick put it, he and his fellow Progressives felt trapped between the unchecked power of the corporation and the expanding population of strangers moving unrestrained on the roads, streets, and streetcars.[17]

Removing the few remaining black voters from the electorate ensured Progressives a degree of dominance over the Democratic Party, which, in turn, provided them with the governmental power to institutionalize disfranchisement and other antiblack measures. By those measures expanding Jim Crow segregation and regulating black labor, the reformers established social controls over the daily lives of African Americans.[18]

In 1905, Populists and Progressives, once polar opposites, were drawing closer through the use of government to regulate race relations, African Americans, and corporations for "the public good." Both wanted to roll back the influence of the Fourteenth and Fifteenth Amendments to moderate the autonomy that industrialization had given to urban workers regardless of race. Both movements claimed these goals represented the desires of "the people." In this context, rural and urban reformers came together in 1904 and 1905 to implement Thomas E. Watson's vision of reform.[19]

The early twentieth-century occupant of Watson's Tenth District congressional seat was Thomas William Hardwick, Georgia's "father of disfranchisement." Hardwick also was the one who cemented the reform coalition of himself, Watson, Smith, and Gray into the political juggernaut of 1906. Violating custom, Hardwick returned from Washington to rush "into the fight." In doing so, he said, he "was guided only by his love for the [white] people ... and inspired by the utter sincerity of his own motives."

Hardwick was born in 1872 in Thomasville, in southwest Georgia. He graduated from Mercer University in 1892 and completed a law degree the following year at the University of Georgia. Like Hoke Smith, admitted to the Georgia bar at a very young age, he represented the new breed of southern politicians who led antiblack and disfranchisement campaigns in the New South during the 1880s and the late 1890s and attained political office as a result of their efforts. These politicians grew up in the post-Reconstruction period and carved out their own business and political careers in the early twentieth century. Assuming that they were qualified to run government efficiently and utilize its regulatory power, these "new men" were determined to correct the mistakes of the Civil War generation.[20]

Hardwick began his political career in 1895 with a two-year term as Washington County prosecutor. He also headed the county's Democratic committee and became a delegate to the 1896 gubernatorial convention. Always a loyal Democrat, Hardwick was an ardent opponent of Populism. He met Thomas E. Watson in 1894, when James C. Black fraudulently defeated Watson for Congress. This election initiated a relationship between the two men that continued until Watson's death in 1922. In 1898, however, Hardwick attacked the Populist agenda in his own successful candidacy for the Georgia House of Representatives. Hardwick took on taxation, appropriations, and prohibition, but made his political reputation in the Georgia legislature advocating black disfranchisement as the solution to political corruption. He was a Progressive Era reformer despite rejecting the label "progressive."[21] The bills Hardwick began promoting in 1899 to terminate black voting rights finally became institutionalized in 1908 as the disfranchisement amendment to Georgia's constitution. Disfranchisement and disdain for corporate exploitation thus bridged the ideological gap between Watson's Populism, Hardwick's Democratic dissidence, and southern Progressivism.[22]

In 1902, when Hardwick ran for Congress, Watson declined to campaign for him but encouraged family members to stump the district for the "Fighting Gamecock." As a Democrat, Hardwick won the previously Populist congressional seat by advocating electoral honesty and revocation of the Fourteenth and Fifteenth Amendments to the United States Constitution.[23]

In 1904, Hardwick and Watson jointly laid the groundwork for the political machine that sustained them for five years. In March and April, Watson used his editorial position to attack former president Grover Cleveland for publicly dining with prominent African Americans Frederick Douglass and C. H. Taylor. Reading Watson's editorials into the *Congressional Record,* Hardwick claimed that Watson had exposed the ex-president's "delight" in knowing "negroes socially."[24] On September 4, 1904, Watson publicly argued that reformers would protect the "white man's interests" and "white supremacy in Georgia" better than "the men who control the democratic machine in Georgia." Shortly after that speech Hardwick met privately with Watson and confirmed before "Almighty God" Watson's commitment to disfranchisement. They sealed their union with simultaneous "All rights." Hardwick recommended that they find a "fearless man to make the race for governor," a person who would "forever put into law the principle of the white primary."[25] Nominating Hardwick would violate Georgia's unwritten political rule that a politician who served in one office did not campaign for another public position from outside the state. Hardwick, therefore, remained the liaison between the Populist Watson and the Democratic Party and volunteered to do the legwork linking Watson to their chosen disciple of disfranchisement, James Pope Brown.[26]

Contemporary journalist Ray Stannard Baker described Pope Brown as "the best type of the new Southerner" who worked to improve his community. He was a "black belt" plantation owner and a veteran state legislator who had served five years as president of Georgia's Agricultural Society and a term chairing the Georgia Railroad Commission. Brown's politics put him squarely in the Watson and Hardwick antiblack camp.[27] He vowed "to come out as explicitly as one could desire on three propositions": the white primary, the Negro question, and the anticorporation line. The *Atlanta Journal* in June 1905 added that Brown possessed the virtues of drive, conscientiousness, executive ability, outspoken sincerity, and honesty, but his most important "virtue" was that he was "not a politician in any sense of the word." In the end, that "virtue" killed his candidacy for governor.[28]

Brown's commitment to Hardwick's "three provisions" thrilled Hardwick and Watson, but Brown's decision to delay a public presentation of "the platform" until October 1, 1905, distressed them. True, the primary would not be held until August 22, 1906, but Watson and Hardwick wanted immediate results or at least a "hot fight." Brown's slow start forced them to seek another "hot candidate."[29]

Atlanta Journal owner James R. Gray wanted reform but not through Pope

Brown. Gray, who initially had endorsed Clark Howell, told Howell he was switching to Hoke Smith to achieve "revolutionary reform."[30] For five years Gray had been using the editorial page of the *Journal* to initiate reform. He called for a county reformatory, better education for Atlanta's white youth, and an end to both convict leasing and child labor. Gray promoted urban growth, including infrastructure improvements, but opposed corporate corruption, especially on the part of the railroads. He argued against the free railroad passes given to public officials, and endorsed public ownership of utilities. Along with his criticism of black political involvement, these positions placed Gray firmly on the side of reformers Hoke Smith and Judge George Hillyer.[31]

In 1905, when Gray became managing editor of the *Journal*, he began to create a political machine as powerful as those of his journalistic predecessors Henry W. Grady and Hoke Smith. From 1900 to 1905, he did not publish Watson's editorials and political statements with the consistency that Watson expected, but in 1905 Gray and Watson became political partners to oppose black political participation and change the Democratic Party.

In May and June 1905, Gray serialized Thomas Dixon's inflammatory new book, *The Clansman*, on the *Journal*'s editorial page. That novel, set in the Reconstruction era, portrayed African Americans as puppets of unscrupulous white northerners who made the black man "the enemy of his former master." It consequently legitimized violence against self-assertive African Americans. Young members of Atlanta's commercial-civic elite such as Aldine Chambers enthusiastically shared the novel with associates.[32]

At first, Gray and Watson worked separately to organize political support against Clark Howell while *Journal* staff member John S. Cohen and former *Journal* editor John Temple Graves served as go-betweens from Gray to Watson and Hardwick.[33] Cohen learned from their "mutual" friend Hardwick that Watson believed in preserving white "racial integrity," an issue "[m]ore dear to us all than silver and gold." Cohen then suggested that if Watson made this attitude public, he could win the electoral support of Georgians. Gray likely had more direct lines of communication with Hardwick and Watson and was a driving force behind the choice of Hoke Smith as their new "hot candidate."[34]

On May 25, 1905, Gray opened the *Journal*'s offices to Hardwick, Watson, Brown, and Smith. The group concluded that Brown needed to withdraw and allow Hoke Smith to replace him. In early June 1905, the *Journal*'s headline read: "Hoke Smith Is Urged to Run for Governor." Nine Hoke Smith clubs appeared immediately, pledging in the words of the Coweta County Club just outside

Atlanta their "support and best endeavor, to secure Smith's election."[35] That same month Hardwick became the liaison between Watson and Smith. Madison, Georgia, was selected as the site of Smith's first speech because the location made it easy for Smith and Watson to meet and establish an understanding on their mutual aims. Hardwick assumed that Smith need only have the "right attitude" about disfranchisement to satisfy Watson, but Watson still resented Smith and Gray's refusal to print his editorials. Hardwick requested that Watson write "exactly what reparation you think Mr. Smith [and Gray] ought to make." The solution was a double-column editorial authored by Hardwick extolling Watson's antiblack answer to Booker Washington's comparison of African Americans and Italian immigrants. Smith's previous opposition to Populism, however, forced Hardwick to justify why Smith was their "hot" property, and this led Watson to delay endorsing Smith until September 12, 1905, when he promised to do so publicly in the October issue of *Tom Watson's Magazine*.[36]

In fact, Smith had been a racial moderate before political opportunity pushed him to embrace the antiblack attitudes of Watson and Hardwick in 1905. According to the black editor of the *Atlanta Independent,* Benjamin Davis, Smith had been a respected advocate for the African American community, but Smith's political ambition changed that in 1905. Smith had fervently opposed disfranchisement as unnecessary given the whites' demographic majority over African Americans. He had condemned lynching and acknowledged that blacks had the right to be free, to work, and to vote if they submitted to white supervision. In 1904 and early 1905, he even had endorsed the Peabody Fund's allocation of monies for black education.

Although Smith, like Watson, never accepted social or political equality, he tolerated black self-assertion as long as white people upheld their moral obligation to educate and govern African Americans.[37] Three years before his first speech of the gubernatorial campaign, Smith had used his credentials as a city, county, and state board of education member to try to get Atlanta University to "conform to the Booker Washington idea of education for the negro." To popular acclaim along the gubernatorial campaign trail, Smith "suggested restricting black education" to make African Americans "more like the higher type of antebellum negroes."[38]

In the shadow of Smith and Howell, there were three additional gubernatorial candidates. John H. Estill of the *Savannah News* did not have a major role in the debate about race. Judge Richard B. Russell Sr. aligned himself with

Howell in arguing that blacks were already disfranchised in practice, so no new laws were needed. James M. Smith, owner of the Smithsonia plantation and private town, represented farmers who wanted to force blacks to pay to "educate Negro children." James Smith followed Watson and Hardwick's belief about disfranchisement.[39] Hoke Smith finally convinced Watson that he also had the "right attitude" on "negro disfranchisement."[40]

Black disfranchisement united the rural and urban reformers in a coalition to take over the Democratic Party just as Watson and Hardwick had bridged the political divisions between the Populists and dissident Democrats. Hardwick was the catalyst who represented a new generation of southern politicians willing to use antiblack attitudes, disfranchisement, and violence to implement southern Progressive reform and keep power in the hands of "the best men." The campaign of Watson, Hardwick, Gray, and Smith mobilized whites in the way the "new men" of North Carolina in 1898 had disfranchised blacks and spawned the Wilmington riot of 1898. Indeed, by combining antiblack attitudes, racial violence, and a reform agenda that included disfranchisement, James R. Gray consciously adopted the Wilmington model to promote reform in 1905 and 1906.

5

"The Seeds of Incendiarism"

THE GUBERNATORIAL CAMPAIGN OF 1905–1906

> Hoke Smith ... proposes to banish the fear of negro domination by disfranchising the negro. If he can do it he will have done a splendid work for Southern independence and Southern progress.
>
> Thomas E. Watson, 1905 editorial

Reform dominated Georgia's gubernatorial campaign in 1905 and 1906. As early as June 1905, the *Waycross Journal* noted that prohibition, regulation of child labor, disfranchisement, and terminating railroad passes were popular among white voters, but *Atlanta Constitution* owner and gubernatorial candidate Clark Howell did not stand right "on any public questions." In July 1905, political independent and federal judge Emory Speer warned Howell to address the political dissent and desire for reform festering among the white Georgians, ruled by Howell's Democrats, or "be shocked ... by a massacre of negroes." Howell met the challenge by declaring himself a "reformer" with a more established record than his new opponent, Hoke Smith.[1]

This chapter examines the campaign for governor between Hoke Smith and Clark Howell, whose longtime political rivalry reached a climax during the gubernatorial debates. Their fight was reduced to a political contest over disfranchisement as the best program for controlling African Americans. In defense of the status quo, Howell argued that measures put in place since 1890, such as the white primary and secret ballot, kept blacks sufficiently regulated. On the other hand, the sort of blatant disfranchisement Smith proposed would lead to racial violence and federal intervention. Smith and the reform coalition of Thomas E. Watson, Thomas W. Hardwick, and James R. Gray had presented black disfranchisement as the panacea for all of Georgia's problems. Pointing to North Carolina's "war" against black political power, the *Atlanta Journal* claimed "revolutionary reform" had reaffirmed white dominance and ensured prosperity for all white North Carolinians. The gubernatorial campaign that culminated in the white primary of August 22, 1906, was thus a referendum on the institutions that defined black and white relations in Georgia.

Clark Howell had begun his political career in the Henry W. Grady machine in the 1880s. In the 1890s, after Grady's death, Howell carved out his own political niche as a "reformer," being elected as "Speaker of the first reform House in [the] Georgia Legislature—the Alliance House of 1890." Never a Populist, the loyal Democrat presided over the Populist-dominated "Alliance House," which passed the first Jim Crow laws in Georgia.

In June 1904, at the Democratic nominating convention for governor, Howell and Governor Joseph Terrell called for "a radical change" in electoral practices to implement "pure elections." During his speech accepting nomination for a second term, Terrell noted that the white primary had "become the most essential part of our party machinery" because "[o]ur nominations are equivalent to elections."[2]

To reinforce the white primary in June 1904, Howell's *Constitution* called "in no uncertain terms" for implementation of the "Australian ballot law" in both primary and general elections. The secret ballot initially had been utilized in 1898 as an "electoral reform" to end corrupt elections. Translated, this meant that even in the hands of "machine" Democrats, it was an instrument for reducing the black vote. The Australian ballot prevented semiliterate voters from identifying their choice of political party by the color of the ballot and so reduced the visibility of the Republican Party and black voting potential, ongoing efforts since the mid-1870s.[3]

Howell felt that his "reform" credentials qualified him for automatic promotion to the governorship as Terrell's successor after 1906.[4] Most people believed that Howell would succeed without opposition because, having attained the power of a political boss, Howell would use county officials, editors, and Terrell to get elected. Howell already had "the vote of all the oil and fertilizer inspectors and city court judges and solicitors." Naturally he was assured that he could ride out "the Smith furor."[5]

Howell's political organization charged Hoke Smith with promoting black "social equality" and being a "negro lover." As secretary of the interior in the early 1890s, Smith had provided federal jobs to Bishop Henry McNeal Turner's sons. Consequently, Howell's supporters charged, Smith now endorsed disfranchisement solely for opportunistic personal gain, not a true reform.[6]

In January 1906, Howell summed up his case against Smith. A reformer "for office only," Smith advocated disfranchisement to frighten whites into panic voting over one concern, "the Negro question." As had past candidates, Smith used the Civil War's "bloody shirt" and black political power, which were symbols of defeat, disgrace, and anger, to dodge the public policy and political questions he was afraid to address. Preying on white "prejudices and passion," Smith threatened Georgia on three levels. First, by claiming that blacks were so far out of control that they invited a violent white response, Smith jeopardized "peaceful relations between whites and negroes." Howell warned in big thick capital letters in one editorial that Smith's fear tactics were "Sowing…The Seeds of Incendiarism," with "The Possibilities of Riot, Bloodshed, and Friction."[7] Second, Smith's anticorporate reforms would undercut city building and industrial development, and finally, his association with Thomas E. Watson resurrected Populism, imperiling the Democratic Party's survival. A Smith victory, Howell concluded, would open Georgia to unimaginable consequences of which violence would be the most destructive.[8]

Howell himself hoped to use the "Menace of [the] Educated Negro" to defeat Smith. He argued that black disfranchisement would introduce literacy tests that, in turn, would lead blacks to pursue educational opportunities. As a result, disfranchisement would encourage "every negro in Georgia…to get out of the cotton patch and into the negro college," signaling the end of "the old time darky" who avoided politics and resurrecting "the dude negro" who represented "negro [political] domination." According to Howell, black working people who had been urged to value education more than white workers would gain undue political influence, and a unified black voting bloc would hold the "balance of power" in 48 of Georgia's 137 counties.[9]

During a debate in January 1906, Howell asserted that the threat of disfranchisement would encourage 93,000 "largely unqualified educated negro voters" to make their voices heard in the upcoming August white primary. In anticipation of the link between literacy and voting rights, black women endured squalor so "that their children may be qualified to kill the white man's ballot." Every hill in the city of Atlanta was "crowned with vast negro colleges, whose combined endowment from northern philanthropy far exceeds the total endowment of every white college in Georgia."

Disfranchisement, therefore, would hurt working-class whites to a greater extent than Smith's promises of liberation could overcome. Yet the white primary already kept educated African Americans in check. Disfranchisement, moreover, made federal interference in Georgia politics a near certainty, along with a return to the dark days of black-dominated Reconstruction. Howell would "protect my own people with my life... [rather] than dodge behind the cowardly expedient of a statute of subterfuge [such as disfranchisement] hatched in fraud." He reminded everyone, "This is a white man's country, and it must be governed by white men."[10]

Atlanta's reformers countered Howell's attacks by appealing to popular reform sentiments. Evangelist and *Atlanta Journal* columnist Rev. Sam Jones called for "a spontaneous uprising... of the people." A "revolt" of "free men" organized to defeat an overwhelming foe, the corporation-controlled government that manipulated black votes. Hoke Smith was "leading a great revolt against... Wall Street" and lighting the way for a white "reconquest" of popular government through black disfranchisement.[11]

According to *Tom Watson's Magazine*, Smith's reform effort was part of the national Progressive movement or a new American Revolution of whites to overthrow the "tyrannical suppression of individuals and classes." Georgia's "revolution," the former Populist's journal claimed, was part of a "people's revolt" against urban populations that gambled, drank to excess, fought in the streets, and got "into trouble with the police." Susceptible to manipulation by "boss regimes" and the "criminal rich," such populations frequented "the saloons, dives, and all the hosts of graft and shady business, [who] hold the balance of power." If not for the revolution, the African Americans who patronized institutions of ill repute would seize that "balance of power" in local politics over such issues as prohibition and urban development.[12]

Hoke Smith opened his reform campaign for governor on June 25, 1905, with the claim that "the people" had "called" him to save Georgia from corporate abuse, "boss rule," and "negro domination."[13] In McIntosh County, where blacks had elected African American county officials and a representative to the Georgia legislature in the early twentieth century, Smith confronted "three thousand Negroes" when he presented his antiblack platform. Described by the press as "the gigantic tribune of white democracy," Smith conspicuously placed a traveling bag on the platform as he delivered his speech. According to Herbert Quick, a contemporary reporter examining Progressivism, the bag contained a revolver that symbolized Smith's commitment to control blacks either by disfranchisement or by bullets.[14]

Smith praised the Georgia General Assembly elected in 1905, whose members were "fresh from the people" and willing to implement their desires. In August 1905, that General Assembly disbanded the state-supported black volunteer militia companies, a sign that Georgia politicians heard the popular outcry arising not only in Georgia but also in Alabama, North Carolina, and Virginia. In those states "reformers" had disbanded their black militia units and instituted the white primary and disfranchisement, using racial violence as needed.[15] In this context, Hoke Smith argued that the next governor of Georgia had to be as committed as the 1905 General Assembly was to controlling blacks.

Reinforcing the white primary with disfranchisement was necessary because whites faced a "new threat" from the Republican Party in 1905 and 1906. The Republicans, Smith charged, promoted "class legislation" that divided "the white vote in national elections" by luring members of the commercial-civic elite to break Democratic ranks and vote in favor of corporate business. In Perry, Georgia, Smith spelled out the rationale for white unity across party and class lines. Utilizing national census data that Congressman Thomas W. Hardwick probably provided, Smith told his audience that blacks made up 44.6 percent of the state's population and had enough votes to return "negro domination" in seventy-nine counties if just a tenth of the white Democrats succumbed to Republican inducements. Disfranchising black voters would preserve the "white man's government" while giving white Republicans the opportunity to vote on issues as independents. Smith's "reform party," as it was sometimes called, claimed to represent "150,000 white men" united in a movement to make Georgia modern.[16] In pursuit of reform, the *Atlanta Journal* and Smith placed more emphasis on controlling the African American vote than on fighting corporate corruption and boss rule, seizing upon Republican postmaster general John Wanamaker's public meeting with Booker T. Washington to rail against "social equality."

For his part, Smith ousted blacks from his political rallies or, as in Calhoun and Baxley counties, ordered them into the balcony. He hired all-white musicians, unlike Clark Howell, who employed a black band from Savannah for his Swainsboro rally. Smith's forces pounced on Howell's "social" error, which the *Griffin Farmer* saw as evidence that Howell would utilize black voters to win the governorship. Nevertheless, the *Farmer* claimed, farmers, the mill people, prohibitionists, merchants, and every lawyer, editor, and doctor solidly opposed further "participation of Negroes at the ballot box."[17]

During the last three months of 1905, the *Atlanta Journal* published an editorial series on the lessons more "progressive" southern states had learned from disfranchising black voters.[18] For example, Maryland Democrats had allowed "the negro" to organize an opposition to disfranchisement. As a result, black voters in Baltimore aligned with Polish and Jewish citizens to defeat disfranchisement. The "Lesson to Georgia," the *Journal* said, was that the "negro should be eliminated from the political situation" as soon as possible.[19]

In contrast to Maryland, North Carolina was the model for Georgians to emulate because North Carolina and Georgia were more alike in their black to white population ratios than Maryland and were politically and economically similar. *Journal* reporter Milt Saul interviewed the leaders of North Carolina's Democratic Party who had successfully led the disfranchisement effort and nurtured antiblack violence in Wilmington, where, on November 9, 1898, local Democrats, supported by state party leaders and white women, had overthrown the legitimately elected, biracial government. Through the long-term benefits of antiblack violence and disfranchisement in 1900, white North Carolinians had secured "a great industrial expansion with "more than three times as many corporations" investing in the state during the last four years.

Racial harmony and contented labor were additional benefits. According to North Carolina's secretary of state, J. Bryan Grimes, disfranchisement made blacks submissive and therefore "much better off." White racial hatred "engendered by fusion" between the Populist and Republican Parties in 1896 and "negro rule" had given way to "friendliness and harmony." Black disfranchisement also ensured a future for large plantation owners, with the restoration of a "contented" black laborer committed to agricultural employment. By removing "corruption" and an "incompetent [black] government," reform produced a stable society, white prosperity, and modern industrial development.[20]

Former North Carolina governor Charles B. Aycock outlined for Saul "How the Tar Heel State Was Redeemed." When whites fragmented politically in 1894, "black rule" resulted in a government that was "incapable of enforcing the law and preserving order." White women regularly were forced to flee from "Black brutes." White North Carolinians consequently determined that they needed "to disfranchise the negro" and purge the state with "streams of blood and agony mountains high." *Journal* owner James R. Gray asked, "Do we want to pass through the same experience that North Carolina passed through?" Ironically, he seemed to answer yes in posing his second query. The violent Wilmington riot in 1898 and disfranchisement in 1900 saved North Carolina from black rule, "so why not Georgia?"[21]

Milt Saul's interviews reiterated the benefits of racial violence. Senator Furnifold Simmons had headed the Democratic Party's state executive committee in 1898 and "the war on negro rule." According to Simmons, North Carolina was plagued by 1,000 governmental officials, economic stagnation, the loss of "millions of dollars" in development, and intolerable social conditions. In Wilmington and New Bern, where large numbers of black officeholders "dominated," the troubles with blacks exceeded "the days of reconstruction," but Wilmington's riot and passage of black disfranchisement vanquished "negro domination."[22]

Simmons's senatorial colleague Lee S. Overman explained that white "revolution" had required a comprehensive societal cleansing in which sex and gender roles, race relations, economic development, jobs, social deference, and politics were all transformed by white violence. In one illustrative public gathering, "a beautiful North Carolina girl, dressed in pure white . . . on a pure white horse [carried a] pure white banner." Following her were twenty more young white women dressed and mounted in a similar fashion. The most important "feature came next. It was a body of thirty stalwart young [white male] North Carolinians each with a Winchester rifle over his shoulder." In rural communities and eastern cities, white men walked around perpetually armed and "[b]lood flowed in many streets. In Wilmington they ordered a gatling gun."[23]

Gray and Saul noted newspapers "led" whites in Wilmington to organize each ward into "white government unions" whose members "publicly 'drummed' out" black officials and burned black press facilities. In Georgia, immediate action for disfranchisement was necessary, given the problems whites encountered in Maryland and North Carolina when they failed to respond promptly. Georgians, in fact, faced "a far more dangerous situation" than Maryland and North Carolina, because it had a larger black population.[24]

Thomas W. Hardwick's letter "To White Voters of Georgia," published in the *Journal* in conjunction with this series, claimed 99 percent of the black voters, whether educated or illiterate, were "absolutely venal." In Georgia's cities and towns, however, they could seize the "reins of power." Atlanta's black electorate of 7,896 made up more than a third of the 23,141 voters in the city. Ten other unnamed Georgia cities had black majorities. White men had to act because "we are walking over a veritable powder magazine ready to explode."[25]

South Carolina senator "Pitchfork" Ben Tillman weighed in with the assertion that Georgia's problem was qualitatively as well as quantitatively greater than North Carolina's. According to Tillman, black Georgians were more resistant and would not submit to white dominance without a struggle.[26]

In May 1906, the *Journal* reprinted Milt Saul's North Carolina "lessons" and added supportive letters from the public in Georgia and other states. Rev. Dr. J. B. Hawthorne, a former Atlantan, claimed that white Virginians, too, had nearly lost the balance of power to an organized black political bloc. Disfranchisement, however, pacified black "passions... [and ensured] the goodwill and friendship of the white man—his superior and his ruler." It also decreased the incidence of "criminal assault," a category of crime the *Journal* had begun to report more frequently (and more sensationally) after Hoke Smith's first campaign speech in June 1905.[27]

On July 2, 1906, a less prominent Georgia editor wrote that violence served a definite purpose, for whites finally had decided to resist black rapists, murderers, and arsonists who committed "crime out of resentment and hatred toward the white man."[28] "Editor Beasley" of the *Lee County Journal* floridly raised the specter of violence—and Wilmington—in an editorial that the *Journal* reprinted, also on July 2. The theme seemed to be "ballots now or bullets later."[29]

In mid-July, Thomas W. Hardwick looked back to the Civil War as a moment when white violence was justified. Resorting to corruption, force, and intimidation, the Civil War fathers had acted with a "heroic patriotism [and] ... a purer pride of race," but in the end "[t]here was no other way open to them and they were right to take it." In Hardwick's view, because white violence struck at the basic structures of modern government, eroding respect for the law, disfranchisement offered a way to avoid teaching lawlessness as a solution to black political power.[30]

In reaching all the way back to the Civil War for his examples, Hardwick gave short shrift to the late nineteenth-century South's penchant for violence. Since "Reconstruction" and "Redemption," white "reformers" repeatedly had used violence to revive the Democratic Party and undermine black voting. One of Milt Saul's prize interview subjects, Ben Tillman, had mastered the use of antiblack violence in Hamburg, South Carolina, thirty-seven years earlier. White Georgians, too, had killed black voters, laborers, and landowners in random and organized acts of violence from 1868 to the end of the nineteenth century. Henry W. Grady in the late 1880s had celebrated the Danville, Virginia, riot of 1883, now recalled by Reverend Hawthrone.[31]

In 1905 and 1906, disfranchisement was the foundation upon which reformers usurped power from the Democratic Party. It was a popular proposal that politicians Thomas W. Hardwick, Thomas E. Watson, Hoke Smith, and James R. Gray used to win the 1906 white primary, promising it would produce "good times" for all whites, but especially for working men. Watson and Hardwick in

1905 recruited Smith and Gray into a coalition that used antiblack rhetoric to rally the Populist remnants and newly emerging southern Progressives with images of North Carolina's "armed revolution."

Clark Howell, Smith's main gubernatorial opponent, claimed that black disfranchisement threatened the resurrection of the "educated negro" and "negro domination" from the mythical days of Reconstruction. Howell argued that blacks had already been disfranchised by the white primary, the Australian ballot, and white solidarity. At the same time, Howell entertained the possibility of antiblack violence should black political power again approach the federally supported "negro domination" of the past. He pledged to man the barricades personally to defend white rights against renewed federal intrusion. Howell, nevertheless, stood for a system that dissident Democrats increasingly viewed as unworkable.

Hoke Smith argued for new methods and new party leadership. Citing North Carolina, he and his backers contended that disfranchisement made blacks return to the land as deferential laborers who worked for whites. It also opened the state to investment and new jobs for whites. Just as Henry W. Grady, Thomas E. Watson, and Clark Howell separately had promised prosperity to white workingmen during the late nineteenth and early twentieth centuries, Hoke Smith in 1906 offered similar promises in exchange for working-class support. For southern Progressives and Thomas E. Watson, reform was a long, hard road littered with the failures of Populism, prohibition, and the 1890 white primaries. Success required what *Atlanta Georgian* editor John Temple Graves called "an illegal revolution." That was the Atlanta riot.

6

The Summer of 1906

> There has never been a race riot in Atlanta.
>
> Thomas Martin, white Atlanta merchant and urban booster, 1902

In the years before the gubernatorial campaign of 1905–6 took shape, elite whites, such as Atlanta merchant and urban booster Thomas Martin, did not believe that their class could create a civic disaster like the bloodbath of September 22–25, 1906. Atlanta was a city known for its tranquillity, profitability, and progress, united by the "Atlanta Spirit" to solve any problem. Nevertheless, it was Atlanta's commercial-civic elite that created the very climate in which the Atlanta riot erupted, playing the dual roles of racial terrorists and peacemakers.

During the summer of 1906, as white Atlantans daily read about the "carnival of rapes" allegedly committed by working-class black men against white womanhood, Georgia's political leaders were wrapping up a two-year fight over the most effective legal, political, and extralegal mechanisms for controlling African Americans.[1] Meanwhile, judges warned that the law had failed to contain blacks, and violence loomed on the horizon. Even after backing the victors in the pivotal white primary of August 22, 1906, white newspapers editorialized that "black assaults" were overwhelming white institutions, requiring extralegal violence as the solution to white powerlessness.[2] As a result, Atlanta followed in the footsteps of cities in the antebellum North and turn-of-the-twentieth-century South that reacted to the presence of free blacks by rioting against them.[3]

In the South, African Americans knew that white violence against them was directly tied to black powerlessness and the decline of the militia as a defender of black political power. In Maryland, Rev. W. J. Winston, formerly a college president, now pastor of the New Metropolitan Baptist Church in Baltimore, presented a public address entitled "Disfranchisement Makes Subject-Citizens Targets of the Mob and Disarms Them in the Courts." Black Atlantan John Hope expressed a similar concern over Georgia's 1877 poll tax, the white primaries of 1871, 1892, and 1897, and disfranchisement debate in the legislature from 1899 to 1906, in the midst of which the "reforming" legislature of 1905 had disbanded the remaining black militia companies.[4]

The Atlanta riot was one of several in U.S. history to combine "reform," disfranchisement, and antiblack violence in order to resist black autonomy and urban community development. In Providence, Rhode Island, black citizenship, home ownership, and crime were irritants that white workingmen fanned into antiblack riots in the 1820s and 1830s after blacks were disfranchised in 1822. Only when the black militia helped put down a labor rebellion for the vote in the early 1840s were African American voting rights restored and the rioting ended for certain. Blacks in Pennsylvania were stripped of their political rights in the 1830s, exposing black Philadelphians of all socioeconomic backgrounds to more than five years of white working-class mob violence.[5]

White violence against African Americans in the pre–Civil War North retaliated against such symbols of autonomy as home ownership or economic success in catering, lumber and coal distribution, and transportation. Other flash points could be public displays of social mixing, the competition for recreational space, abolitionism, or attempts to reform the drinking behavior of the working classes of both races.[6]

Southern urban antiblack political violence in Danville, Virginia, in 1883 and in Wilmington, North Carolina, in 1898 coincided with the reformation of the Democratic Party. In those states, young members of the white elite sought to reaffirm their racial, political, and economic dominance. In Danville and Wilmington, as later in Atlanta, where the press had publicized their example, urban antiblack violence united all the strands of the white elite and the working classes to reaffirm white supremacy.[7]

Riots occurred in cities where white confidence in the institutional structures of white dominance had been eroded by black autonomy, urbanization, and industrial development, as well as by the perception, often deliberately manufactured, that black crime was out of control. In Atlanta, the influential judges Emory Speer and George Hillyer accepted violence as the alternative to a legal system they deemed to be broken. Real justice, they argued, was "swift, sure violence" unhampered by the "legalities" that sent an unclear message to blacks about who was in charge of the "power struggle among men."[8] In July

1905, Speer warned in a personal letter to Clark Howell that a "generation of Southern [white] manhood ... now living" under the "nervous terror of the criminal negro" was not convinced that the legal system worked. These men were being driven to "something like [a] St. Bartholomew['s Day]" massacre by the delay in strengthening "our miserably inefficient laws for the apprehension of criminals."[9]

Judge Hillyer's editorials in Atlanta's newspapers had sounded the call for judicial reform as early as 1894. If Georgia's criminal laws were not amended, "lynching would never be stopped," Hillyer warned. Of course, the laws he wanted strengthened were not directed at members of a lynch mob; the real issue for Hillyer was that African Americans insisted on equal justice under the law. Antebellum rapists, Hillyer argued, had few rights, and criminals did not have access to the appeal process. Nevertheless, in 1906 as the alleged crime wave of black assaults carried the city inexorably toward violence, Hillyer urged white leaders to make sure that "nobody hurt any of the peaceable and good negroes, but rather commend and encourage them."[10]

Rape criminally violates its female victims, but Speer and Hillyer were concerned with the interaction between the rapist and the victim's male guardians. For them, and for generations of men before them, the punishment of rape determined who possessed the highest level of dominance and control. During wars, when men used women as symbols of victory and defeat, owning or controlling women determined who held power and who did not. Similarly, in the post–Civil War South, punishing black men for alleged sexual violence and denying them the role of protector over black women eroded their newly won citizenship, public power, and self-realization. Thanks to the two judges, in twentieth-century Georgia due process thus became a casualty of the "power struggle" between black and white men.[11]

Although the white newspapers began cataloging the alleged assaults by black men against white women in June 1905, J. Max Barber's *Voice of the Negro* was offering an alternative perspective by October. For instance, "a Negro named Jim Walker did assault a white woman near Brookwood." Because of universal agreement about Walker's limited mental capacity, however, white leaders feared that "a committee of colored physicians" might derail white justice by pronouncing Walker insane, so several white doctors "left church on Sunday to examine him and pronounce him sane." Walker was legally executed in December 1905.[12]

The "three ... most distinguished lawyers of Georgia" had served as Walker's defense team: Judges George Hillyer, W. R. Hammond, and Howard Van Epps. According to the *Atlanta News*, Walker "voluntarily plead[ed] guilty to a capital offense whose fixed punishment was death." After urging Walker to reconsider, Walker's all-jurist counsel acceded to his wishes to waive a formal trial and, as the *News* put it, voluntarily place his neck in the hangman's noose. Hillyer's contribution was a tearful request that law officers carry out the death sentence. Fulton County sheriff John W. Nelms had promised to turn over the execution to the victim's husband, but that would circumvent the legal process and sanction an extralegal lynching.[13] As noted earlier, the right to punish rape had come to symbolize the highest level of dominance and control. Therefore, Atlanta's commercial-civic elite wanted to make sure that reserving the privilege for white men did not confer it on all white men, regardless of class or background.

For over a year, from June 1905 to September 1906, the white press and politicians convinced the whites of Atlanta and Fulton County that they had suffered twelve horrific "assaults" on white womanhood. According to journalist Ray Stannard Baker's investigation, only two of the twelve were real assaults, including the one Jim Walker so readily admitted. Baker argued that three incidents before the riot of September 22, 1906, could be classified as "aggravated attempts at rape." Three others "may have been attempts, [but] three were pure cases of fright." Among the "fright" cases was that of a woman who claimed assault to cover up her "attempted suicide." Southern reformer A. J. McKelway reported three additional "assaults" not noted by Baker on July 20, August 15, and August 24, 1906. African American editor J. Max Barber considered only the Walker case a "real attack" and attributed the rest to white women who were seeking to avoid public intrusion into their personal problems. Whites in general were easily persuaded by their own editors and political leaders that black men indeed were assaulting white women with a vengeance.[14]

On July 31, 1906, Fulton County whites lynched Frank Carmichael for the alleged rape of thirteen-year-old Annie Laurie Poole. A mob of "citizens" marched with dogs through the woods until late afternoon when "one of the dogs belonging to the posse was found standing near a Negro cabin." Of the four black men and one woman inside, Carmichael admitted muddy shoes in a corner of the cabin belonged to him. When the alleged victim "identified" Carmichael as her "attacker," the mob "shot [him] on the spot," even though his clothing did not match the description provided by his accuser. Fulton County police officers arrived after the execution. The suburban or semirural mob had usurped the elite's prerogative to protect white womanhood, but *At-*

lanta News editor Charles Daniel praised the men for exercising their "right" to defend white women and white supremacy.[15]

An alleged assault on August 20, 1906, convinced J. Max Barber that the Atlanta riot was a planned affair. Just two days before the white primary on August 22, two white girls, Mabel and Ethel Lawrence, were "brutally assaulted on the outskirts of Atlanta." Because police and an armed posse accompanied by bloodhounds lost "the trail ... at a white man's door," according to Barber, the "white man had blacked his face and committed this deed either out of sheer lust or as an emissary of Hoke Smith to help inflame the voting whites against blacks." Alleging that "white men with blackened faces have been killed in South Carolina, Kentucky, and Texas and one is now in jail in the district of Columbia for playing [a] negro while committing [a] crime," Barber contended that *Atlanta Georgian* editor John Temple Graves acknowledged just after the riot that none of the precipitating assaults was a real criminal assault or rape.[16]

Regardless of any link between Hoke Smith's candidacy and the reported assaults, the hysteria did not abate after the primary. In late August, Judge George Hillyer headed a group of commercial-civic elite members who urged Atlanta's white press to mount a crusade against black crime. Hillyer's colleagues included businessman and newspaper board member Joseph Hirsch, attorney Linton Hopkins, riot reconstructionist L. Z. Rosser, Rev. C. B. Wilmer, and retailer George Muse, who wrote the postriot investigation report. They "demand[ed] that the police force[s] be increased ... for the enforcement of the law" and, along with Atlanta's white clergy, called "for the elimination of all low dives" that served black clients.[17]

The *Atlanta Georgian*, from August 22 to 24, published a three-part series of editorials on "The Reign of Terror for Southern Women." The first addressed the alleged August 20 assault in suburban Atlanta of Ethel and Mabel Lawrence, the fifth "open and monstrous attempt at rape within the last four weeks." Stressing that white people could not "wait for the slow process of the law" and that lynching had failed to prevent rape, the *Georgian* proposed "personal mutilation of the rapist" to create a deterrent mystique of terror. The second editorial, "The Way to Save Our Women," asserted that black autonomy "must be met until it is finally answered in the only and inevitable way." Blacks had tried white patience to its breaking point of "wild ... retaliation." "The 'Reign of Terror' Must End" counseled white restraint but threatened "by the Goddes [*sic*] of liberty" to use "stronger means."

Atlanta Journal owner and editor James R. Gray asserted that to "intimidate" blacks as "thoroughly" as possible, white men should "teach their wives and daughters and sisters how to become reasonably expert with" a pistol. Further, every white man in "Fulton county should be made a deputy" armed with "the power [to use] his discretion to prevent these unspeakable crimes," and "the mobs . . . scouring" metropolitan Atlanta should "strike terror" in blacks.[18]

The two afternoon newspapers, the *Atlanta News* and *Atlanta Georgian*, were far more aggressive than the *Journal*, where their editors had learned the value of "yellow journalism." Now Charles Daniel of the *News* and John Temple Graves of the *Georgian* used antiblack attitudes, editorials, and sensationalism to advance their position against the *Journal* for control of the afternoon market. Both supported "reform" by employing the *Journal*'s antiblack techniques.[19] Originally the two had cooperated in founding the *News* in 1902, but in April 1906, Graves defected, to create the *Georgian* with former New Jerseyite F. L. Seely.[20] As partners and as rivals, Daniel and Graves focused their reform efforts on restricting blacks and conceded gubernatorial politics to the *Journal* and *Constitution*.

Before the riot, members of the commercial-civic elite provided financial and social support to the two new papers, but especially to the *News*. On primary day, August 22, 1906, the James W. English family and other board members of the Fourth National Bank, including James R. Gray and Joseph Hirsch, lent their financial influence to the *News*. James W. English Jr. became president of the Publishing Company, and his brother Harry joined him and Hirsch on the company's board of directors. According to Daniel, English, who belonged to the chamber of commerce, connected the *News* with the most successful young businessmen in Atlanta.[21]

Another *News* director, young lawyer Charles T. Hopkins of John L. Hopkins and Sons, was from a family involved in black education setting racial policies in Atlanta. Yet Charles, who had supported Clark Howell's candidacy, was silent when Daniel attacked blacks in his August and September editorials, becoming an advocate for racial "peace" only after the September 22–25, 1906, riot.

Other prominent members of Atlanta's commercial-civic elite endorsed Daniel's leadership and editorials. Fulton County officials made the *News* the "Official Organ of Fulton County" for legal, ordinary, and clerk's notices, and Sheriff John W. Nelms appointed Daniel "a special deputy sheriff in Fulton County." In return, the paper provided the county with "a pack of bloodhounds to be used in running down and capturing criminals who attack white women."[22]

With support from the commercial-civic elite, Daniel and Graves escalated the discussion of blacks and deference. Daniel campaigned for a white liberation army reminiscent of Reconstruction and the Ku Klux Klan and sponsored a reward for the capture and conviction of black men accused of attacking white women. He claimed "several hundred of the best and most successful citizens" had signed a petition for a mass meeting to revive the KKK.[23]

In July 1906, the *News* had proclaimed that the "bestial idea of social equality" was behind "all lustful assaults upon white women." Any black man who "lays his fingers upon a white woman" violated the white male's privilege to defend "their property and homes as well as 'our women.'" Some of the responsibility now fell on the previously irreproachable woman, in particular, the transit rider, Daniel argued in August. White females had to keep "a proper distance" between themselves and black men to maintain the social structure of white dominance, wrote Daniel, who invoked the image of a "black fellow jammed against a white woman in ... an overloaded streetcar."[24]

On the other hand, the *News* quoted the Atlanta Ladies of Lithia Springs, Georgia, who criticized white men for their failure to protect white women from "diseased" black men on streetcars. The ladies asked if white female virtue should be sacrificed for the cost of a nickel streetcar ride and claimed corporate greed had superseded southern racial etiquette. They called upon white men to act with legislation or violence to end white women's ordeal with black men.[25]

As to legislation, Daniel recommended that the mayor and general council not be concerned about violating African American rights when they considered "passing an ordinance preventing the arming of Negroes." Mrs. Lugenia Burns Hope, wife of Atlanta Baptist College president John Hope, recalled years later that "Negroes [were] not able to buy firearms for months before the Riot," hindering their efforts to defend themselves. Her husband turned to out-of-town "friends" who shipped weapons to Atlanta in "coffins" and "soiled laundry" before the riot.[26]

When Daniel and Graves demanded that blacks surrender their autonomy and submit to law and order,[27] working-class whites showered them with supportive letters to the editor. An unnamed Atlantan who congratulated Daniel suggested burning in answer to the cry for mutilation instigated by Graves.[28] Another wanted to change the Constitution to protect only white rights. Letters from outside Atlanta called for "forcible deportation" if not the annihilation of African Americans.[29]

Increasingly, in August and September 1906, the white press attacked black working-class recreational sites. It defined black part-time workers and dance hall patrons as vagrants and charged that "negro restaurants are in reality nothing but saloons and loafing places" for the "criminals, and half-way criminals that have been causing all the trouble in this community lately." Armed with the new definition, the police resurrected an antivagrant policy dating back to 1900 with an expanded aim "to rid this community of tramps, vagabonds, and well known criminals."[30]

Clark Howell and the *Atlanta Constitution* called for "relentless war ... against vagrancy and the dives." According to the *Constitution,* black men on Decatur Street worked "only four days." Saturday was payday; Sunday was "the day of rest," followed by "blue Monday" when blacks "loitered" on Decatur Street. Whites were powerless because "no law" dictated when and how blacks worked and "brute force" was the "only influence that they comprehend and respect." City officials needed to give "idle" blacks an ultimatum: "Leave the city and county or be sent to the chain gang."[31]

In August 1906, the Atlanta press was able to reinforce its chronicle of alleged local violence with news of national events. In that month, the all-black U.S. Twenty-fifth Infantry Regiment launched a retaliatory raid against white harassment in Brownsville, Texas. As a result, the *Constitution* proposed that the federal government terminate the "negro militia" just as Georgia had done in 1905. Daniel of the *News* lent his voice to Howell's.[32] Together, the two editors attacked any institution that provided African Americans with autonomy, the vote, political influence, the opportunity for patriotic service, the right to work, or the independence to pursue personal recreation.

Recognizing that the potential for white violence was rapidly on the rise, members of Atlanta's African American elite tried to save what they could of black autonomy and lead the black working classes to respectability—from a secure distance. The Ministers Union of the African Methodist Episcopal Church passed resolutions on August 30, 1906, endorsing "law and order" and advising "the people to be sober, industrious, and economical." The clergymen resolved "to preach and practice" the patience of Job while encouraging cooperation between white employers and black workers. Members of their own class, they noted, already were patriots, loyal and law-abiding.[33]

Likewise in late August, the Rev. Henry Hugh Proctor promoted the First Congregational Church as the institution that might instill "respect" in the black working classes and forestall white violence. One of his sermons outlined "The Protection of Womanhood." In it, Proctor stated that only "outcasts" living outside the influence of "our churches and schools" attacked white women. He asked "good [elite] men of both races" to "prevent disorders."[34]

White editors rejected the black elite's overtures. Instead, they demanded concessions that African Americans could not provide, such as "clear[ing] Decatur and Peters Street[s] of every barroom, clubroom, and restaurant."[35]

In light of the mandate handed Smith for Progressive reform on September 18, 1906, after twenty days of hiring new police officers and a municipal investigation of black dives, the city council passed an ordinance also endorsed by Proctor, restricting dive operators of both races who served black clients. Police Chief Henry Jennings completed his evaluation of Decatur Street establishments on Friday, September 21, failing 22 of the 260 "Negro Restaurants" examined. License Inspector Richard Ewing toured Decatur Street uncovering dives and "negro clubs" and confiscating the liquor bottle advertisements of "nude white women." Ewing recommended that "every [closed black] club [pay] a license of $1,000 to the city," because "few if any of the 'vile' establishments can afford such a tax." City council members and the police sought to force black dive owners to regulate black working-class behavior and report criminal activity in order to receive a favorable license review. Black proprietors Rosa Edwards, T. W. Jackson, P. A. Keith, and J. T. and Emmie Dobbs were listed in the white newspapers as subject to the new standards.[36]

At the same time, the white papers told their readers that the new measures were too little, too late. By now, African Americans supposedly were experts at evading the law by manipulating "technicalities." For instance, many worked just enough to satisfy the legal standards regulating vagrants.[37] Black autonomy operated far beyond the reach of the control mechanisms provided by government and white employers. In the growing city, there seemed to be a whole separate world many whites believed they did not control.[38]

As the summer of 1906 came to a close, Atlanta joined a statewide, regional, and national debate over the "proper" public status of African Americans. After the August victory of Hoke Smith secured the governorship for the white reformers, the nominating convention that followed in mid-September verified that the August white primary was the "revolution" whites had awaited for more than forty years to reaffirm their dominance over blacks. Smith's election and black disfranchisement marked the "popular" retaking of government by "the people." African Americans in Georgia lost any remaining political power they had possessed. By making them vulnerable to white violence, Progressive reform negated Thomas Martin's 1902 boast that Atlanta had never had a race riot. Atlantans now expected a riot.[39]

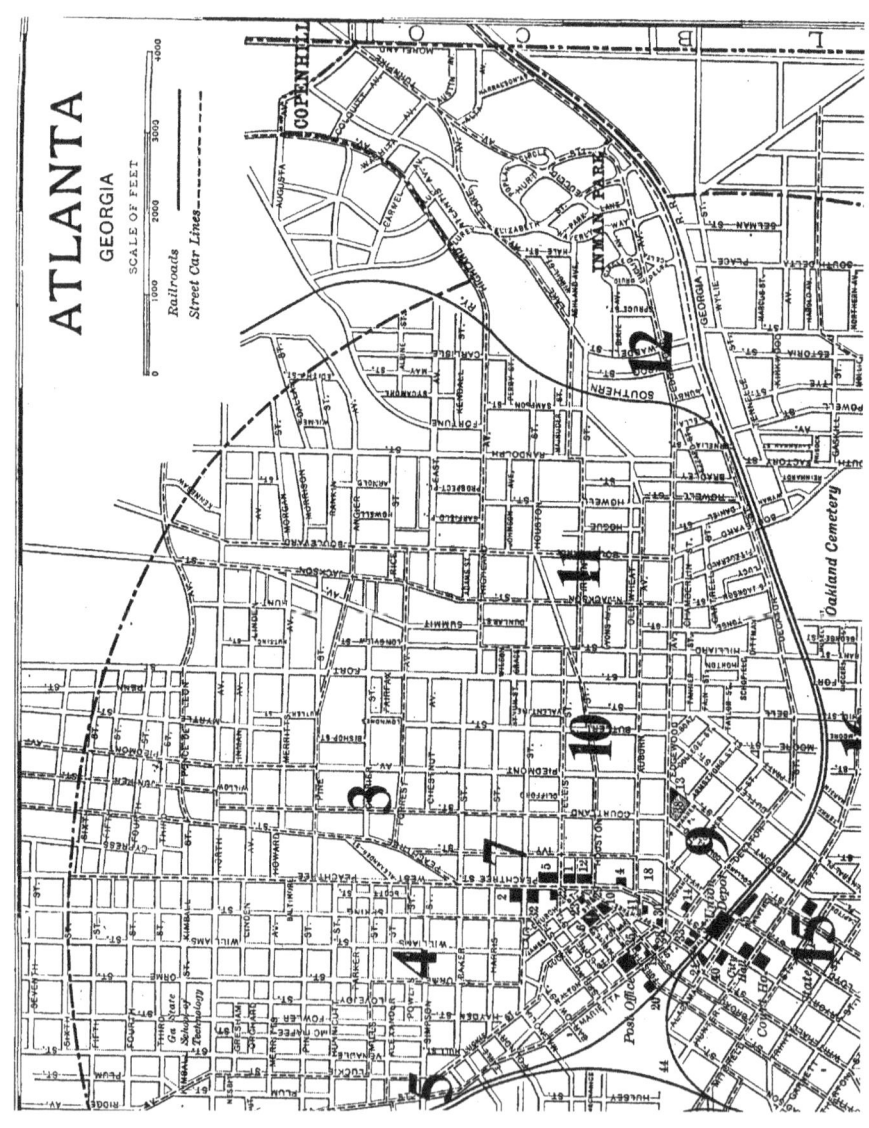

Map 6.1. Mabel and Ethel Lawrence reportedly were assaulted by a black man in Copenhill on August 20, 1906. Police and an armed posse accompanied by bloodhounds lost "the trail ... at a white man's door." (Map by O. F. Kauffman, C.E., Atlanta, 1905, courtesy Georgia Archives, Atlanta.)

Part Three

7

Riot

> The curtain rises on a veritable devil's cauldron. An atmosphere overhead, usually resplendent with electric lights, blackened by a sheer swirling dust and powdersnake, beneath, the faint glitter of blue steel, the brandishing of dirks, the dull thud of wielded clubs, the whir of stones, the crash of glass, and the deafening report of guns, . . . the dreadful faces of . . . an organized . . . mob; who having seen it, can never forget?
>
> J. Max Barber, *The Voice of the Negro*, November 1906

The "true picture" of Atlanta on the night of Saturday, September 22, 1906, wrote African American editor J. Max Barber, was "primal savagery," as enraged white men attacked and destroyed black dives, poolrooms, restaurants, barbershops, and human lives. One of their many victims, Mrs. Mattie Adams, barred the door to the restaurant she had operated for twenty years, hoping to defend it against a gang of white men led by George W. Blackstock of Decatur, Georgia. Earlier that night, Blackstock boarded a streetcar in Oakland City, the site of a black man's "assault" upon a white farmer's wife, Knowles Kimmel, two days earlier. His sole reason for traveling into Atlanta's central business district, Blackstock later admitted, was "to hurt niggers." Armed with a battering ram, Blackstock led rioters into Adams's restaurant. They beat her and her daughter with wagon wheel spokes and made her grandson "dance" by firing bullets at him. All three survived their injuries, but everything in the restaurant was destroyed.[1] Other victims fared even worse.

On Peachtree Street, across from the Federal Building, where a well-known black barbershop served a white clientele, the mob bricked its windows and rushed in carrying "heavy clubs, canes, revolvers, [and] several rifles." According to the *Atlanta Constitution,* both barbers were working at their respective chairs, and neither attempted to resist the mob. One held up his hands just before "a brick caught him in the face" and guns discharged. When the black men fell, the rioters proceeded to ransack the shop and mutilate the barbers' faces. They kicked and disrobed the black victims on a floor "wet with puddles of blood" so that they could take the barbers' "shirts and clothing home as souvenirs or wave them over their heads to invite further riot." Then they dragged the bodies across the street and deposited them in an alley. Capturing another black man outside the barbershop, the rioters clubbed and shot him and left his body with those of the barbers, in the shadow of the Henry W. Grady statue, a monument to the spirit of the New South.[2]

The Atlanta riot was an outburst of antiblack violence involving the full social and institutional spectrum of white society. Its instigators or perpetrators included the press, elements of law enforcement, state and local governmental agencies, and white-collar as well as industrial workers. As the culmination of the "reform revolution" to reaffirm white dominance and black deference, violence was directed, above all, at getting "the negroes off the streets."

The press accounts reported that white anger started to coalesce around 6 p.m. Saturday as a group of white men began congregating in the central business district along Peachtree and Decatur streets.[3] Three hours later, the riot began when "several thousand people of all classes driven by frenzy because of repeated assaults on women of Fulton County by negroes mobilized" on Marietta, Peachtree, Whitehall, Decatur and Broad streets. Armed with sticks, rocks, guns, and other weapons of violence, they "made war upon the negro population" until after midnight.[4]

The *Atlanta Journal* contended that Mayor James G. Woodward restrained a crowd of angry whites until 9:30 p.m. before news of "another assault" destroyed any calm Woodward had hoped to achieve. Woodward, former police commissioner James W. English Sr., members of Atlanta's city council, and leaders of the police and fire departments tried to disperse the thousands of white men congregating in Atlanta's central business district. Standing in front of Hoke Smith's Piedmont Hotel with English, Woodward condemned Atlanta's white newspapers for circulating the extra editions that inflamed the crowd. Pleading with the crowd not to commit any acts of violence, Woodward urged its members to consider how violence might stain Atlanta's reputation. The mob responded with a "Bronx cheer," followed by the exchange of "Hurrah for Woodward" and "To hell with the niggers." English, a city father since Reconstruction, was called "a nigger lover" and told to "shut up." Soon the announcement of a new "assault" on a white woman mobilized 100 armed white men and boys to march on Decatur Street.

Saturday night's riot would be confined within the city limits despite the *Atlanta Constitution*'s reports that it spread to Bellwood, Reynoldstown, Edgewood, and Oakland City. In fact, white men and boys flocked to Atlanta by streetcar from those outlying districts, and at 10 p.m., when the bars closed, more white men poured onto Atlanta's downtown streets.[5]

The *Constitution* stated that "the first disorder" occurred at Pryor and Decatur streets, where white youths assaulted a black bicycle messenger, who was then rescued by the police. Some white men also chased "negroes along Decatur and Pryor streets and Central Avenue until the fire department" sprayed the mob of 2,000 at 10 p.m. The African Americans who entered downtown Atlanta unaware of the emerging violence were gainfully employed blacks carrying out their appointed duties. The *Constitution* complained about the white "boys and youngsters" who wanted to "kill every damned nigger in the town." Rather, the purpose of the riot was only "getting the negroes off the streets." The *Atlanta Journal* explained that as emotions increased, however, all blacks came to look alike, and not even black women were spared by white male rioters.[6]

Mayor Woodward opened the alarm box at Decatur and Ivy streets to declare a "general alarm." He also ordered Fire Chief W. R. Joyner, who was the mayor-elect, to direct fire hoses at the mob along Decatur Street between Ivy and Peachtree streets. Five minutes later, the mob regrouped at Edgewood and Pryor streets beyond the reach of the water, laughing.[7] Chief Joyner ordered six hoses turned on another set of rioters. After they dispersed beyond the range of the water stream and shouted out regret for having elected Joyner mayor, the chief did not order another hosing of infuriated whites. Instead, firemen turned down Decatur Street to confront several hundred blacks, placing Joyner's official power on the side of the rioters.

At Ivy Street, the powerful streams of water drove blacks "like cattle . . . up Decatur Street into the open plaza at Marietta, Peachtree, Edgewood, and Decatur," where blacks and whites engaged in combat. The firemen's high-pressure hoses were reported to have instantly killed a black man, identified by the *Atlanta News* as Henry Welch. On the other hand, the *Journal* asserted that Welch died in the Cuban Pool Room on Peachtree Street when the mob discovered his hiding place and shot him to death. The *Constitution* claimed that rioters "cut [Welch] to pieces." He died at Henry W. Grady Hospital.[8]

On Central Avenue just off Decatur Street, the police "protected a skating rink which housed probably five hundred negroes." The police, the press reported, then saved a crowd of white rioters who wanted to continue pursuing blacks "below Central avenue [where] they would have encroached upon the most densely populated part of the street and encountered thousands of half drunken negroes." Eventually the mob's "attention was drawn by a baggage wagon bearing two darkies." For the most part, white rioters had no desire to confront African Americans as one opposing army engaging the other. In Saturday's riot, large numbers of white men and boys overwhelmed small groups or individual blacks, making examples of them.[9]

Three hundred police officers were mobilized. Although solitary officers were able to save black victims, mass police efforts to maintain order usually were overwhelmed by white power. At Pryor Street, Captain William Mayo commanded twelve officers who kept enraged whites confined on Decatur Street, saving them, the *Journal* applauded, from rushing headlong into a black neighborhood known as "Rusty Row." Captain Mayo lost control of the crowd when a "boisterous drunken" black man blundered into the district and was trampled by the mob. From that point on, running fights occurred on the mob's route to Decatur Street as white men hit any African American unfortunate enough to be on downtown streets.[10]

On Peachtree Street near the Piedmont Hotel, Officer Carson witnessed the convergence of two white mobs bringing together 1,000 men armed with bricks, sticks, and other improvised weapons. When the rioters caught a black streetcar patron after he escaped from the trolley, Carson fought through to extract the black victim. Carson would return to the streets just as the mob expanded its attacks upon streetcars at the intersection of Peachtree and Luckie streets, "fighting as best he could single-handed," the *Journal* recounted.[11]

At 10 p.m., on Peachtree and Marietta, new police chief Henry Jennings attempted to prevent white rioters from beating a black man with sticks, and he arrested W. G. Shepard, a white steamfitter. Jennings "managed to beat the mob off" while securing Shepard at the police station. On Decatur, in front of the Star Theater, other officers held their position for five minutes, until the mob spotted a solitary black man inadvertently entering the riot zone.

Some police officers, however, did not execute their responsibilities. Police commission member J. J. Woodside charged that he personally observed officers who failed to do their "duty." Mayor Woodward received reports that officers permitted "the mob to attack negroes without interference." Patrolmen also stood by while Atlanta's hardware stores did a brisk business with white rioters. One store sold $16,000 in weaponry; others were looted without police resistance.¹² Fulton County sheriff John W. Nelms called for an end to general gun sales, but selectively distributed hundreds of gun permits to "respectable [white] citizens."

Whatever their level of dedication to duty, the police lost control of Atlanta's streets between 10 and 11 p.m. By midnight, frustrated with their inability to stem the ever-expanding waves of white men who were chasing blacks, officers just "sat upon their horses as the race for life went on."¹³

The riot began as an assault upon the unregulated black entertainment district along Decatur and Peters streets, but shifted to new targets between 10:00 and 10:30 p.m. after the mob swelled to 10,000 with the closing of saloons, clubs, and theaters. This new set of white working-class rioters attacked black deliverymen and messengers. Between forty and fifty white workers were arrested for rioting on September 22, 1906, and an untold number of white workers were hospitalized. Among them was A. C. Moore, a lineman for the Georgia Railway and Electric Company and a neighbor of cabinetmaker Frank Arnold, "shot by a negro at the junction of Bellwood Avenue and the Southern Railway yards."¹⁴

At 10:15 p.m., white workingmen were enraged by the rumor that G. C. Tomlinson had been "badly cut by a negro" just as the bars closed on Decatur Street below Pryor Street. A mob of perhaps 400 to 500 white men armed with sticks, guns, and rocks solidified behind Randall Brothers Coal Company foreman T. F. Clements, armed with a brick, and surged along Decatur Street toward the Piedmont Hotel. At the Piedmont, the *Journal* reported, white rioters "enacted a scene never witnessed before in Atlanta," the merciless torment of a defenseless African American captured in retaliation.¹⁵

The streetcars entering downtown Atlanta were symbols of corporate refusal to enforce Jim Crow segregation with separate vehicles for each race. Moreover, unwilling to lose black fares, the corporate owners inconsistently regulated the black passengers, who rode the same cars as whites. White violence against the downtown streetcars and their black patrons raged between 10 and 11:45 p.m. when service ended. African Americans boarded streetcars on Decatur Street unaware of the violence exploding in the central business district. White rioters took control of the streets, tracks, and overhead wires, separating the trolleys from their power source. At Peachtree and Luckie streets, rioters pulled black passengers through the windows and from the front and rear platforms of fifteen disabled streetcars. Using sticks, they inflicted head wounds on victims who "showed fight."¹⁶

Pursuing a black person down Peachtree Street toward Edgewood Avenue into the most congested part of Atlanta, white rioters also overwhelmed streetcars at that intersection. There, police officers saved two African Americans "cut bloody" by covering them on the car's floor until the vehicle regained power and moved out of harm's way. When another streetcar entered the central business district with black men sitting near white women, rioters boarded the streetcar near Five Points, allowed white passengers to depart, and proceeded to attack blacks regardless of gender, pulling six black women and four black men off the streetcar and beating them "with bludgeons or anything that could be wrenched off a building, including iron bars."

According to the *Constitution*, the black women defended themselves with umbrellas and hat pins, because they "were fighting for their lives, and knew it." The mob pulled the remaining African Americans through the shattered windows and "almost disrobed" the black women, whom they cuffed on the head and allowed to escape.

White men and teenagers armed with sticks beat the black men. Half of the black victims found safety in Atlanta's side streets. A black youth named Evans, around eighteen years old, challenged whites, only to be "knocked down" and bloodied over and over by the mob. After attempting to defend himself with a knife, he was run down by twenty men on Forsyth Street between Blumenthal's and the side door of Richard's, a barbershop, "and he was dead within three minutes."[17] Although the police had only their physical strength to remove the rioters from the streetcar, the motorman finally managed to climb up on top of the vehicle and reattach the streetcar to its overhead wire, enabling it to move the victims out of reach of the mob. The police reported three black women had been killed in the confrontation.[18]

Yet another streetcar entered the riot zone. Its black passengers, too, were pulled through broken windows and beaten with sticks and fists. Then the rioters tossed the men off the Forsyth Street viaduct onto the railroad tracks ten feet below and shot them, killing three. In a similar incident on the West Fair line, white rioters assaulted three African Americans with brass knuckles and clubs.[19]

Frank Smith, a barber employed at Cooper's on Broad Street and a resident of Summerhill, fell victim to the mob at 11 p.m. on the Forsyth Street bridge above Marietta Street. "Neatly dressed" and light skinned, Smith was removed from the Marietta streetcar and chased to the bridge, where rioters sliced his chest open. Young men and boys, no more than twenty years old, the *Journal* reported, shot two other blacks to death after extracting them from the Forsyth

Street streetcar near Alabama Street. A third African American was beaten to death beside the Henry W. Grady memorial, where he had been attempting to hide.[20]

The hospital named for Grady treated a number of additional victims of the streetcar violence, including Ed Watson with "a deep gash" in his forehead, Ben Nelson, whose left eye was nearly "punched out" and head "badly cut," Roy Thomas with a slash wound from shoulder to shoulder and a head wound, and James Davis, whose mouth was beaten "to a pulp."[21]

The *Journal* noted that a "crowd" of African Americans along Edgewood Avenue fired fifteen to twenty shots at one streetcar emerging from the downtown riot district. Georgia Railway and Electric Company superintendent Nym Hurt told a *Journal* reporter that this was one of only two streetcars damaged by blacks. White rioters, however, damaged at least six streetcars and killed ten or eleven passengers.[22]

Decatur Street was the home of black recreation, where blacks and whites met as equals despite the segregation laws. Rioters wrecked the Detroit, a popular black barbershop on Decatur Street, "with a volley of rocks" that injured black clients. Of black entrepreneur Alonzo Herndon's three barbershops, the largest at 66 Peachtree Street served white patrons. Herndon's own records contradict the popular assumption that Saturday night's mob destroyed one or more of the Herndon shops. According to the ledger books, every man employed by Herndon was back at work after the riot, but Saturday night's antiblack violence caused a distinct decline in Herndon's barbershop revenues. *Atlanta Independent* owner and editor Benjamin Davis insisted, however, that after the mob smashed the front window of the Peachtree Street establishment, four barbers "in the shop were shot" and a "boot black was kicked to death." Henry A. Rucker's Decatur Street barbershop likewise does not appear in the historical record as a casualty of white rioting.[23] The barbershop inside the prominent Kimball House Hotel in downtown Atlanta was open for business when the riot began. After the mob spied the African American bootblacks on the Wall Street side of the Kimball House's "magnificent plate glass window," the rioters attempted to get the bootblacks by breaking the window with rocks. On Peachtree, the mob uncovered a black man hiding in a barbershop and shot him, fatally by some accounts.[24]

Across from the Kimball House's more successful rival, Hoke Smith's Piedmont, rioters on Peachtree Street chased a black man "through the plate glass door to the tailoring house of Tom Weaver." In the *Journal's* version, the fleeing man entered "the refreshment stand of Eunice Moore ... opposite the Prudential building." Misreading Moore's efforts to close for the night as an attempt to defend the escaping black man, the mob destroyed Moore's shop and lacerated her right arm.[25] According to the *Constitution,* the mob attacked a Greek merchant's combination fruit stand, cigar store, and soda fountain in the belief that he and his three Greek assistants had tried to defend the black man and the fruit stand by placing chairs and stools in the mob's path. The rioters wounded Eustace Brown, a young Greek boy, who fought the invaders. The black man escaped.[26]

The mob broke up into four units during and after the streetcar attacks and the fire department's hosing. Each group patrolled one of the following sections of downtown Atlanta: the area around Old Union Station, Peachtree Street and the National Cash Register building, Central Avenue, and Peters Street. The groups that ravaged the Union Station and Peters Street areas attacked the black entertainment district on Peters as well as federal property. At Union Station, a mob pulled a dozen black porters off their trains and chased them down the tracks, killing three, injuring numerous black railway employees, and breaking windows in the train cars.[27]

At midnight, 75–100 white men and boys broke off from the Union Station mob to march on Peters Street. After these rioters assaulted restaurant owner Mattie Adams and her family, they encountered "a negro with a pistol" and "quickly killed" him. But another black person fired a shotgun from a window into the mob, wounding a rioter. The rioters then broke into the Pearson and McCarley hardware store at the corner of Walker and Peters to steal ammunition and weapons. The *Journal* and *Constitution*'s accounts diverge at this point.

The *Constitution* reported that the Peters Street mob intended to "visit Pittsburg," the site of the deadly May 1902 "Pittsburg riot" involving African American Will Richardson, the police, and white citizens. The Peters Street rioters seemed to consider the "Pittsburg riot" a defeat that whites needed to avenge. Having taken knives, pistols, one gun, and a large hammer from Smithers's pawn shop, they took ammunition, five rifles, two shotguns, and six or seven pistols from the hardware store.

By all accounts, machinist J. W. Briggs challenged his fellow rioters not to vandalize a white business, but the mob reacted so severely that rioter C. N. Walker had to rescue Briggs. Three police officers were attempting to restore order when "a negro [Milton Brown] emerged from Castleberry Street." Brown tried to run, but twenty steps later "a fusilade [*sic*] of forty or fifty bullets" brought Brown's flight "to a sudden halt." He died at Grady Hospital from head and torso wounds. His sudden appearance had diverted the mob from confronting a black community instead of solitary individuals.[28]

Governor-elect Hoke Smith did not join local efforts to quell the riot. At 12:10 a.m., Smith was waiting at the new railroad Terminal Station to meet a friend. By the time Smith returned to his horse-drawn cab fifteen minutes later, the black driver had disappeared. Soon Police Chief Jennings, accompanied by a squad of mounted officers, "rode through" the lobby "and out to the floor over the train shed," driving all before them and arresting six men, possibly including Smith's cab driver.[29]

The mob that moved toward the Forsyth Street viaduct fired at a black man. As the man left the bridge, "a man stepped from the shadow ... came down upon the negro's skull with a club, the sound of contact being heard for a block. The black man dropped like a shot." Subsequently, "two or three members of the mob standing directly over the body ... [poured] the contents of their revolvers into it."[30]

The mob was substantially young and lower class, but storeowners, businessmen, students, craftsmen, and white-collar workers helped to assault blacks. As a Southern Railway official put it, "members of the best families" rioted. Dr. R. R. Kline contended that "respectable saloons" and lower-class dives alike were rallying points for white rioters. "Hundreds of witnesses watched" a few white men stab two African Americans in front of the Piedmont Hotel. Arthur Hoffman, a visiting white minstrel employed by Field's Minstrel Show, saw well-dressed men, women, and children offer their support for the attacks upon black Atlantans. Elite white men joined the rioters and later returned to the sidewalk. To amuse the sidewalk spectators, trapped blacks were given "a five yard start," then chased by men with knives and clubs.[31]

Some whites with long-established relationships to black employees protected their deferential and reliable black workers. Because the riot in part was an attempt to restore black deference in place of black autonomy, businessmen were inclined to defend their "steady" black workers in a paternalistic, or even possessive, way. J. D. Belsa of the Bijou Theater reached his baggagemen at about the same moment as the rioters. Locking his charges in a safe place, he stood guard over them with a shotgun for the rest of Saturday night. The owner of the largest downtown stable saved two black assistants by standing before the mob with a shotgun and "great presence of mind." On Marietta Street, the white driver of an undertaker's barouche drove through the mob with three blacks in the back, almost running over Walter White and his father. Presumably after walking home, Hoke Smith, who employed whites at the Piedmont, also saved "his negroes," Ray Stannard Baker reported. Other whites, especially women, gave "their negroes" weapons, but armed black men did not live long in riot-torn Atlanta.[32]

Those African Americans who armed themselves did survive the riot better within black neighborhoods. Some cases of resistance can be reconstructed from the fines levied by local authorities. At least sixty-eight blacks, including six women, were arrested for what the courts would define after the violence as "rioting." Jane Simon was fined twenty-five dollars for "flourishing a pistol." A young female "firebrand" had paraded on Cain Street, inciting black men to avenge the race. Another woman served time in jail "for helping a male friend organize" a resistance group.[33]

In one of the more densely populated black areas, shots were fired into the Inman Park streetcar near the intersection of Butler Street and Edgewood Avenue as it returned to Atlanta from the suburbs filled with white passengers around midnight. No one suffered any injuries. Eleven men of Georgia's militia apprehended "the whole bunch of seventeen" black alleged assailants, some of whom "talked impudently." Other African Americans "hidden from view" fired into additional streetcars, making Edgewood Avenue the focus of black retaliation. At Whiteford Avenue and McClendon Street, blacks also rocked and waylaid the streetcar. On a motorman's complaint of gunfire, police surrounded a residence at Edgewood Avenue and Fort Street and captured nine blacks but found no guns or ammunition.[34]

While blacks openly defended themselves in their own neighborhoods, those completing their shifts at work were exposed to white rage on the way home. The *Atlanta Constitution* proudly illustrated how the power of the paper's reputation protected its black delivery boys. Western Union messengers lived to work another day. In contrast, African Americans who "fled to the post office for protection believing themselves safe on federal property" were killed. Just seventeen days earlier, the reformers had publicly proclaimed at the state Democratic nominating convention that whites no longer need fear federal protection of black rights. In this sense, the riot was the implementation of Southern Progressive reform.[35]

On Saturday night, Henry A. Rucker, collector of internal revenue for Georgia since 1897, moved with his son into the old post office at the corner of Marietta and Forsyth streets, where he had an office. The female members of the family remained at the Ruckers' Piedmont Street home. The Ruckers lived in a predominantly Jewish neighborhood with an interspersion of native white southerners and German immigrants. These white Atlantans did not participate in the riot nor did they take any action to aid Annie Eunice Rucker or the two other black families in the neighborhood bracketed by Piedmont and Houston streets and Auburn Avenue, two blocks north of "Darktown" (map 8.3). Henry Rucker went home to gather his family on Sunday, when the riot partially abated. He took them by train to Macon, Georgia, his wife's hometown, where they arrived in the middle of Macon's violent streetcar strike but encountered no further difficulties. Rucker immediately returned to Atlanta, and his family spent a week in Macon waiting out the riot.[36]

Another segment of black Atlanta remained outside the riot area. Kathleen Redding Adams recalled hearing shots around 11 p.m. Saturday. But accustomed to hearing loud commotions every Saturday night, Adams remembered the riot as no more than the usual disturbances. She consequently believed the historical legacy of the riot was exaggerated. Her father, Wesley C. Redding, also noted the sound of gunfire Saturday night but remained totally unaware of the riot until Sunday morning following worship services at First Congregational Church.[37]

According to arrest records and newspaper accounts, the white rioters were clerks, bookkeepers, common laborers, factory operatives, a fireman, skilled craftsmen, a soldier in the Seventeenth Regiment, boarders, and three juveniles. These men overwhelmed the police and ignored white authority. They killed at least twenty-five respectable African American working people and up to ten more black victims mentioned in contested newspaper reports. Most of the black fatalities were in downtown Atlanta.

White rage was focused upon three public areas where blacks and whites interacted as equals on streetcars and in the two entertainment districts on Decatur and Peters streets. Overall, white rioters destroyed an unreported amount of property. Barbershops, a major form of black business enterprise and a symbol of black political power, were singled out by the mob.

Only one white fatality was reported. He was killed by a black man at the Seaboard Airline freight depot. Thus, with minimal loss of life, white men had used "revolutionary reform" to drive "the Negroes off the street." Their victory bell was the riot bell that summoned the all-white Georgia state militia not to quell white anger but to prevent a black counterrevolution on Sunday, September 23, 1906.[38]

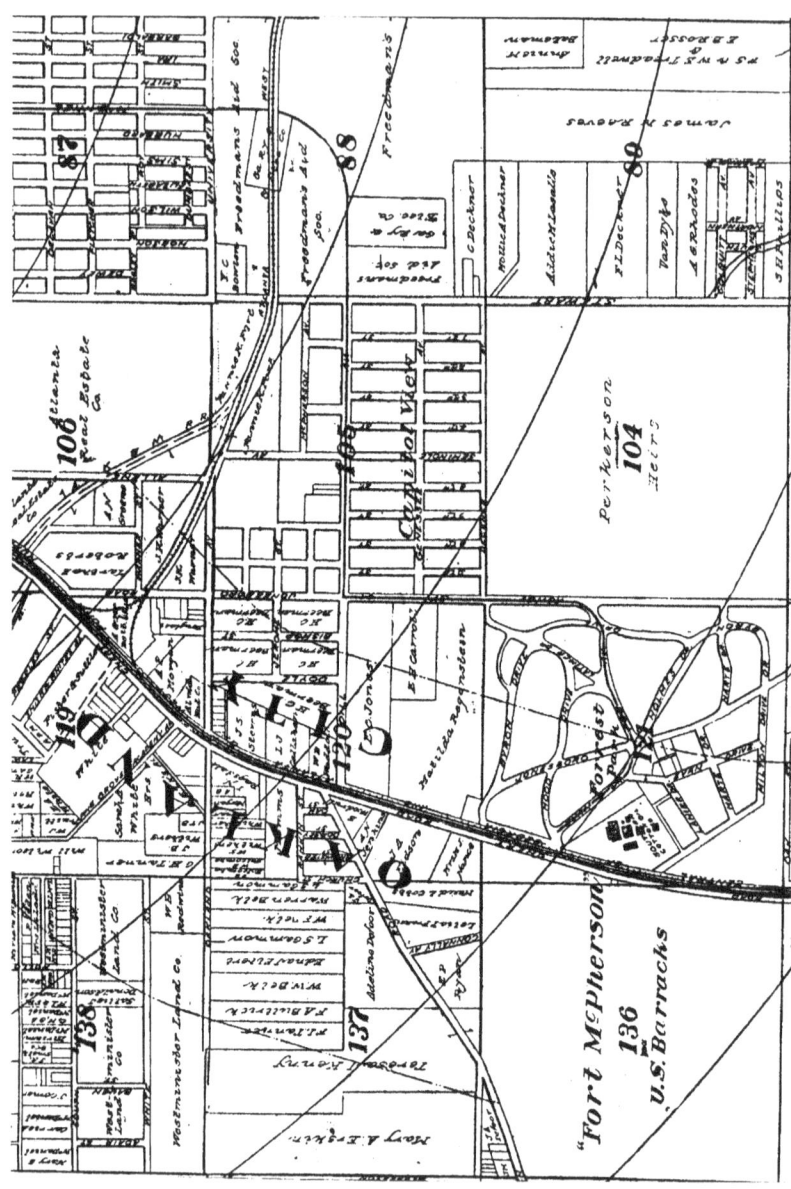

Map 7.1. Knowles Kimmel resided with her husband, John, on an isolated suburban farm in Oakland City, "a mile beyond the end of the streetcar line" (120). After her encounter with a black stranger on Thursday, September 20, infuriated mobs captured several black men. But either Kimmel could not identify them as her assailant or the captives were rescued by their employers or law enforcement officers before they could be lynched. No one was charged with the assault. Governor Joseph Terrell ordered three state militia companies to report to Fort McPherson. (Map by O. F. Kauffman, C.E., Atlanta, 1905, courtesy Georgia Archives, Atlanta.)

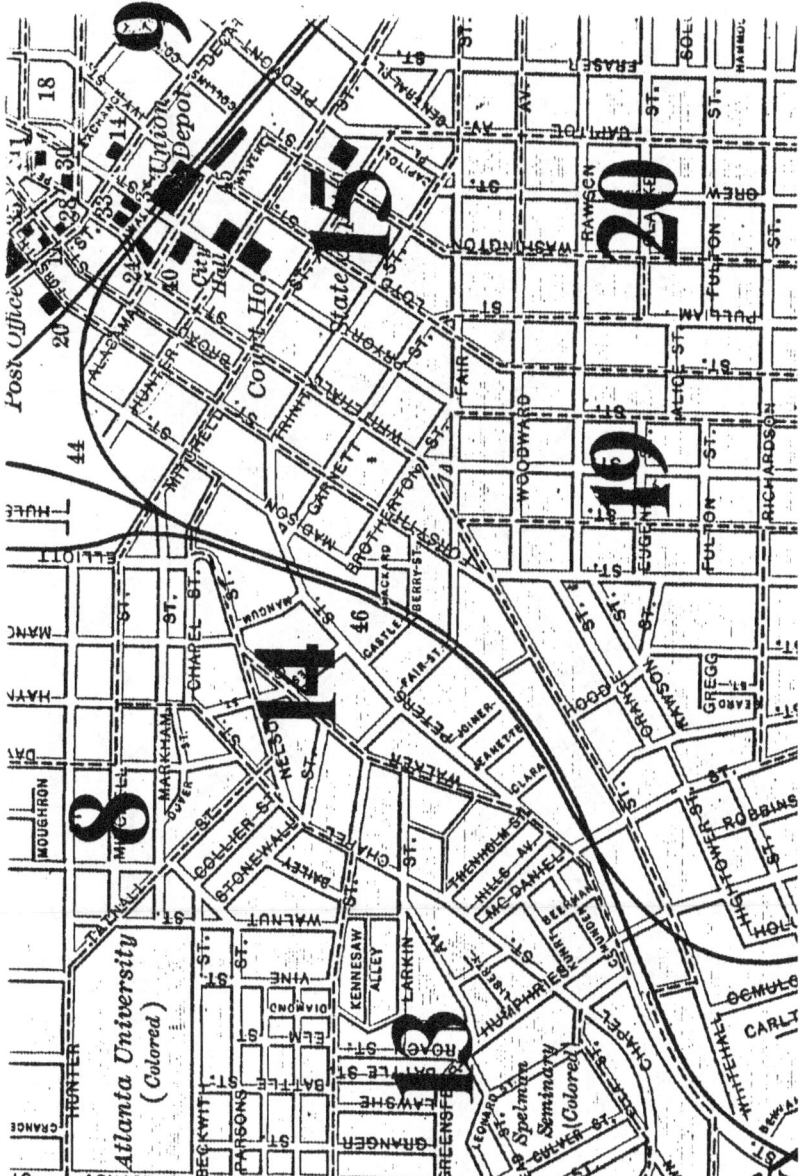

Map 7.2. On Saturday night, a mob progressed down Pryor Street (9, 15), up Alabama Street one block, down Whitehall Street and past Madison Avenue to the Peters Street entertainment zone (14). George Blackstock led the assault on Mattie Adams's restaurant at the intersection of Fair Street and Peters. The mob then looted the Pearson and McCarley hardware store at the corner of Peters and Walker Street. At Castleberry Street (14), Milton Brown died of forty or fifty gunshot wounds to the head and torso. A Macon militia company relieved Atlanta militiamen patrolling Spelman Seminary, Atlanta Baptist College, and Atlanta University (13). Soldiers also protected a brewery at the intersection of Peters and Walker. (Atlanta City Map 1902, courtesy Georgia Archives, Atlanta.)

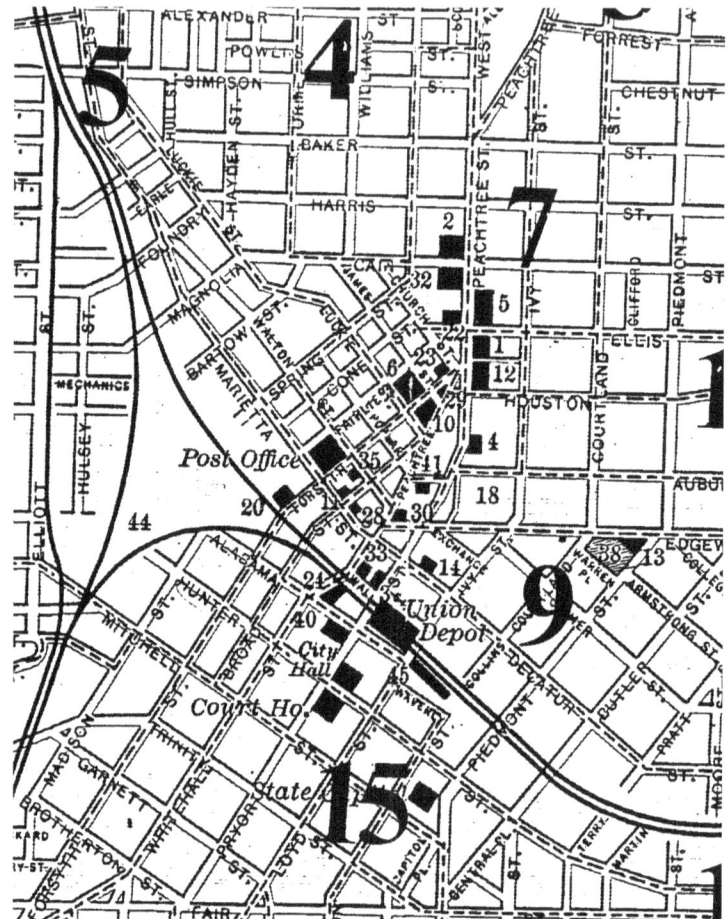

Map 7.3. Luther Frazier, "a sinister looking negro 21 years of age attempted a brutal attack" upon Orrie Bryan on Friday night, September 21. Frazier was apprehended by neighbors soon after he broke into Bryan's home at 232 Courtland Street (between 7 and 9 on map). At 6 p.m. Saturday, whites gathered along Peachtree and Decatur in downtown Atlanta (33). By 8:30 p.m., there was "much angry shouting about 'vengeance' on the [black] rapist," and rioting began minutes later. Mayor Woodward and former police commissioner James W. English sought to defuse tensions in front of the Piedmont Hotel (30), but 100 men and boys marched down Decatur. They assaulted a black bicycle messenger and chased blacks along Decatur and Pryor streets and Central Avenue. Woodward opened the general alarm box at Decatur and Ivy (14). The Atlanta Fire Department turned fire hoses on white rioters at Marietta and Peachtree, prompting the mob to retreat down Edgewood and Pryor. Fire Chief W. R. Joyner ordered the hosing of several hundred blacks at Ivy Street (14) and herded them "like cattle up Decatur Street into the open plaza" at Marietta, Peachtree, Edgewood, and Decatur streets (33). At Central Avenue just off Decatur (9), Atlanta police protected a skating rink that "housed probably five hundred negroes." Captain William Mayo and twelve police officers kept the mob in check at Decatur and Pryor (33). Officer Carson saved a black streetcar patron along Peachtree Street near Piedmont Hotel as the mob headed toward Auburn Avenue (41). G. C. Tomlinson was "badly cut by a negro" on Decatur below Pryor Street (33). At Union Station (3), a mob pulled a dozen black porters off their trains and chased them down the tracks, killing three. (Atlanta City Map 1902, courtesy Georgia Archives, Atlanta.)

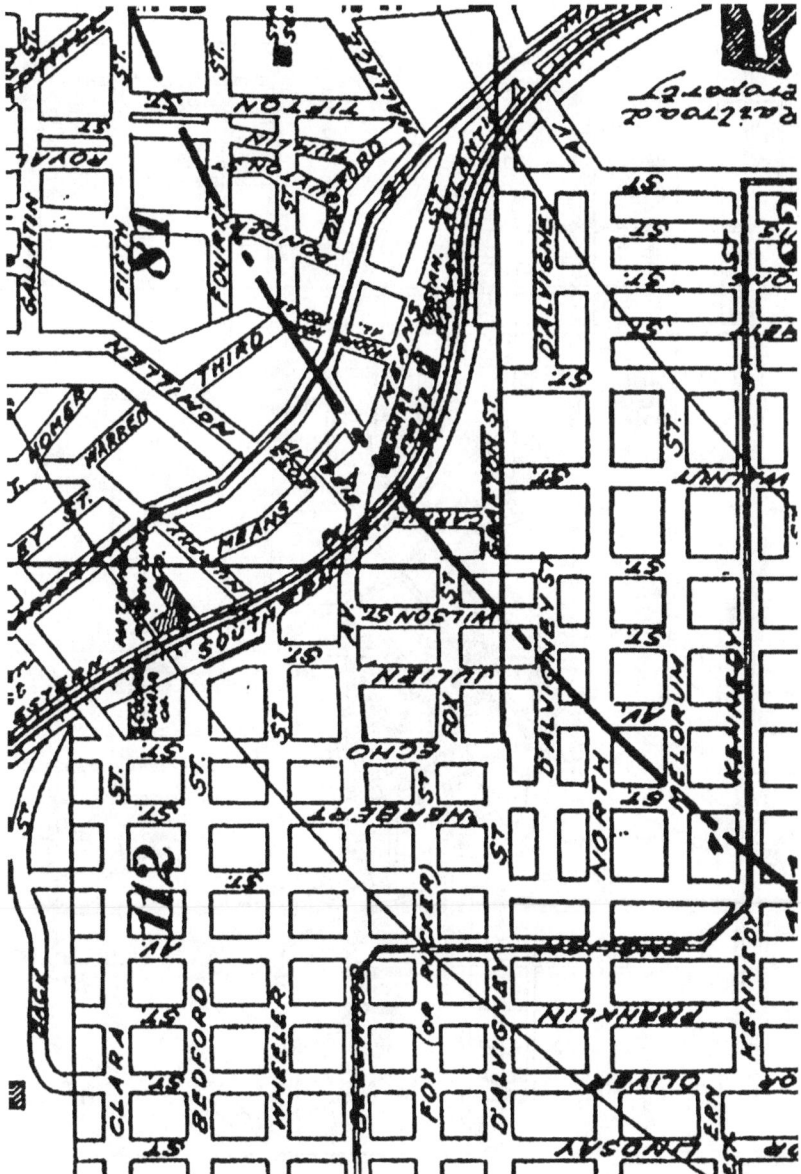

Map 7.4. The home of Mrs. Mattie (Frank) Arnold, "assault" victim, at 127 Julien or Julian (112). A. C. Moore, Georgia Railway and Electric Company lineman, was "shot [and wounded] by a negro at the junction of Bellwood Avenue and the Southern Railway yards" (112). Jim Middlebrooks and Luther McGhee, black residents of West North Street in the Bellwood section, were pelted and beaten by Fulton County sheriff John W. Nelms's "elite deputies," who formed a "posse." See North Street south of Julien Street. (Map by O. F. Kauffman, C.E., Atlanta, 1906, courtesy Georgia Archives, Atlanta).

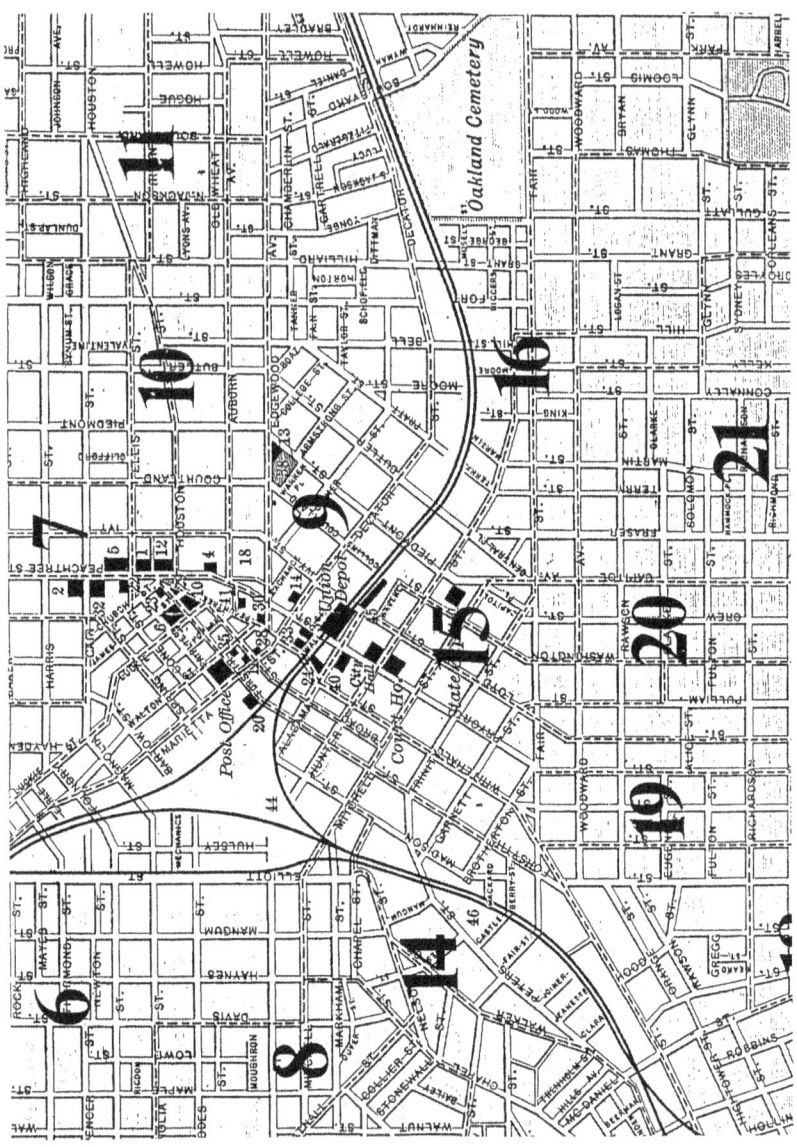

Map 7.5. White rioters boarded streetcars near the post office on Saturday night, dragging black passengers through shattered windows and murdering them. Blacks threw rocks and fired guns at streetcars on the Edgewood Avenue and Lloyd Street lines (9 and 15) as well as on Auburn Avenue (10) and in the Pittsburg community (14, 15, 19). A young woman paraded along Cain Street (7), inciting black men to avenge their race. (Atlanta City Map 1902, courtesy Georgia Archives, Atlanta.)

8

"Off the Streets"

> For the first time in the history of Atlanta, the two riot calls
> on the fire bell were rung. . . . About 11 o'clock . . . it was decided
> to summon every police man. . . . Shortly after 12 o'clock fifteen taps
> were sounded on the fire bell. That was a call for the military.
>
> *Atlanta Constitution,* September 23, 1906

White members of the Georgia militia responded to the "fifteen taps . . . on the fire bell" shortly after midnight on September 23, 1906. Georgia had disbanded its black militia companies over a year earlier.[1] Although trained to combat "riots," Georgia's state militia was mobilized in anticipation that African Americans would counter white violence with violence. City Court Judge Andy E. Calhoun, who fifteen years earlier had upheld streetcar segregation in Atlanta, made the requisite official request for militia assistance.[2]

Although the governor's mansion was located in the downtown district, lame-duck governor Joseph Terrell was oblivious to the riot until 11 p.m., when a representative of the *Atlanta Constitution* informed him. Terrell's chief of staff, Colonel James W. English Jr., was on a two-month European vacation. Not awakened until white rioters already had overwhelmed the police, attacked streetcars, destroyed private property, and killed nearly thirty African Americans, Terrell drafted a proclamation giving the Georgia militia immediate blanket authority.[3] But unnamed prominent citizens drew the line against martial law. The ensuing debate delayed the governor's mobilization of the militia for forty minutes.[4]

This chapter examines the Atlanta riot's second and third days, Monday and Tuesday, September 23 and 24, and the end of the riot on September 25. After some units of the Georgia militia mobilized on Sunday to join the "war" against blacks, on both Sunday and Monday Atlanta's white newspapers and militiamen assured whites that they controlled Atlanta's streets and that blacks had been conclusively subdued by white power. Testing and proving this assertion, bands of white men invaded black neighborhoods Sunday and Monday. The commercial-civic elite also organized to end the violence and take over responsibility for Atlanta's governance from the city's municipal authorities.

A second riot call was sounded Sunday at 12:20 a.m. as Colonel Clifford L. Anderson renewed his efforts to contact the Fifth Infantry Regiment's staff, infantry, cavalry, and artillery units. At least one militiaman, Dr. W. A. Jackson, encountered what the white press characterized as "a band of negroes" as he made his way from his home on Forest Avenue for the one-block walk to his neighborhood armory and returned home, dazed.[5] Heavy rain between 2 and 3 a.m. Sunday further delayed deployment but did the police and militia's work of dispersing 10,000 white rioters. Anderson preferred to credit the militia's reputation. The full regiment of 600 men, mostly infantry and single companies of artillery and cavalry, was prepared to confront the riot late Sunday morning.[6]

With the primary purpose of protecting white people from black retaliation, the mobilized troops joined not only the Atlanta and Fulton County police, armed with Winchester rifles, but also armed white civilians. The militia's leadership declared as early as Sunday that the riot had achieved its goal of "terrorizing" blacks and convincing them to submit or "be severely punished." The militia pledged to protect "good" African Americans "so long as they conduct themselves properly."[7]

Sunday morning, Atlanta's whites were the ones not behaving properly, even toward the all-white state soldiers. Atlantan A. J. McKelway reported that at 10:30 a.m. militiamen near the Piedmont Hotel "were rushed upon . . . hissed at spat on and hustled from one side of the street to the other" by "menacing jeering thousands" at whom they leveled their guns. With howling voices, the mob of "men and boys" reassembled and marched up Peachtree Street. Men who had remained in Atlanta's central business district Saturday night joined the "formidable though leaderless band." Back at the hotel, someone proposed entering to lynch black waiters. The militia stepped in to protect the governor's private property just as members of the mob were diverted by the chance to pursue, stone, and club two black men.[8]

Colonel Anderson requested reinforcements at 11 a.m., and Governor Terrell agreed, contacting Marietta, Cedartown, Rome, Lindale, Griffin, and Macon for 200 more militiamen. The full force of eighteen infantry companies, an artillery battery, and a troop of cavalry came together at midnight.

Anderson had called Colonel Walter Harris, primary officer in charge of the Second Infantry National Guard of Georgia in Macon at 12:40 p.m., and Harris's three companies had assembled from church or work by 2:30. Before they departed, however, the mayor demanded that one company remain in Macon because of an ongoing streetcar strike. Convincing them to stay was not easy, so Harris had the company captains "draw lots."[9] Bitterly disappointed, the officers left behind with the losing company felt their personal honor was being jeopardized. Some believed that suppressing blacks overrode military discipline, and they left for Atlanta on their own, without authorization.[10]

Macon's companies were ready to serve Colonel Anderson by 9 p.m. They kept "the crowd moving along Peachtree and Whitehall streets up to the viaduct." Some also patrolled the area from the Aragon Hotel to the State House and Governor's Mansion, and others patrolled Spelman Seminary, Atlanta Baptist College, and Atlanta University, as well as Peters and Walker Streets and the area near Pittsburg.

Militia deployment around the colleges and especially around Pittsburg, scene of the 1902 "riot," reflected white fears of armed black resistance. One of many rumors suggested "that the negroes were forming a military company and arming at Pittsburg for an advance upon the soldiers of the city." The assertion proved erroneous, as "the negroes in the vicinity . . . were all closely locked in their houses." Just to be sure, the white militia and 300 police officers armed with Winchester rifles shot at black Atlantans who ventured out on Sunday. According to even Atlanta's white newspapers, "[w]henever a negro happened to pass along the streets," white authorities "pounced" on that person and "woe betide the negro if he carried a pistol or dirk for he was summarily rushed off to prison and locked up."[11] Although there never were any signs of an organized, violent black response, the militia obviously had been called out to alleviate white fears of uncontrollable black violence.[12]

Meanwhile, whites on Atlanta's periphery complained about Colonel Anderson's tactical decisions. They argued that militiamen were "bunch[ed] too much" in the central city. The "real danger" was in suburban Atlanta, where black "assaults" on white women allegedly had occurred before the riot.

Shortly before 6 p.m. Sunday, Governor Terrell ordered Adjutant Burton Smith, Hoke Smith's brother, to tell Anderson "to spread the troops over the city." Anderson then found himself besieged "on all sides by citizens" across Fulton County pleading for troops or the "authority to secure ammunition" themselves. As did these civilians, the colonel believed violence would only end when "negroes ... stop their attacks" and "act accordingly."[13]

Sunday, Atlanta police officers rounded up what the *Constitution* called "practically all the vagrants in Atlanta." The police concentrated on those who patronized "negro dives," which were "the source" of black crime and "assaults" upon white women. Late Sunday afternoon, Mayor James G. Woodward closed all businesses selling alcoholic beverages. In addition, Colonel Anderson tried to persuade the newspapers to stop publishing "extra editions."[14]

Sheriff John W. Nelms, a resident of Atlanta's elite suburban West End, claimed deliberately severed telephone wires prevented him from learning about the riot until past midnight. On Sunday, Nelms joined the effort to control blacks by deputizing the "leading business and professional [white] men" of Fulton County against "negroes ... in a mighty ugly humor."[15]

Some of Nelms's new elite "deputies" formed a "posse." Seeking the African Americans suspected of attacking white women before the riot, they captured a man accused of the attempted assault on Mrs. Mattie Arnold at 127 Julian Street in Atlanta's racially mixed Bellwood section. The black prisoner, however, diverted the buggy transporting him into the path of a streetcar and, after the collision, escaped back into Bellwood. Another group of deputies beat and pelted two black male residents of West North Avenue with an umbrella and a thrown object.[16]

Not every white neighborhood believed the riot to have been an instant success in removing blacks from the streets. Five-year-old Margaret Mitchell, the future author of *Gone with the Wind,* lived on Jackson Street, a mile from downtown's rioting. There, future governor John Slaton advised his anxious neighbors to arm and prepare for black retaliation. Mitchell's father, Eugene, who did not own a gun, secured an ax and a heavy water key to guard his family until they saw Georgia's militia "march up the street."[17]

Despite attacks on isolated blacks and sounds of "musketry,"[18] the "presence of the military" generally provided whites with "a sense of security." According to the *Atlanta Constitution,* white people who rioted Saturday night returned to Atlanta's streets Sunday afternoon as "law-abiding citizens." They "laughed and chatted," finally freed from the plague of "too many negroes crowding into the trolley cars on Sundays." On the other hand, black cab drivers "declined to take any chances" on Atlanta's streets, messenger services lacked black bicyclists, whites had "no negro boys to carry their grips," and restaurants with no cooks had to serve "cold breakfasts."[19]

African Americans did not retaliate with massive violence as whites feared, but immediately challenged white control with work stoppages that lasted until whites guaranteed them a safe environment.[20] At the same time, the limited use of violence reinforced the "strike." For instance, getting to work on time was hindered because white streetcar motormen and conductors on lines traversing such black communities as Pittsburg, Auburn Avenue, and Houston Street feared to complete their routes. Transit company superintendent Joel Hurt reported African Americans fired into streetcars on Auburn Avenue and stones were thrown on other routes. At 8:30 p.m. the Magnolia Street car was shot at by "an unknown negro." Conductor C. L. Donaldson was wounded. Another white transit employee charged two fired black employees burned his home with kerosene Sunday evening, causing $500 in damages.[21] Atlanta's police arrested three black men carrying "concealed weapons" on Sunday night. In suburban East Pointe, an African American who boasted that he was armed was arrested by the police but kidnapped and lynched by a "posse" late Sunday night.[22]

Before the militia was called up, white rioters hesitated to confront concentrated groups of African Americans, but during the second and third nights of rioting, white mobs invaded the black neighborhoods of Darktown, Auburn Avenue, and suburban South Atlanta. There blacks were mobilized to defend their homes. Sunday, on Auburn Avenue African Americans attacked the streetcars traversing what was about to become the new black central business district. That same night, white rioters made their presence felt. The family of Kathleen Redding Adams had been completely isolated from the first night's violence, but on Sunday night, Adams recalled, white textile workers marched three abreast along Auburn Avenue with scowls on their faces to intimidate blacks sitting on their porches.[23] Postal clerk John Wesley Dobbs was armed with his federally issued Colt revolver to defend the home he had just purchased that summer at 446 Auburn Avenue. He watched the white mill hands march past by "torch light." He would live for years with guns and ammunition at the ready in case of another white assault upon black Atlanta.[24]

The family of thirteen-year-old Walter White, the future leader of the National Association for the Advancement of Colored People, lived in Darktown. Saturday night, "white skinned" blacks including the men in Walter White's family, had used their "mask of invisibility" to purchase weapons and ammunition. They were able to move through the riot district, helplessly watching the mob chase, club, and kill a lone bootblack but rescuing a black female cook from the mob between Marietta Street and Five Points in downtown Atlanta.[25]

Sunday night, as a mob moved toward the home his family owned, the very light skinned Walter came to understand his identity: "I was a Negro, a human being with an invisible pigmentation which marked me a person to be hunted, hanged, abused, discriminated against, kept in poverty and ignorance." He was pursued so "that those whose skin was white would have readily at hand a proof of their superiority, a proof patent and inclusive, accessible to the moron and the idiot as well as to the wise man and genius." It allowed any white man, regardless of circumstance, to "hold fast to the smug conviction that he was superior to two-thirds of the world's population. For those two-thirds were not white."[26]

A white boy with skin no lighter than White's led the mob. He was the son of a grocer with whom White's family had traded for years, but he screamed, "That's where the nigger mail carrier lives! Let's burn it down! It's too nice for a nigger to live in!" White and his father took aim, as he "wonder[ed] what it would feel like to kill a man." Before White completed the thought, however, "a volley of shots," fired by friends of White's father from a nearby two-story brick building, stopped the mob in its tracks. When another volley caused the mob to retreat up Houston Street, White was relieved that he was not "one of those made sick and murderous by pride" and that African Americans had an "opportunity to write a record of virtue as a memorandum to Armageddon."[27]

Walter White's sister, later Mrs. Eugene M. Martin, was seven or eight years old when her brother and father guarded their two-story home against the white rioters. She recalled hearing, "Let's get that White nigger" as they "came down Houston Street and started in our gate." Although Walter White remembered that black neighbors dispersed the rioters with gunfire, his sister recalled the kind of distraction that sometimes occurred in Saturday night's violence. A solitary black victim, driving an ice wagon, inadvertently attracted the mob's attention. Pursued by the mob, he hid under a nearby house all night. Martin's recollection, though it differed from her brother's, concurred in refuting white newspaper accounts of a "quiet" day.[28]

Also on Sunday, Colonel Anderson assigned Atlanta militiamen to the west side, where black faculty and staff guarded Spelman College, Atlanta Baptist College, and Atlanta University. No students were present because of summer recess, but John Hope, Atlanta Baptist's first black president, patrolled the campus armed and recognized faces from the previous night's mob among the militiamen. Challenged by one of the troops, Hope stepped forward with his hands raised, disarming the militiaman with a smile and an invitation for a cup of coffee in Hope's home, which the guardsman accepted.[29]

Unlike Hope, Rev. H. H. Proctor and Dr. W.E.B. Du Bois were both out of town, but their families still were in Atlanta. A mob entered the yard of First Congregational Church and looked through the windows while Proctor's children peeked out of the shuttered parsonage at the entire scene. No one there or belonging to that congregation was hurt throughout the riot. Du Bois returned from a research trip to Alabama after Sunday's violence. Having written the famous "Litany of Atlanta," a condemnation of the riot and the city, he joined colleagues in armed protection of the Atlanta University campus and his family.[30]

On Atlanta's periphery, in Summerhill, blacks organized near the local school to detain and search whites entering the area. Determining that white insurance collector Ed Schloss carried no weapons, blacks allowed him to proceed, but the *Constitution* claimed that a "big burly negro" took offense at his comments, cornered him, and pounded him before one of a "shower of stones" hit Schloss in the head. Hiram Myers, collecting payments for a Mitchell Street furniture store, experienced a similar frisking but no beating as he did not respond impudently when asked his purpose in Summerhill. In the Fourth Ward, a quartet of African Americans "attacked two white men" and "ran two white women from their homes." Monday night, on McDonald Road fourteen members of a white family named Hicks were driven from the community under gunfire.[31]

The story was different in South Atlanta's upper-class African American suburb of Brownsville, home of Gammon Theological Seminary and Clark College. On Sunday night, Gammon president John Wesley Edward Bowen pleaded with Atlanta authorities for militia and police protection. His request was ignored, although Bowen had been cooperative with white Atlanta's leaders and there were no saloons or dives in the community. Journalist Ray Stannard Baker characterized the residents as "industrious" with "the best reputation among white people who know them." Despite their reputable image, however, Brownsville residents did not get along well with their white neighbors across Lakewood Park in South Atlanta as whites unsuccessfully attempted to prevent them from using the park and swimming in its lake.[32] Consequently, when the riot began, African Americans organized to defend themselves, led by South Atlanta's postmaster and storeowner L. J. Price, who distributed his weapons collection and ammunition. Monday night, both Gammon Theological Seminary and Clark College, patrolled by armed blacks, opened their doors to the Brownsville population. Mrs. Ruby Owens, a young wife and mother, remembered that men were stationed on one side of the street and women on the other to warn against white invaders.[33]

As Brownsville residents took refuge on the campuses, the white newspapers endorsed the overall result of violence: Atlanta's streets were cleared of blacks. On Sunday, the *Atlanta News* had extolled the riot itself as a "just war" to force blacks to "remain at their homes and be quiet," and the next day, while three of the four white papers appealed for the restoration of law and order, the *News* continued its quest to eclipse them as the dominant evening paper and Atlanta civic leader.

The *Atlanta Constitution* said that whites were beginning to view the violence as "deplorable," so "clear headed" citizens needed to lead the city into the care of "the strongest best elements of Anglo-Saxonism." The *Atlanta Journal* wanted a return to stability with black bellboys and porters back at their posts, urging in its headline "Get Back to Business." The *Atlanta Georgian* counseled legal authorities to retake control of the city. In that spirit, the Recorder's Court started to levy fines on white rioters, including mob leader T. F. Clements, who received thirty days and a fine for "intent to murder and ... rioting."[34]

Public opposition to the *News* also began to emerge on Monday. The *Journal* blamed its afternoon rival for igniting the riot with inflammatory editorials and extra editions. Attorney Aldine Chambers observed that the "Atlanta News is being almost universally censured here," especially "for the trouble ... Saturday night." Even the grand jury condemned the *News* as it lost the approval of Atlanta's leaders when the violence waned Monday.[35]

Monday, the *Constitution* claimed, was not a typical "Blue Monday" when as many as 1,500 African Americans idled "half-drunk" in Decatur Street dives. Now there were "only eight negroes" on Decatur Street and the "same wonderful metamorphosis" on Peters Street.[36]

Constabulary authorities reinforced the idea that whites were at last safe from black crime by returning to legally recognizable methods. The grand jury presented "true bills" charging Robert Branham with "assaults" upon Mabel and Ethel Lawrence in the Copenhill area August 20, 1906, and Luther Frazier for entering Thomas L. Bryan's home to attack his daughter, Orrie, on September 20. Sheriff Nelms also continued deputizing prominent white citizens, 150 in the West End alone.[37] The *Constitution* incorrectly announced that "Federal Troops [Were] Ready to Help" prevent black retaliation. They would report to Georgia militia commander Clifford L. Anderson and so be under state control, the erroneous *Constitution* article reassured white Atlantans.[38] In fact, as the *Georgian* reported, the troops had been marching back to Fort McPherson from training in Tennessee since September 13 and were en route to Cuba.[39]

Dr. A. R. Holderby, pastor of Moore Memorial Presbyterian Church, voiced the consensus of the white clergy that the riot had been inevitable because of "the weakness of the law" which "does not protect the people," specifically "wives and daughters and sisters." Pastor John E. White from Second Baptist Church, Bishop Kelley from Sacred Heart Roman Catholic Cathedral, and Dr. W. W. Landrum from First Baptist Church all condemned the riot but as the final stage in a collapse of law and order. Other ministers also asserted that the riot was preordained, but they blamed the white leadership and newspapers as well as the legal system for a collective failure. According to Rev. A. C. Ward from Temple Baptist, the experience showed that racial segregation was the only answer.[40]

Events on Monday evening and Tuesday morning brought the riot to a conclusion in South Atlanta, where Brownsville's blacks had been bracing for white violence all weekend. On a tip from unnamed informants, Fulton County police, supported by armed local white citizens, marched into Brownsville and "began arresting negroes for being armed." The white forces captured Sam McGruder and Wiley Brooks and herded them onto a streetcar. Left behind, one unit of five white men "was ambushed," including Fulton County policeman James Heard, son of North Fulton County Judge John S. Heard. In the ensuing gun battle, glorified by the white press, Heard and twelve African Americans were killed, and four whites were wounded. The *News* accused Gammon president Bowen of luring the police into the ambush by requesting their protection. All denials were futile.[41] Before word of any ambush could have spread, a mob at Jefferson and Crew streets pulled Brooks and McGruder from the streetcar and shot them to death on the front porch of Park Commissioner R. Manley's home. Mrs. Robert P. Thompson, a neighbor who witnessed the episode, died instantly of heart failure, the third white casualty of the riot.[42]

Heard's death forced Colonel Anderson to mobilize a segment of the militia Monday night to protect white people after Monday's calm was disrupted by "a conflict between a band of negroes and a squad of county policemen." This statement from Anderson's official report did not mention that armed white citizens were in Brownsville accompanying the police.[43] Neither did Anderson report that the police and their "deputies" assisted the cavalry troops he sent to invade Brownsville Tuesday morning.

Members of the reinforced military unit searched every black home in Brownsville. Facing the combined armed might of the militia, Fulton County police, white citizens, and even a Gatling gun with 1,000 rounds of ammunition, Brownsville's nearly 300 black men and boys could not resist white efforts to take them to Atlanta's stockade. Mrs. Ruby Owens saved her husband from capture by hiding his pistol and disguising him as a woman, but Mr. Owens's brother, along with Postmaster L. J. Price and most of the other adult black males of Brownsville, went to jail in Atlanta. Individuals "found with guns, razors and pistols" were immediately placed on waiting streetcars. The unarmed were forced to sit on the ground.[44]

During the house-to-house search, more white violence occurred. Fulton County police found a black man in bed named Lewis, who had been "badly wounded the night before." They "opened his shirt, place[d] their revolvers at his breast, and in cold blood shot him through the body several times in the presence of his relatives." Left for dead, "he . . . recovered." One officer hit John W. E. Bowen "over the head . . . with his rifle butt." Sixty of the 100 black men arrested during the Brownsville raids, Ray Stannard Baker reported, were "charged with the murder of Officer Heard." At least five more black men were killed in the raids.[45]

Elsewhere in Atlanta Tuesday morning, white police officers and blacks exchanged shots at the intersection of MacGruder and Randolph streets. Although the three patrolmen were "ambushed," the press claimed, they killed two of the three blacks who had been "shooting at passing white citizens." The *News* announced, "5 Blacks Dead for Sure; 12 Believed Killed."[46]

As the incidents continued on Tuesday, Sheriff Nelms also continued recruiting new deputies from the ranks of the "prominent and conservative." Having petitioned Governor Terrell, Nelms had received assurances that his needs for weaponry would be met. As a result, Nelms swore in 300 additional deputies to "visit every negro section and arrest negroes found armed." The *Atlanta Journal* characterized his actions on Tuesday as "one of the wisest moves that could be made by the authorities." When Nelms attempted a mass deputizing of 1,000 more white men on Tuesday, however, Mayor Woodward and Captain English told the crowd to go home, for they now sought to end the violence.[47] Whatever the extent of his ambitions had been, Nelms quickly withdrew, leaving English to rule Atlanta as the chairman of the Committee of Ten, the new government of Atlanta that directed the postriot reconstruction.

The three-day riot ended Tuesday, September 25, 1906. It had claimed between twenty-six and forty-seven black lives, by varying newspaper estimates. A united front of white people—the military, police, press, commercial-civic elite, and working classes—had utilized the violence to drive African Americans from Atlanta's streets. But after the violent "revolution," this white solidarity splintered. Segregation then affirmed the commercial-civic elite's rule over everyone else.

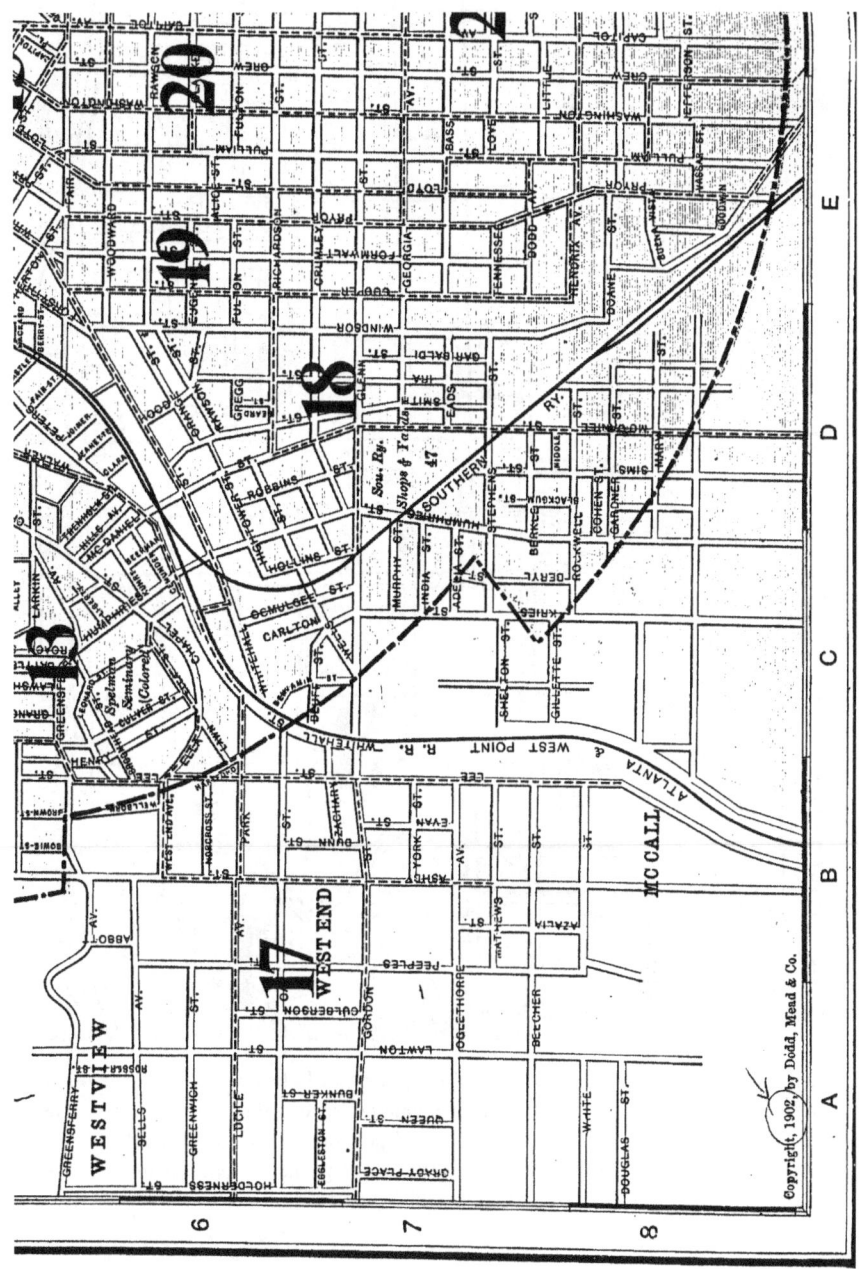

Map 8.1. Sheriff John W. Nelms deputized the "leading business and professional men," 150 in the West End alone (17). (Atlanta City Map 1902, courtesy Georgia Archives, Atlanta.)

Map 8.2. On Saturday evening, Martha Holcombe screamed when she "saw a Negro" on the sidewalk outside her home at 275 Magnolia. One hour later, Alma Allen reportedly was "grabbed" briefly as she washed her hands on a dark porch at 182 Davis Street. Shots were fired into streetcars at 8:30 p.m. Sunday at the intersection of Magnolia and Vine. (Atlanta City Map 1902, courtesy Georgia Archives, Atlanta.)

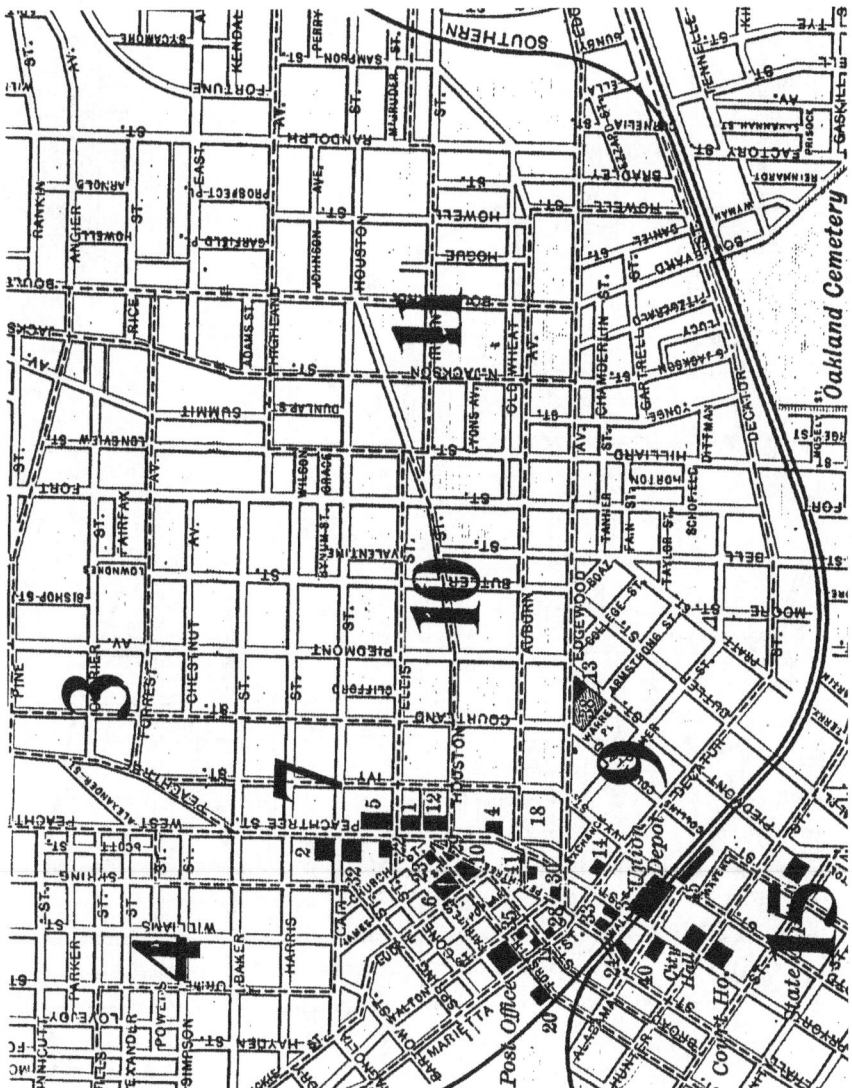

Map 8.3. A riot call was sounded at 12:20 a.m. Sunday. Militia member W. A. Jackson left his home on Forest Avenue (3), rushing to his assembly point at the local armory one block away, but he encountered "a band of negroes" and returned home. Militia headquarters was located at the intersection of Peachtree and Marietta streets (33). At 10:30 a.m. Sunday, a mob assembled at the intersection of Auburn Avenue and Peachtree Street (41, 4) after "hustling" militiamen "from one side of the street to the other" in front of the Piedmont Hotel (18). White textile workers invaded Darktown (11) and proceeded east along Auburn. Rioters approached Walter White's home on Houston Street (10), but neighbors' gunshots prevented them from attacking. (Atlanta City Map 1902, courtesy Georgia Archives, Atlanta.)

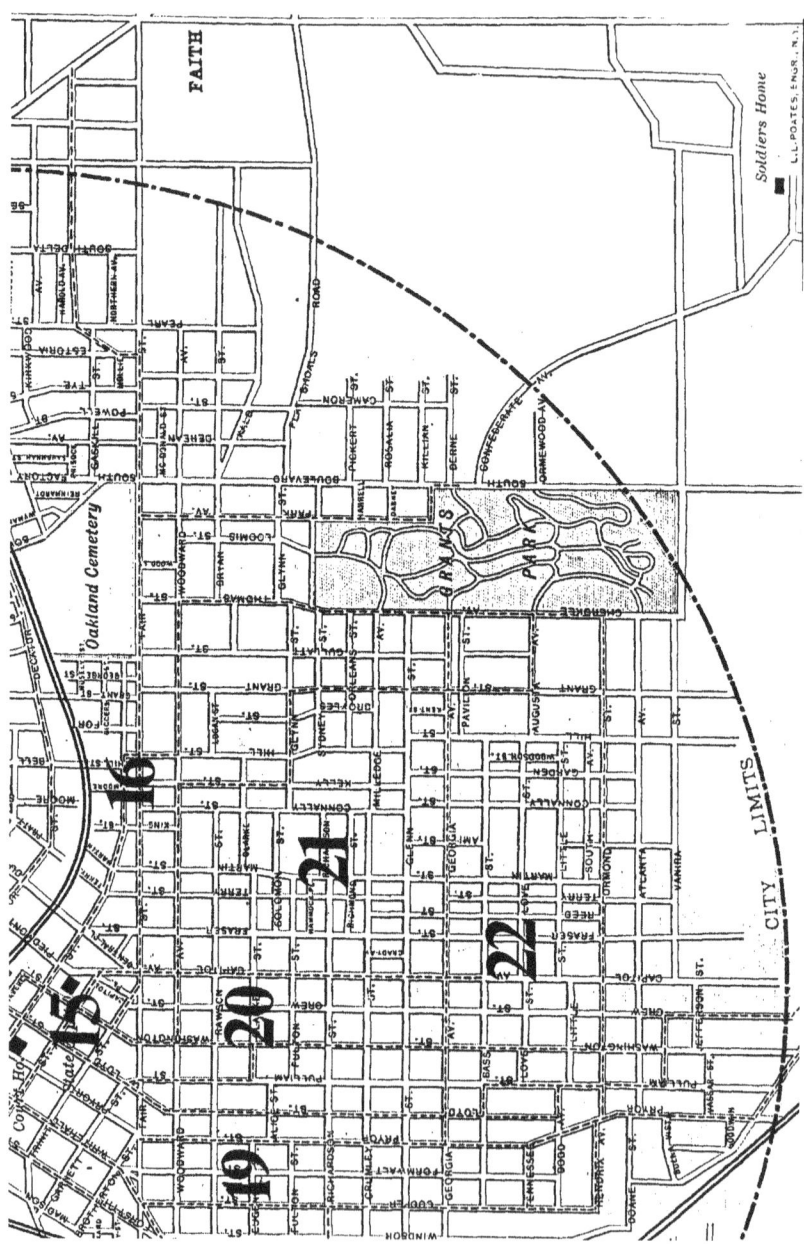

Map 8.4. Lizzie Chaffin, who resided at Sugar Creek near the Soldiers Home, reported she had been approached by a black man on Saturday afternoon. Summerhill (21), a community of black property holders, organized a defense on Sunday and searched all whites who entered the community. On Monday, on McDonald Road, southeast of Oakland Cemetery, blacks fired at fourteen members of a white family named Hicks and drove them from the community. A white mob pulled Sam McGruder and Wiley Brooks off the streetcar from South Atlanta at the intersection of Jefferson and Crew streets, just north of the city limits. (Atlanta City Map 1902, courtesy Georgia Archives, Atlanta.)

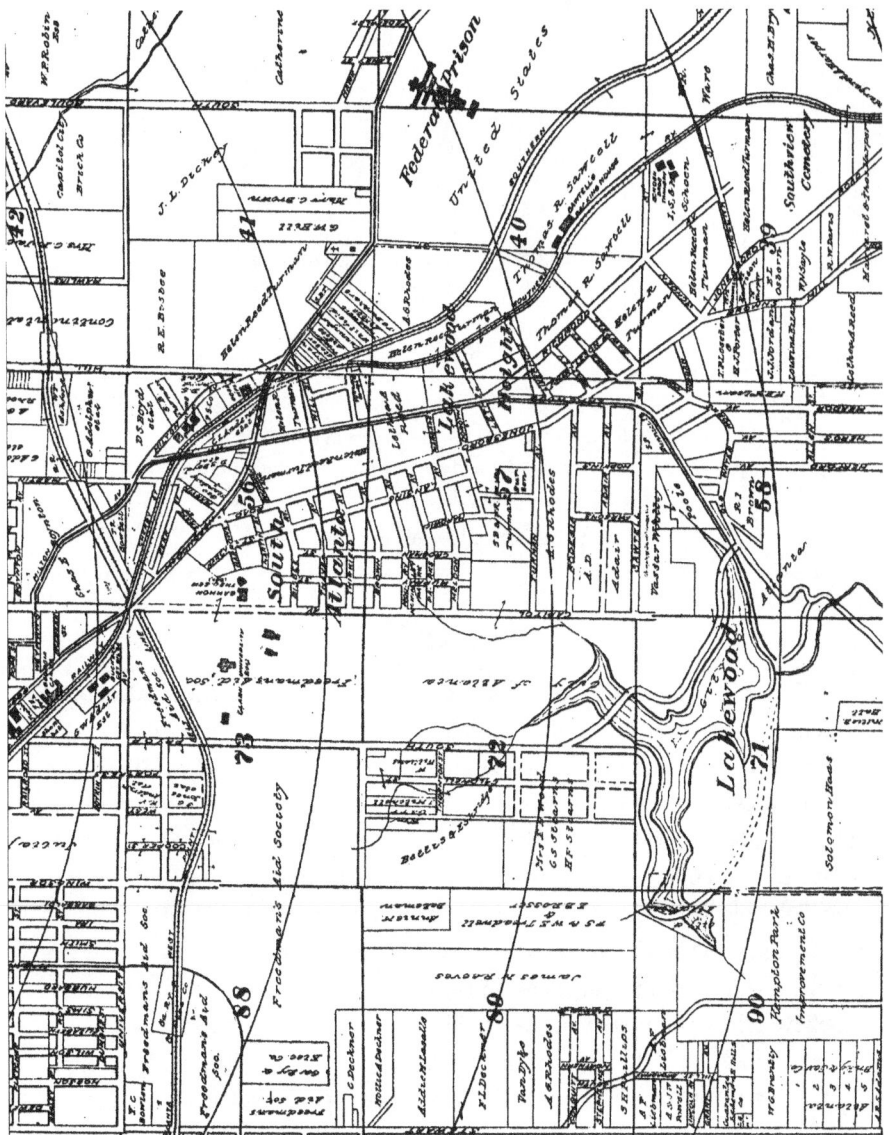

Map 8.5. The South Atlanta black suburban community of Brownsville was home to Gammon Theological Seminary and Clark College (73). Postmaster L. J. Price lent his weapons collection and ammunition to black neighbors in the community of Lakewood as white mobs attacked (71). (Map by O. F. Kauffman, C.E., Atlanta, 1905, courtesy Georgia Archives, Atlanta.)

9

Reconstruction: The Illusion of Hope

> St. Bartholomew's Day was not an explosion that came out of nowhere.... The powder had already been accumulating for years and it had been touched off several times already.
>
> Barbara Diefendorf, "Prologue to a Massacre"

The Atlanta riot of 1906 occurred within a context of politics, urban development, industrialization, and social change created by the migration of blacks and whites to the city. Atlanta's commercial-civic elite actively initiated the antiblack violence of September 22–25, 1906, by manipulating the press to create the popular belief that white institutions were being overwhelmed by black "assaults." Members of the class themselves remarked on the parallels with the St. Bartholomew's Day Massacre in sixteenth-century Paris. Both then and in 1906, the urban leadership used violence as a means of control to secure their hold and impose their agendas on the city. Although most white Atlantans believed their riot merely had restored southern social etiquette between the races,[1] it was, in fact, part of a long tradition of antiminority urban violence in Europe and all sections of the United States. Time and again, not just in Danville and Wilmington, but also in Paris, Providence, Philadelphia, and now Atlanta, a dominant elite responded to problems of urban development and contested visions of the city, by violently making an autonomous minority powerless.[2]

This chapter examines the white commercial-civic elite's efforts to reap what it really had sown and reconstruct Atlanta's social parameters after the riot. In the now-segregated city, that elite, including publishers, militia leaders, businessmen, and politicians, attempted to install at least two types of racial paternalism. The chief advocate of one type, former governor William J. Northen, led the Business Men's Gospel Union, which tried to revive one-on-one relations between the white and black elites. Attorney Charles T. Hopkins spearheaded the new paternalism's second branch. A member of a postriot chamber of commerce subcommittee, Hopkins promoted the racially separate, but coordinated, white elite Civic League and Colored Cooperative League. Both the Civic League and the Business Men's Gospel Union were subcommittees of the powerful Committee of Ten, the new governing body of postriot Atlanta. In other words, they were intended to solidify race relations in terms of white superiority and black deference while refashioning Atlanta's image as a city that used segregation to ensure racial peace and its embrace of development.

Atlanta's black elite viewed the postriot period as an opportunity to seek concessions from the white commercial-civic elite.[3] Black leaders hoped that whites might at last recognize the class differences among blacks in Atlanta and distinguish "law abiding" blacks from the "criminal elements" of both races. While many African Americans rejected both types of white paternalism by voting with their feet, believing that the riot was another manifestation of white repression and that no changes were in the offing, some members of the black elite continued to believe that they could be equal partners with the white elite in shaping Atlanta's development because they viewed the violence as an opportunity to redefine black and white relations using class as demarcating difference. Immediately after the riot, these leaders hoped to insert class as a marker of separation. But to do so, they had to deal with white perceptions.

On September 29, 1906, the *Atlanta Georgian* published T. J. Eady's letter arguing that white rioters had "take[n] things in their own hands to regulate" blacks. He concluded that, as a result, "good negroes" had to align with white people to make the "sorry negro" act predictably or to erase the "bad negro" from the South.[4] Another writer, Myrta Lockett Avary, supported the *Georgian*'s demand that black leaders cooperate with whites in re-creating the "safe days" of slavery. She wanted the "better class" of blacks to step forward to serve white women as "a mighty constabulary force" in the way loyal slaves supposedly did.[5] Meanwhile, the *Georgian*'s editor, John Temple Graves, argued that the "sensational and revolutionary" political campaign preceding the riot was no more extreme than campaigns that had less violently instituted segregation in at least five other states. Nevertheless, the superiority "of the white man in arms" had given white Atlanta "absolute control of all the avenues of force" and blacks "a powerful and convincing ocular demonstration" of that control.[6]

At 4 p.m. on Tuesday, September 25, 1906, white "men from every walk of life" convened in the Fulton County Court House to reassert their power over Atlanta. Chamber of commerce president Sam D. Jones had summoned white men representing every business, factory, financial institution, and church, to create the Committee of 1,000 for reconstructing postriot Atlanta. Members included Charles Hopkins, Coca-Cola chairman Asa G. Candler, businessman and police commissioner James W. English Sr., *Atlanta Georgian* executives F. L. Seely and John Temple Graves, Judge George Hillyer, Clark Howell, clothing store owner George Muse, and Fire Chief W. R. Joyner. Howell, Hopkins, James R. Gray, and John S. Cohen of the *Journal*, along with members of the clergy, drafted proclamations and initiated a riot victims' fund, generating $4,387.

Such "substantial colored citizens" as businessman Alonzo Herndon, Rev. Henry H. Proctor, Bishop Henry M. Turner, Colored Methodist Episcopal Bishop Lucius H. Holsey, and editor J. Max Barber and his assistant Willie Murphy pledged their support "in suppressing disorder." They said they "would be glad to be directed and advised by the committee as to the course the negroes should pursue ... to bring about a restoration of good order."[7]

The most important subcommittee, called by the press "the committee of safety," was the Committee of Ten. It was to be "advised by" both the Committee of 1,000 and the chamber of commerce. English chaired the Committee of Ten, and lawyer W. D. Ellis served as secretary, but Hopkins assumed a vital role that elevated him beyond the committee. The remaining seven members were Sam D. Jones, wholesale grocer H. Y. McCord, capitalist John E. Murphy, board of education chairman and antidive reformer Luther Z. Rosser, lumber merchant A. R. Steele, railroad executive M. Lamar Collier, and real estate developer Forrest Adair.[8]

Sensitive to national criticism, the Committee of Ten sought to show the world outside Atlanta "that the people are not in sympathy" with the riot. The committee advised judicial officials to direct the "grand jury as to its duty" to prosecute both white and black rioters. English encouraged court recorder Nash R. Broyles and Judges John T. Pendleton and Leonard S. Roan, whose courts were directly responsible for prosecuting rioters, to spare no effort. English also directed outgoing governor Joseph Terrell to create a fund for the apprehension of rioters. Hopkins, McCord, and Jones led a delegation "advising" the city's newspapers of their proper role in publishing news for domestic and national consumption. English even had the militia commander, Colonel Clifford L. Anderson, Mayor James G. Woodward, and Sheriff John W. Nelms "appear and confer with the committee" at English's offices in the Fourth National Bank. Usurping municipal, county, and state authority, English made the Committee of Ten a clearinghouse of expertise and authority over every segment of the postriot reconstruction. Mayor Woodward and other municipal leaders pledged their cooperation, agreeing to close the dives for "as long as it is necessary."

Mayor-elect W. R. Joyner led the subcommittee administering the riot relief fund, assisted by merchant George Muse and chamber of commerce secretary Walter G. Cooper. The same three also investigated the riot. In the context of efforts to prevent future violence, the subcommittee in charge of compensating victims reduced the official number of riot fatalities by two-thirds to no more than twelve deaths: ten black and two white. The subcommittee also acknowledged a low total of seventy individuals injured.[9]

The African American elite split in response to the actions of the Committee of Ten. On one side were those who perceived limits in the relationships developing between the elites of the two races; on the other were those who believed the day had at last arrived for both elites to unite in elevating the lower classes to a more civilized stage of racial cooperation. In other words, African Americans believed the riot had opened the door to a class unity that transcended race, but others were skeptical that white leaders sincerely wanted to work with them as coequals.

Rev. Henry H. Proctor, J. Max Barber, and W.E.B. Du Bois listened to the speeches and observed the actions of Charles T. Hopkins and William J. Northen. Of the two, Hopkins seemed more cognizant of black concerns and Northen more interested in black deference. Yet each independently advocated an alliance of the religious and business communities with local authorities to resolve the race question. To permit the elites to work together, the lower classes of both races would be blamed for the riot.

Black writers for the *Bulletin of Atlanta University* reported after the riot that "numerous members of the mob have been arrested and sent to the stockade for thirty days." Some white rioters went before the grand jury for further punitive action. From September 29 through Thanksgiving, Judge Pendleton and the grand jury "conscientiously ... probe[d] to the bottom of the rioting." As a result, lower-class white rioters such as George W. Blackstock and Herbert Talley were indicted for "assault with intent to commit murder" on Peters Street. But businessman L. E. Fain went free.[10]

A biracial meeting in city council chambers on September 25 was attended by upper-class African Americans. Lawyers H. L. Johnson of the firm Johnson and Malone and T. H. M. Johnson blamed the riot on "assaults" by lower-class blacks against white women. According to H. L. Johnson, "Every place of business run by a negro man ought to be closed ... and ordered closed until quiet is restored. And every negro ought to be made [to] go home and stay there." In response, Police Chief Henry Jennings had black businesses closed even in Darktown, and the *Atlanta Journal* commended the Johnsons for their cooperation. Proctor advised African Americans not to resist the police or militia.[11]

Likewise, *Voice of the Negro* owner J. Max Barber cooperated with the white elite immediately after the riot when no African Americans felt safe or secure. He attended the city council meeting with the Johnsons intending to depart Atlanta if blacks of "good reputation" were not guaranteed protection. Although a militant defender of black rights as a member of the Niagara Movement with Du Bois, Barber wanted to stay in the city and work through its problems in the "Atlanta Spirit" of united community effort. Barber's belief that a biracial elite would reconstruct Atlanta, however, was dashed by John Temple Graves's public justification of the riot in the *New York World* on September 24, 1906.[12]

In "Separation of the Races Is the Inevitable Solution," Graves called the riot a legitimate defense of white womanhood. It had "whipped" blacks into submission and cleared the "atmosphere" between the races enough to "keep the negro in order for five years." But Graves contradicted himself by adding that if "another wave of crime [emerged] next summer," whites were ready to mobilize "the mob" again. To prevent that, northern whites had to accept the South's use of segregation, the only sure path to racial peace.[13]

Barber telegraphed the *World*, demanding and receiving the opportunity to rebut Graves as "A Colored Citizen." Barber charged that "no 'carnival of rapes'" provoked the riot, only a "frightful carnival of newspaper lies" concocted and spread by Graves and *Atlanta News* editor Charles Daniel. The owners of the *Atlanta Journal* and *Atlanta Constitution* were equally responsible for the riot, for the *Journal* mimicked the *Georgian* and *News* while the *Constitution* "was mum."

Barber also blamed the riot on Hoke Smith's "Negro hating platform," which inflamed antiblack violence by "the snarling riff-raff." According to information Barber obtained from an unnamed "prominent banker," Smith's political emissaries even "blacked their faces, knocked down a few white women and fled," aggravating white fears of black crime. Barber also asserted that several times on September 22, 1906, "trusted" black workers had been advised by white employers "to go home" because of the impending antiblack violence. This advance knowledge, Barber said, showed Hoke Smith's political campaign was involved.[14]

The Committee of Ten characterized Barber's editorial as the "horrors of exaggeration." Chairman English summoned Barber to a closed-door meeting that Barber described as a "star chamber session." Charging Barber with slander, English demanded that the *Voice of the Negro* owner "straighten [himself] out with ... white people at once." Given a choice of exile or a grand jury conviction and time on the chain gang, Barber departed into permanent exile.[15]

Atlanta University professor W.E.B. Du Bois joined in an open discussion of race relations with white Atlanta Episcopal minister Cary Breckenridge Wilmer in January 1907. Du Bois, like Barber, sought avenues to black and white elite cooperation and "wanted to join the Colored [Cooperative] League as soon as [he] heard about it." Invited by League chairman Henry H. Proctor, Du Bois attended executive committee meetings. Charles Hopkins, who addressed one or more of the meetings, "spoke to us, [with an attitude of] impatience and ... carelessness" that caused Du Bois to leave the meeting "with the same sinking of heart again that I have come out of so many meetings." His conversation with Wilmer was equally frustrating. Both Wilmer and Hopkins seemed dedicated to convincing the black elite to endorse segregation as the solution for avoiding another riot.[16]

According to Wilmer, the "Southern White man" was under attack by black liberty, crime, the vote, and a doctrinaire black elite. Black employees needed to submit to white employers with "honest labor in the lower walks of life." Since this "class" had been empowered with the "free gifts" of the vote and freedom, they engaged in crime and refused to work. The black elite, Wilmer also noted, was too aggressive. They needed to ignore "the occasional injustice arising from" segregation. Eventually, the clergyman informed Dr. Du Bois, a professor of history and sociology, that African Americans were a "child race."[17]

The Du Bois–Wilmer "colloquy" in early 1907 only increased white efforts to discredit Du Bois as a black leader. Responding to Ray Stannard Baker's compilation of the colloquy manuscript, Wilmer made "points that ... mainly [stressed] the bad effect of Du Bois's principles on ... [black] domestic service." White male employers, Du Bois had contended, sexually exploited black domestics. In January 1908 Wilmer wrote Baker again to attack Atlanta's black leaders but especially to "hit the nail on the head so far as such men as Du Bois are concerned."[18]

J. Max Barber monitored the Committee of Ten's reconstruction efforts from his exile in Chicago. The committee had promised blacks more security by restoring law and order in the city, but "sixty or seventy colored people" were jailed for the death of one police officer and only "sixteen white [rioters were jailed] for the whole riot." According to Barber, "five thousand of the city's most industrious [black] citizens" departed immediately after the riot.[19]

The *Atlanta Georgian* confirmed the exodus, reporting that "Hundreds of Negroes Are Leaving Atlanta." The white press noted that black students, laborers, sanitation workers, the best mechanics, and the most prominent "colored citizens" all left Atlanta in late September and early October 1906. The wife of Republican Party leader Henry P. Farrow observed the phenomenon among her black domestics. Her maid, Carrie, was "ready to pull out for Greenville" [South Carolina] on Monday. Carrie's sister Fannie and her children "were run out of their home" Tuesday night and were forced to seek "protection" from Farrow. Waiter Jim Hearnshaw was ready to leave Atlanta for the safety of one of the other Farrow homes in Gainesville, Georgia. The violence, however, had forced Farrow's black workers to be more "respectful" and, it appears, more dependent upon her benevolence. Newspapers in Anniston, Alabama, also reported "scores of fleeing negroes from Atlanta passed through here Sunday and Monday," September 23 and 24.[20]

Two hundred forty black sanitation workers may not have possessed the resources to leave the city, but they did protest against the riot with absenteeism. Sixty or more street sweepers, paid $1.15 a shift, had refused to report for night duty until "the trouble is over for good." Board of Health president C. F. Benson proposed, as a long-term solution, requesting enough funds "to employ white men only." Sanitation chief John Jentzen also hoped to transform a black job into a white position, arguing, "We are employing the scum of God's creation . . . and I know we can get good white labor."[21]

Atlanta Independent editor Benjamin J. Davis sent a letter to the *Atlanta Georgian* invoking the "Atlanta Spirit" and urging African Americans not to flee.[22] Personally ambitious, Davis wanted to be seen as the foremost responsible black leader in Atlanta. He was most unhappy about Henry A. Rucker's domination of Georgia's black Republicans, which Davis felt had prevented him from carving out a prominent position for himself. Nevertheless, after the riot Davis did seek to defend the race from white impositions and uphold the black elite's belief in equality before the law. At the same time, he subscribed to many ideals of the white elite. For instance, the antidive campaign of the city council and the Committee of Ten targeted almost exclusively black establishments, but Davis challenged officials to close every business selling alcohol to the lower classes, regardless of race. He also criticized the black laboring classes for a lack of reliable work behavior. Davis's aims were to fill the void left by J. Max Barber and to continue building the *Independent*'s reputation among blacks as their voice.[23]

On September 29, 1906, Mayor Woodward encouraged black students and "better class" blacks to return to study and work. Proctor, however, believed that Davis's efforts and the start of the fall semester at the colleges were what brought African Americans back to their pursuits in Atlanta. President John Hope said parents were confident their children would be safe at Atlanta Baptist College.[24] Davis, Du Bois, and perhaps Hope wanted to prove that African Americans still had a vital role to play in Atlanta's development.[25]

The sixty black men charged with Officer James Heard's death gradually gained release from Atlanta's stockade. Some remained in prison as late as November 1906 and, with 500 prisoners arrested for rioting, had been forced to pave six streets and grade sidewalks. But by November, Alex Walker would be the only black man convicted for Heard's death. Judge Leonard S. Roan, former law partner of Luther Z. Rosser of the Committee of Ten, sentenced Walker to life imprisonment rather than the traditional death penalty. Although the decision was touted by the white elite as a triumph of the "rule of law," no white rioter received a sentence as severe as life imprisonment for killing a black person during the riot.[26]

While the preoccupation with "due process" was still in the air, in a case unrelated to the riot, black farm worker Joe Glenn was tried in November 1906 for assaulting a white woman, Mrs. J. W. Campbell. Elite members of both races worked together to make Glenn's trial an exhibition of fairness, in a stark contrast to the hasty Jim Walker trial a year earlier (see chap. 6).[27]

Glenn received a defense coordinated by the Committee of Ten, which even met with the presiding Judge Roan. Rosser, Hopkins, and J. E. McClelland represented Glenn. The jury was culled from the defense team's peers on the Committee of 1,000, and the police investigation continued throughout the trial. At the eleventh hour, the police arrested Will Johnson, a black man "who tallied exactly" with Campbell's description. Johnson would be executed in January 1907. Meanwhile, Glenn's own attorneys had him put in jail for protection from whites until they could send him south "to a safe house in Alabama." With a new suit of clothes and a train ticket, however, Joe Glenn headed north.[28]

Whites generally hoped that blacks had learned something from the riot. That lesson was their need for paternalistic white "guardianship," as in the antebellum era when blacks were required to maintain a "face-to-face" relationship with a white benefactor who guaranteed that they were "honest, sober, pious, respectful, and hard working." Postriot leaders Charles T. Hopkins, Rev. C. B. Wilmer, and former governor William J. Northen were among those who sought to re-create the "guardianship" through segregation. To that end, Wilmer worked at reforming whites, Hopkins promoted the Civic League, and Northen championed the Business Men's Gospel Union.[29]

The Business Men's Gospel Union mobilized against "disorder" seven days after the riot began. Northen met with a "representative body of colored ministers and colored laymen" at the Colored Young Men's Christian Association. He shared the ambivalent feelings many in the commercial-civic elite held about the Atlanta riot: white violence served as a "positive" check upon blacks, but in this case it had exceeded the boundaries of civilized behavior. The Gospel Union was intended to keep whites from jeopardizing the image of a modern New South freed from the problems of slavery. If white violence again got out of hand, it could damage white supremacy as well as southern development.

Following the model of Atlanta's postriot white leadership, Northen created three committees. Most of the Gospel Union's power was held by his Committee of 1,000 and the Committee of Ten while African Americans were to organize a black Committee of Ten to cooperate with its white counterpart in educating the races about law and order and finding mechanisms to control the lower classes. Within the boundaries of the legal system, Northen hoped to use the law, segregation, and an aggressive "antebellum" Christianity to rein in both black autonomy and the antiblack violence of lynching and riots.[30] Perhaps because Northen was so immersed in the past, he did not get the elite Committee of Ten's endorsement or the support Charles Hopkins received for his Civic League.

A member of the *Atlanta News* board of directors and legal counsel for the newspaper, Hopkins represented a new generation seeking to shape race relations in Atlanta. Having served with his father, John L. Hopkins, as counsel for Atlanta University, the black collegiate institution, Charles T. Hopkins was legal representative for two Atlanta institutions on opposite sides of the riot question. He had remained silent during August and September 1906, when the *Atlanta News* published the antiblack editorials that did so much to spark the riot. After the riot, however, Hopkins became a vocal leader and something of a conduit between the races through his membership on the powerful Committee of Ten and his leadership of its subcommittee, the Civic League, and the Colored Cooperative League.

W.E.B. Du Bois's critical observations suggest Hopkins was only partially successful because he maintained the position of white master. Despite his service to Atlanta University and meeting with Colored Cooperative League members, immediately after the riot, Hopkins "was astonished" by the black elite's "intelligence and diplomacy." Saying "those negroes understand the situation better than we did," Hopkins claimed he "didn't know that there were such negroes in Atlanta." He added that they "never refer[red] to the riot: they were looking to the future." The Civic League and its African American subsidiary were made permanent by the cooperation of Hopkins and Proctor in the defense of Joe Glenn. With the resources and institutional endorsement of the Committee of Ten, Hopkins sent 3,000 invitations to a Thanksgiving meeting at the Jewish Temple that had been built in 1902 on Pryor and Richardson streets. The continued teamwork of Proctor and Hopkins helped create the Commission on Interracial Cooperation in 1919 to challenge racial violence in the South. But violence was one thing; segregation and even "cooperation" were others. Charles Hopkins, journalist Ray Stannard Baker reported, endorsed segregated streetcars after the riot, for he and his family belonged to a white elite that unanimously believed segregation was the best public policy for maintaining peace between the races.[31]

As leader of the Colored Cooperative League in 1906, Henry Proctor published articles in the *Bulletin of Atlanta University* praising both Hopkins's Civic League and Northen's Business Men's Gospel Union for their efforts to reestablish law and order. Proctor also commended Rev. Dr. Len G. Broughton, pastor of the Baptist Tabernacle, for reviving the Anti-Saloon League and eventually for winning the fight for prohibition in Georgia two years later. Proctor believed denying alcohol to the working classes and criminal element marked the "dawn of a new and better day." In December 1906 Proctor wrote, in an article entitled "Interracial Cooperation in Georgia," that the riot "awaken[ed] the better element from its lethargy," mobilizing them to make definite changes in Atlanta's racial climate. Leaders of both races concurred that the absence of industrial training caused lower-class blacks "to deteriorate into crime" and unpredictability. By contrast, Proctor noted, college graduates dominated the Colored Cooperative League. The majority of members were alumni of Atlanta University, while Proctor himself had graduated from Yale University and W.E.B. Du Bois had graduated from Fisk and Harvard. Leaders and members of the league, therefore, would represent Du Bois's "talented tenth" of African Americans who connected the black and white worlds.

Initially, under the auspices of the Civic League and Colored Cooperative

League, the elite of both races appeared united in the movement to uplift the lower classes. The Civic League for example, wanted a "competent lawyer to defend Negroes arrested" by the police. It also proposed, as Henry A. Rucker and other black leaders had in the 1880s, that the police department hire black officers to "uphold the law in Negro communities." The Colored Cooperative League, led by Proctor and his First Congregational Church, did its part for the elite coalition by opening the church to the working classes as what was called at the time an "institutional church," with an employment bureau, library, kindergarten, and other social welfare activities in addition to religious services. Members of the white elite contributed financially to a new First Congregational Church building for the expanded mission.[32]

Segregation, however, defined the long-term aftermath of the Atlanta riot. Cooperation with Hopkins and the Civic League did not progress to the new day that Proctor and other upper-class African Americans had anticipated. While black neighborhoods remained intact, the black central business district was scattered to other parts of the city, such as "Sweet" Auburn Avenue. Members of the black elite were not incorporated into the rebuilding and urban planning efforts. Instead, they were excluded and isolated from Atlanta's urban redevelopment projects, including a new city hall and an auditorium-armory built to accommodate conventions and reward the militia's work during the riot. Similarly, progress toward racial peace did not materialize from the work of any organizations that emerged after the 1906 riot. African Americans continued to be lynched in Atlanta into the 1920s. Black police officers did not walk the city's streets until the late 1940s, and then they were confined to black neighborhoods.

On the contrary, law and order reinforced segregation and, with it, the economic dominance of Atlanta's white commercial-civic elite. The economic and institutional development nurtured by segregating black businesses on Auburn Avenue did not lead to black participation in any chamber of commerce activities. Rather, the long history of relegating most urban African Americans to unskilled and semiskilled labor as well as domestic service was perpetuated. The commercial-civic elite paid whites higher wages than they offered blacks and combined with the white workers to deny black employees access to job tracks that offered chances for upward mobility.[33]

The political disfranchisement promoted by Thomas E. Watson, Thomas W. Hardwick, James R. Gray, John Cohen, John Temple Graves, Hoke Smith, and Rev. C. B. Wilmer was made part of the 1908 Georgia Constitution. As a result,

Atlanta's leaders could safely ignore African Americans' need for paved streets, sanitation, street lights, parks, schools, health care, and fire and police protection. These repercussions multiplied as black Atlantans remained essentially politically powerless until the 1940s, when postal clerk John Wesley Dobbs helped organize a voter registration campaign for a mayoral election. Only then did the black elite begin to realize the postriot Colored Cooperative League's goal of a working alliance with the white commercial-civic elite.[34]

The immediate impact of the Atlanta riot of 1906 had been to define the black elite's role for ensuing decades as a rubber stamp of the commercial-civic elite.[35] At first, there had been false signs that the violence of September 1906 had transformed the white elite's attitude in favor of working with its African American counterpart. In reality the white commercial-civic elite reaffirmed not only white supremacy and its own dominance but also institutionalized segregation and antiblack political reform. Du Bois articulated this reality in 1907, and Henry Proctor verified it in 1919 when he accepted a pastorate in Brooklyn, New York.[36] The Atlanta race riot of 1906 allowed some African Americans to envision law and order as a means of uniting the black and white elites by class. African Americans, however, had to wait more than half a century for the civil rights movement to experience any benefits from law and order or to see the white commercial-civic elite cooperate with the black elite in fact.

Conclusion: Urbanization, Segregation, and Violence

The Atlanta riot of 1906 was a seminal moment in race relations. It marked the end of the personal paternalism that had characterized antebellum and some post–Civil War race relations in Atlanta. It opened instead a new era in which urban race relations were defined by legalized segregation and antiblack violence. Urban growth had brought together the conflicting agendas of four social groups in Atlanta: the white commercial-civic elite, the white working classes, elite African Americans, and the black working classes. The visions of each group with regard to city building, politics, and social questions were not coordinated or unified by the legendary "Atlanta Spirit." So they collided at a moment in Atlanta's history when change itself already was unsettling relations among the races and classes. Urban development, industrialization, and segregation allowed the city's white commercial-civic elite to polarize race relations from 1865 to 1908. To effect that polarization, the elite used forty years of electoral "reform" to blunt black and white working-class efforts to shape Atlanta's development. As a consequence, working-class political cooperation between the races began to collapse in the 1890s. White reformers carried the breakdown into the new century, uniting with the growing ranks of white workers created by development of the textile industry to exploit the social and political backlash of Prohibition's failure and to end black political participation. In this way, Atlanta's antiblack violence was a direct consequence of urban growth, industrialization, and political discontent.

The Atlanta riot was part of a regionwide effort to make blacks politically vulnerable and then to terminate their access to power. The riot occurred when blacks had been stripped of the vote and protection from a state militia or federal troops. Electoral reform had gradually reduced black political participation to a small remnant, surviving primarily on federal patronage. The Georgia gubernatorial primary of 1906 certified the return of home rule for whites as the foundation of southern Progressivism. Home rule would translate into the disfranchisement of African Americans. Almost immediately it meant whites were free to impose deference upon African Americans through antiblack violence, without federal intervention.

Georgia's rural and urban reformers alike defined their movement in terms of restructuring race relations, controlling blacks, ending black political power, changing white political leadership, moderating corporate power, and expanding local and state governmental regulation. On these issues, Thomas E. Watson and Thomas W. Hardwick had formed the political management team that undermined Clark Howell's control over the Democratic Party. Their aim was to combine rural protest against corporate abuse with the ambition of urban leaders to replace Howell. Black disfranchisement was the instrument that brought the two constituencies together across the urban-rural divide and united Watson and Hardwick with their former rivals, James R. Gray and Hoke Smith. Moreover, in Atlanta disfranchisement, along with segregation, even allowed Hardwick and Watson to gain control over the socially disruptive white laborers.

In the wake of the reformers' victory, however, the white press legitimized antiblack violence, not the panacea of disfranchisement, as the linchpin to white men's role as protectors of women and defenders of property and status. Both the reformers and the white newspapers took advantage of black political powerlessness to unite whites across class divisions and mobilize them to seize control of the political and social spheres by attacking blacks.

For African Americans, Atlanta seemed to be a place where an elite could emerge, grow, and mature. But in the aftermath of the riot, white Atlanta obstructed black elite aspirations to cross the racial divide. The black elite's exclusion from Atlanta's commercial-civic elite was highlighted by the frustrated departures to the North of W.E.B. Du Bois in 1910 and Rev. H. H. Proctor in 1919.

Before the riot, the African American working classes of Atlanta had developed an urban culture of their own. Besides supporting the black elite, this culture enabled the working classes to resist white efforts to establish a predicable work routine and social hierarchy in the industrializing city. Instead, the working classes embraced the city as a place of entertainment and geographical mobility but limited social and economic opportunity. Black men, especially, traversed metropolitan Atlanta in an ongoing search for jobs that provided a living wage and working conditions they hoped to control. What they already had given up seeking in the late nineteenth century was even limited political opportunity. From 1868 through the riot of 1906 to disfranchisement in 1908, the white commercial-civic elite used "reform" to blunt any attempts by the black and white working classes to shape Atlanta's political and economic development.

White opposition to every aspect of black freedom and autonomy provoked the Atlanta riot of 1906. Just as the end of slavery had earlier been met with antiblack violence aimed at regaining control over the freedmen, urbanization and industrialization were accompanied by more violence aimed at reining in the autonomy that African Americans found in cities. In attacking black autonomy, the Atlanta riot itself paralleled the antiblack riots of the antebellum North, although the consequences for its victims were characteristic of the New South.

The riot installed disfranchisement as the capstone to four decades of political reform and institutionalized segregation as the dominant form of race relations. In the economic sphere alone, the ramifications of segregation marginalized the black business district and its proprietors and relegated black workers to the most subservient positions. This, in the end, was the urban ethos of the commercial-civic elite that took advantage of every opportunity, including the deadly riot, to make Atlanta a prototype metropolis of twentieth-century America.

Notes

Abbreviations for Archival Collections

ACP—Aldine Chambers Papers, Atlanta History Center
ARVF—Atlanta Riot vertical files, Special Collections, Woodruff Library, Atlanta University Center
CHPUGA—Clark Howell Papers, MS 818, box 3, Special Collections, University Libraries, University of Georgia, Athens
HSC—Hoke Smith Collection, MS 82/sc/17, Richard B. Russell Memorial Library, University of Georgia, Athens
LAS—WRFG Radio, "Atlanta Race Riot of 1906," Living Atlanta series, produced and researched by Harlan Joye and Barbara Joye et al., radio re-creation, Atlanta History Center
PRSB—Papers of Ray Stannard Baker, microfilm, Ohio State University, Columbus.
TEWPR—*Thomas E. Watson Papers: Research Collections in American Politics* (Bethesda, Md.: University Publications of America, 1991)

Introduction

1. *Atlanta News*, 1 July 1906, 1; "Social and Political Equality," *Atlanta Journal*, 1 August 1906, 8; Garrett, *Atlanta and Environs*, 2:500; Deaton, "Atlanta during the Progressive Era," 186.

2. Garrett, *Atlanta and Environs*, 2:499; "In Race Riot Many Negroes Are Killed and Scores of Both Races Are Injured; Atlanta under Control of State Militia," *Atlanta Journal*, 23 September 1906, 1.

3. There are no clear estimates on fatalities. The general range by contemporaries and scholars is 10–25 or more deaths.

4. Greenwood, *Bittersweet Legacy*, 1–4. Greenwood finds alliances among the elite across the racial divide that were destroyed by white southern racist attitudes in the 1890s. Atlanta blacks did not have this alternative. They sought alliances that did not materialize, but as in Charlotte, Atlanta's African Americans were important participants in shaping their city. See Bayor, *Race and the Shaping of Twentieth-Century Atlanta*, chaps. 1 and 2.

5. Dailey, "Deference and Violence"; Gilmore, *Gender and Jim Crow,* chaps. 2–4.

6. Brownell coined the term *commercial-civic elite* in *Urban Ethos in the South,* xvi–xx, 126–27, 188. It generally defines the business leadership of a southern city and its auxiliary members including clergy, newspaper editors, and civic leaders. See also Hunter, *Community Power Structure: A Study of Decision Makers,* and a follow-up study by Hunter, *Community Power Succession: Atlanta's Policy Makers Revisited,* examining this group in the twentieth century. For urbanization and industrialization's impact, see Rabinowitz, *The First New South, 1865–1920,* 48–71; Rabinowitz, *Race Relations in the Urban South, 1865–1890;* Woodward, *Origins of the New South,* 20–22; Doyle, *New Men, New Cities, New South,* 87–103; Greenwood, *Bittersweet Legacy,* 1–7.

7. Brownell, *Urban Ethos in the South,* xvi–xx, 13–14, 35–38, 84–86, 99–102, 105–11; see Brownell's patterns of urban development in chapter 1 for the "zones of deterioration." See also Russell, *Atlanta, 1847–1890,* 5, 65, 72, 86–89, chap. 6; Bayor, *Race and the Shaping of Twentieth-Century Atlanta,* chap. 2; Goldfield, *Cotton Fields and Skyscrapers,* 103; Friedman, *White Savage,* vi–vii.

8. Friedman, *White Savage,* 9–11, 15, 17, 20, 32, 43, 50, 67, 70–71. Friedman argues that the white search for "peace of mind" spanned 1865–1913.

9. Hunter, *To 'Joy My Freedom;* McKiven, *Iron and Steel,* introduction and chap. 3.

10. Gilmore, *Gender and Jim Crow,* chaps. 1–4; Gaines, *Uplifting the Race,* preface, introduction, chaps. 1 and 2; Dorsey, "To Build Our Lives Together."

11. Newby, *Plain Folk in the New South,* 33–50; Kuhn, "'A Full History,'" 34–88; Brownell, *Urban Ethos in the South,* 35–36, 105–11.

12. Anderson, *The Education of Blacks in the South,* 88–101; Woodward, *Origins of the New South,* 221–34, 360–66; Williamson, *The Crucible of Race,* 212–13, 291–94; J. William Harris, "Etiquette, Lynching, and Racial Boundaries"; Goldfield, *Black, White, and Southern,* 1–22, 48–56.

13. For models of political reform and home rule, see Friedman, *White Savage,* chap. 3; Prather, *We Have Taken a City;* Dailey, "Deference and Violence"; Gilmore, *Gender and Jim Crow,* 92, 96–98, 106–17; Edmonds, *The Negro and Fusion Politics in North Carolina,* chaps. 10 and 11; Grantham, *Southern Progressivism,* 10–14, 36–53; Crawford, "The Warriors of Civilization," 1, 5–9; Williamson, *The Crucible of Race,* 180–224.

Prologue: White Elite Control, Black Urban Mobility, and Working White Women

Epigraph. Ray Stannard Baker, "The Atlanta Riot," *American Magazine,* April 1907, 4–5.

1. "Here Are 'Extras' Issued Saturday," *Atlanta Georgian,* 29 September 1906, 11. The *Georgian* published this collection of headlines in response to a Fulton County grand jury's unanimous decision blaming "the sensational manner in which the afternoon newspapers of Atlanta . . . presented to the people the news of various criminal acts recently committed in this county." The afternoon papers "largely influenced the creation of the spirit, animating the mob last Saturday." See "Fulton Grand Jury Fixes

Responsibility for Recent Rioting," *Atlanta Georgian*, 29 September 1906, 10. The *Atlanta Journal* and *Atlanta News* were made the primary culprits by the *Atlanta Georgian*, even though it, too, was published in the afternoon. The *Georgian* published a two-page blowup of its response to the grand jury and the panorama of headlines with the juxtaposition of the *News* and *Journal*'s "Extras" versus the *Georgian*'s "Extras."

2. See "Woman Fights Off Negro Man; Puts Him to Flight with Pistol," *Atlanta Georgian*, 21 September 1906, 1; "Facts of Last Night's Reign of Terror," *Atlanta Constitution*, 23 September 1906, 1; Crowe, "Racial Massacre," 152–57; Baker, *Following the Color Line*, 5–6; "Militia Guard Negro Suspect from Violence," *Atlanta Constitution*, 21 September 1906, 1. Atlanta's newspapers also recorded her name as Mrs. Kimball and Mrs. Kimble.

3. "Woman Fights Off Negro Man; Puts Him to Flight with Pistol"; "Mrs. J. A. Kimble Is Brutally Attacked by a Black Fiend," *Atlanta Journal*, 20 September 1906, 1; "Militia Guard Negro Suspect from Violence," *Atlanta Constitution*, 21 September 1906, 1, 3. The *Georgian* and *Constitution*'s accounts vary in their use of details. The *Journal*'s description appears to be a summary that focused on the *Georgian*'s more detailed report.

4. "Mrs. J. A. Kimble Is Brutally Attacked by a Black Fiend"; Baker, *Following the Color Line*, 5–6.

5. "Militia Guard Negro Suspect from Violence." Fort McPherson was home to the Seventeenth Infantry Regiment of U.S. Regulars.

6. "Militia Guard Negro Suspect from Violence"; "Governor Terrell Extends Welcome to Commoner," *Atlanta Journal*, 21 September 1906, 4; "Hoke Smith Responded to Call for Speech," *Atlanta Journal*, 21 September 1906, 4; "Government Ownership Discussed by Bryan in His Banquet Speech," *Atlanta Journal*, 21 September 1906, 5; "Four Hundred Leading Democrats Enjoy . . . Dinner at Piedmont," *Atlanta Journal*, 20 September 1906, 3; "A Great Day for Democracy," *Atlanta Journal*, 21 September 1906, 8.

7. Baker, *Following the Color Line*, 6.

8. "Assault Is Attempted on Miss Orrie Bryan near Center of City," *Atlanta Constitution*, 21 September 1906, 1, 3.

9. *Atlanta News*, 23 September 1906, 1; Rainey, "The Race Riot of 1906 in Atlanta," chap. 2.

10. *Atlanta News*, 23 September 1906, 1; *Atlanta Constitution*, 23 September 1906, 1; 1907 Atlanta City Directory, Atlanta History Center, 243, 775, 1094.

11. Baker, *Following the Color Line*, 6–9. The *Atlanta News* "published five . . . extras, and newsboys cried them through the city: 'Third assault.' 'Fourth assault.'" Both Baker and the *Atlanta Georgian* provide copies and facsimiles of the headlines from the *Atlanta Journal* and *Atlanta News*. See picture between page 6 and 7 of Baker, *Following the Color Line*, and *Atlanta Georgian*, 24 September 1906, 4.

12. *Atlanta News*, 23 September 1906, 1; *Atlanta Constitution*, 23 September 1906, 1; 1907 Atlanta City Directory, 427, 960; Rainey, "The Race Riot of 1906 in Atlanta," chap. 2.

13. *Atlanta Journal*, 23 September 1906, 1; "Facts of Last Night's Reign of Terror," *Atlanta Constitution*, 23 September 1906, 1; WRFG Radio, "Atlanta Race Riot of 1906," side 1, LAS; Crowe, "Racial Massacre," 152–57; Baker, *Following the Color Line*, 9–10.

14. Brownell, *Urban Ethos in the South*, xvi, xviii, 58–60, 86.

15. Ibid., xvi, xix–xxi, 145–46; "Negro Disfranchisement," *Atlanta Journal*, 25 November 1905, 6; "The Negro and the Ballot," *Atlanta Constitution*, 6 June 1906, 6; McCurry, "The Politics of Yeoman Households," 22–38; Maclean, "Gender, Sexuality, and the Politics of Lynching," 158–88.

Chapter 1. Atlanta: The City of Progress

Epigraph. Emory Speer to Clark Howell, 27 July 1905, CHPUGA, folder 1906–9.

1. Stone, *The Story of Dixie Steel*, 5–6, 44–45; Brownell, "The Urban South Comes of Age," 142; "Work Pledged for Auditorium," *Atlanta Constitution*, 12 July 1905, 11.

2. Brownell, *Urban Ethos in the South*, xvi, xix; "Work Pledged for Auditorium"; Orum, *City-Building in America*, 9, 13–20, 195–96, 198, 200. Brownell provides a broader context of city building in the South. Orum's analysis of capitalist influence is important along with his definitions of city building. Class, race, and gender are neglected components of city building. See Thomas and Ritzdorf, *Urban Planning and the African American Community*, introduction.

3. Brownell, "The Urban South Comes of Age," 142; "Work Pledged for Auditorium"; "Candler Wants Big Auditorium," *Atlanta Constitution*, 9 July 1905, C7; Cooper, *Official History of Fulton County*, chap. 42, "Municipal Government"; Doyle, *New Men, New Cities, New South*, 143–44.

4. Russell, *Atlanta, 1847–1890*, 2–7, 10–11, 260–64; Doyle, *New Men, New Cities, New South*, 87–103, 138–39, 144–57; Stone, *The Story of Dixie Steel*, 14; Larsen, *The Urban South: A History*, 2, 35, 67–68; Larsen, *The Rise of the Urban South*, ix–x, 26–28, 69–86, 91, 94–95, 145; Goldfield, *Cottonfields and Skyscrapers*, 85–89; Watts, *Social Bases of City Politics*, chaps. 2 and 6. For an in-depth examination of urbanization and the Civil War, see DeCredico, "Image and Reality: Ken Burns and the Urban Confederacy," 387–405.

5. Russell, *Atlanta, 1847–1890*, 187–91, 217, 222, 228, 255–56; Doyle, *New Men, New Cities, New South*, 189–91; Atlanta Chamber of Commerce, *Souvenir Album*, 10, 28; Atlanta Chamber of Commerce, *Atlanta: A Twentieth-Century City*, 11–12; Orum, *City-Building in America*, 195–96. For a discussion of Atlanta's post–Civil War efforts, see *Souvenir Album*, 12–16, and *Atlanta: A Twentieth-Century City*, 5–7, 10, 24–25; Sidney Ormond, "Captain Howell's Work for His City and State," *Atlanta Constitution*, 7 October 1906, 2.

6. Russell, *Atlanta, 1847–1890*, 187–91, 217, 222, 228, 255–56; Doyle, *New Men, New Cities, New South*, 189–91; Atlanta Chamber of Commerce, *Souvenir Album*, 10, 28, and *Atlanta: A Twentieth-Century City*, 11–12; Orum, *City-Building in America*, 195–96. See Knight, *History of Fulton County Georgia*, and Garrett, *Atlanta and Environs*, for local capital and urban development efforts.

7. "Aldine Chambers," *History of Georgia*, 2:352–53; "Life Story of Chambers: People's Friend, Atlanta Leader, Georgia Cracker," James Francis Aldine Chambers, Personal Profile, Atlanta History Center; "Progressivism," in *Major Problems in the History of the*

American South, 2:204–10, 217–19, 226–60; Williamson, "Wounds Not Scars," 1237, 1252; Simon, "The Appeal of Cole Blease of South Carolina," 375–77.

8. "Progressivism," 2:205–10, 217–19; Gilmore, *Gender and Jim Crow,* chaps. 2–4; Edwards, *Gendered Strife and Confusion,* chaps. 5 and 6.

9. Greenwood, *Bittersweet Legacy,* chaps. 3–6; Hanchett, *Sorting Out the New South City,* chaps. 1, 3–6. For similar social and political processes in the North, see Miggins, "Between Spires and Stacks," 193, 197; Kusmer, "Black Cleveland and the Central-Woodland Community," 269, 271–72.

10. Doyle, *New Men, New Cities, New South,* chaps. 2–4 and 6–11; Doyle, *Nashville in the New South,* chaps. 3 and 6; Harris, *Political Power in Birmingham;* Wilson, *America's Johannesburg: Industrialization and Racial Transformation in Birmingham,* 1–5, 32–34, 153–56, 171, 174–75, 178; McKiven, *Iron and Steel,* 1–6; Simon, "The Appeal of Cole Blease of South Carolina," 375–77; Greenwood, *Bittersweet Legacy,* chaps. 3–6; Hanchett, *Sorting Out the New South City,* chaps. 3–6; Gilmore, *Gender and Jim Crow,* chaps. 1–4.

11. Doyle, *New Men, New Cities, New South,* 260–69 and chaps. 7, 10, and 11; Jenkins, *Seizing the New Day,* xv, chap. 1; Bacote, "The Negro in Atlanta Politics," 333–42; Bacote, "Negro Proscriptions," 471–98.

12. Cooper, *Official History of Fulton County,* 755; Davis, *Henry Grady's New South,* 25–27, 61–66, 117, 129–31.

13. Cooper, *Official History of Fulton County,* 835–36; Friedman, *White Savage,* 41–44, 48. For parallel examples of white political leaders' manipulation of race relations, see Simon, "The Appeal of Cole Blease of South Carolina," 375–80; Rosen, "'Not That Sort of Women'"; Edwards, "The Disappearance of Susan Daniel and Henderson Cooper," 294–312; Zipf, "'The WHITES shall rule the land or die'"; Waldrep, *Roots of Disorder,* chaps. 5–7 and conclusion.

14. Cooper, *Official History of Fulton County,* 835–36; "Speeches by Henry W. Grady on the New South," and "From Grady's Speech 'The South' Delivered to the New England Club in New York, 1886," *Major Problems in the History of the American South,* 2:71–73; Grady, *The New South: Writings and Speeches,* 119; Friedman, *White Savage,* 41–44, 48.

15. Grady, *The New South: Writings and Speeches,* 11, 22, 24, 105, 139. The assertions made here are summations of public speeches and editorials Grady made between 1886 and 1889. He addressed whites during this period in New York City, Boston, Dallas, Augusta, Ga., and Elberton, Ga. Grady told his audiences that the "weaker" races included yellow, red, and black. For an example of the post–Civil War origins of white resistance to black freedom, see Zipf, "'The WHITES shall rule the land or die,'" 500–503; Simon, "The Appeal of Cole Blease of South Carolina," 375.

16. Grady, *The New South: Writings and Speeches,* 20–24, 47–52, 73–85, 91–92, 95, 99, 102, 136–38, 141–43; Simon, "The Appeal of Cole Blease of South Carolina," 375–81. For a discussion of corporate and federal influence and their application in the South and other emancipated societies, see Cell, *The Highest Stage of White Supremacy,* x, 14–20, 25, 57–58, 81–87, 104, 149–50, 174–81, 190–91; Foner, *Nothing but Freedom,* chap. 1; Ambrose,

Henry Hughes and Proslavery Thought in the Old South, 1, 3–7, 184–89; Du Bois, "Reconstruction and Its Benefits," 53–55; Gilmore, "When Jim Crow Had Wings"; Lorini, *Rituals of Race,* 25–27.

17. For a description of how Grady balanced modernization and tradition, see Bryan, *Henry Grady or Tom Watson?* Populist Thomas E. Watson opposed Grady despite the similarity of their efforts to reconcile tradition with dramatic change. For Grady's comments, see Grady, *The New South: Writings and Speeches,* 85, 100–101, 140. For an evaluation of Grady's role in defining the South and race relations, see Friedman, *White Savage,* chap. 3; Gaston, *The New South Creed,* 124–25, 130–35, 140, 143. See also Williamson, *The Crucible of Race,* for fractious debate among whites concerning black status. See Grady, *The New South: Writings and Speeches,* 19, 47–49, 72, 77–78, 91, 98, 138.

18. Friedman, *White Savage,* chap. 3; Gaston, *The New South Creed,* 124–25, 130–35, 140, 143; Bryan, *Henry Grady or Tom Watson?*; Williamson, *The Crucible of Race*; Grady, *The New South: Writings and Speeches,* 20–24, 47–52, 73–85, 91–92, 95, 99, 102, 136–38, 141–43. See *Atlanta Journal* and *Atlanta Constitution,* July/August 1897 and "Georgia Politics," Long-Rucker-Aiken Family Papers, Atlanta History Center, Political Material 1900–1916, 1957–65, box 12, folder 3, Republican Party 1900–1912. Note that as of summer 2000 the Long-Rucker-Aiken Family Papers have been reorganized. The above notation is from the old finding aid.

19. Grady, *The New South: Writings and Speeches,* 10, 17–18, 47, 50–53, 73–85, 95, 99, 102, 108–10, 136–38, 141–43.

20. Grady, *The New South: Writings and Speeches;* Davis, *Henry Grady's New South,* chap. 5.

21. Confederate veterans W. A. Hemphill and Evan P. Howell shared ownership of the *Constitution* with Grady during his era of political dominance. "Henry Grady's Greatest Work for Georgia and South," *Atlanta Constitution,* 7 October 1906, 2; Knight, *History of Fulton County Georgia,* 465; Candler and Evans, *Georgia,* 2:313; "Over 1,100 Voters Enroll Their Names in Fulton Hoke Smith Club before It Rounds Out Its First Day," *Atlanta Journal,* 29 April 1906, 2; Cooper, *Official History of Fulton County,* 757, 830–36; Davis, *Henry Grady's New South,* 25–27, 61–66, 117, 129–31. Howell acquired Hemphill's stock to gain complete ownership with one other partner. For the Howell machine, see Thos. W. Loyless to Clark Howell, 25 January 1905, 1–3, CHPUGA, folder 1905. See 2–3 for hints at freight rate manipulation. The machine secured public offices not only for Howell but also for Confederate general John B. Gordon, Populist governor and postriot personality William J. Northen, Confederate official Alfred Colquitt, and George Hillyer, a Confederate veteran and an inflammatory voice leading to the riot.

22. Grantham, *Hoke Smith,* chap. 3.

23. Ibid., 14–24; Cooper, *Official History of Fulton County,* 844.

24. Grantham, *Hoke Smith,* 17–18, 23–24, 26–36, 39, 78–79, 93, 131–32, 145, 158–59; Davis, *Henry Grady's New South,* 54; Cooper, *Official History of Fulton County,* 759, 844–45; Fort, "History of the *Atlanta Journal,*" 6–21. The relationship between Grady, Howell, and Smith dissolved over Smith's support for Grover Cleveland. His commitment to Cleveland would last well beyond the Cleveland presidencies in the 1890s.

25. Grantham, *Hoke Smith*, 25–31; Fort, "History of the *Atlanta Journal*," 13–15, 24, 26–38. The members of the group that purchased the *Journal* with Smith were Henry H. Cabaniss, Josiah Carter, Charles A. Collier, Jacob Haas, "Captain" Henry Jackson, W. H. Parsons, R. M. Pulsifer, and Frank P. Rice.

26. Grantham, *Hoke Smith*, 54, 67–70, 76–94, 114; Simon, "The Appeal of Cole Blease of South Carolina," 375. Bishop Turner considered Smith a racial moderate when he was secretary of the interior. Smith would retain this image until 1905.

27. Fort, "History of the *Atlanta Journal*," 13–15, 24, 26–38; Grantham, *Hoke Smith*, 29–31, 76–94. See Grantham, 113–15, for purchase of the paper. The group included James R. Gray, Morris Brandon, and H. M. Atkinson, a utility magnate.

28. Cooper, *Official History of Fulton County*, 761; *Georgia*, 151–52; Fort, "History of the *Atlanta Journal*," 40. The law firm of Ellis and Gray was led by Judge W. D. Ellis and his son, W. D. Jr. In 1881 Gray married May Inman, daughter of Walker P. Inman, one of Atlanta's most important capitalists and cotton producers. He and Samuel M. Inman were Atlanta city builders in the 1860s–90s. See Garrett, *Atlanta and Environs*, 2:141, 180, 513; *Georgia*, 151; Fort, "History of the *Atlanta Journal*," 41. John Temple Graves, Thomas W. Loyless, Henry Richardson, Major John Cohen, Tilden Adamson, and Robert Adamson served as editors during the interim between Smith and Gray.

29. Rainey, "The Race Riot of 1906 in Atlanta," chap. 5; Candler and Evans, *Georgia*, 1:674–75.

30. Knight, *History of Fulton County Georgia*, 244, 247; Stone, *The Story of Dixie Steel*, 34; Candler and Evans, *Georgia*, 1:670–75; Stone, 51–53; Cooper, *Official History of Fulton County*, 630, 852–53, 857. Hunter, *To 'Joy My Freedom*, 88–97, provides a detailed account of one event involving a strike by black laundresses during English's mayoral term. For English's career with the police department, see Mathias and Anderson, *Horse to Helicopter*, chap. 2; "With Our Millionairs [sic] Atlantans Who Have Grown Rich since the War," *Atlanta Constitution*, 7 April 1889, 14; Doyle, *New Men, New Cities, New South*, 93–95; Knight, *History of Fulton County Georgia*, 248; Garrett, *Atlanta and Environs*, 2:476–80.

31. Rainey, "The Race Riot of 1906 in Atlanta," chap. 5; Candler and Evans, *Georgia*, 1:674–75.

32. Knight, *History of Fulton County Georgia*, 144, 157, 160–61; Garrett, *Atlanta and Environs*, 2:87–88, 220; Davis, *Henry Grady's New South*, 18–20, 195–97; Cooper, *Official History of Fulton County*, 631–33.

33. Knight, *History of Fulton County Georgia*, 179.

34. Doyle, *New Men, New Cities, New South*, xi, xv, 17–19, 87–103, 136–58, 189–222; Russell, *Atlanta, 1847–1890*, 7–10; Dittmer, *Black Georgia in the Progressive Era, 1900–1920*, 12; Watts, "Black Political Progress in Atlanta, 1868–1895," 286; Bacote, "The Negro in Atlanta Politics," 333–34.

35. Garrett, *Atlanta and Environs*, 2:400.

36. Hunter, *To 'Joy My Freedom*, 85–97; Dorsey, "To Build Our Lives Together," chap. 6; Bacote, "The Negro in Atlanta Politics," 333–41; Walton, *Black Republicans*, 49–55.

37. "Rucker Goes In; Downs Maj. Smyth," *Atlanta Constitution*, 24 July 1897, 5; "John

Temple Graves," *Atlanta Journal*, 7 August 1897, 2; "John Temple Graves," *Atlanta Journal*, 17 August 1897, 4; Bacote, "Negro Officeholders in Georgia under President McKinley"; Mixon, "Politics and Race: Henry A. Rucker and Aldine Chambers during the Era of the Atlanta Riot," 15–31; Walton, *Black Republicans*, chap. 3; Bacote, "The Negro in Atlanta Politics," 335–41.

38. Inman, *Inman Diary*, 5, 7, 33, 43–51, 56, 61, 64–67; Grantham, *Hoke Smith*, 70, 122, 149, 159, 178; Williamson, *Crucible of Race*, 115–18, 121–22, 127–29, 212–15; "Smith Speaks at Hogansville," *Atlanta Constitution*, 6 August 1905, C3; "Smith Speaks at La Grange," *Atlanta Constitution*, 10 October 1906, 3.

39. Grantham, *Hoke Smith*, 131–32, 134–35; Fort, "History of the *Atlanta Journal*," 28, 46–50.

40. D'Avino, "Atlanta Municipal Parks, 1882–1917," 11, 31–34, 42, 46; Bolden, "The Political Structure of Charter Revision Movements," 1–6, 11–22, 67–68; Cooper, *Official History of Fulton County*, 630–47.

41. Bolden, "The Political Structure of Charter Revision Movements," 27, 29, 30–41, 46, 49, 58, 64–68, 268–73, 336–41. See also Mathias and Anderson, *Horse to Helicopter*, chap. 2 for police board interference in the department. The black population in the Third and Fourth wards nearly doubled between 1890 and 1910. See Slade, "The Evolution of Negro Areas in the City of Atlanta," 40–41, Special Collections, Atlanta University Center, Woodruff Library. In 1901, James W. English Sr. dismissed twenty-two police officers. He replaced them with his appointees. The terminations helped initiate a crusade to revise the city charter. City council's police committee voted to abolish the police board, but the full council ignored the recommendation and remanded the proposal back to the committee. City council's failure sparked a call for a new city charter.

42. Hoke Smith to Fulton Colville, 20 May 1902, Letterbook 10 May 1902–27 August 1902, p. 56, HSC, box 63, Letterbooks 10 May 1902–5 March 1903; Bolden, "The Political Structure of Charter Revision Movements," 34–37; McCombs, "Pittsburg: A Sociological Study of a 'Natural Area,'" 42–43; Mathias and Anderson, *Horse to Helicopter*, 43; Brundage, *Lynching in the New South*, 123–27.

43. Smith to Colville, 20 May 1902; Atlanta—City Limits, Wards, ACP, box 1, folder 1. North Atlanta, Copenhill, and Reynoldstown were annexed in 1904. See Bolden, "The Political Structure of Charter Revision Movements," 49, 58, 60, 64–68, 73–76; Mace, "The Black Population." Expansion would not be taken up again until the next attempt at charter reform in 1909 when Oakland City, a site of a preriot "assault," became part of the city. Bolden suggests that both Smith and Howell fought for dominance and control in each of these contests even though issues were not always clearly identified with them specifically.

44. "One Duty of the Convention," *Atlanta Constitution*, 1 June 1904, 4. The *Atlanta Constitution* heavily favored disfranchisement in 1901–4 and opposed it in 1905–6. "Terrell Renominated for 2nd Term; Celebration Erupts," *Atlanta Constitution*, 2 June 1904, 3; "Address of Clark Howell Candidate for the Democratic Nomination for Governor as Delivered in Joint Debate at Columbus, Georgia, with Hoke Smith," 3–7, Clark Howell Collection, Woodruff Library, Emory University, Atlanta. See Niswonger, *Ar-*

kansas Democratic Politics, 1896–1920, 17–24, for use of Australian ballot as a means of reducing the black electorate. For the evolution of the white primary, see Dittmer, *Black Georgia in the Progressive Era, 1900–1920*, 94–97; Woodward, *The Strange Career of Jim Crow*, 84–85. For Smith's views, see *Atlanta Journal*, June 1905–October 1906.

45. Simon, "The Appeal of Cole Blease of South Carolina," 375; Cook, *The Governors of Georgia*, 186. My thanks to Dr. Timothy J. Crimmins.

Chapter 2. "If Folks Don't Treat Me Right": Atlanta's White Working Classes

Epigraph. "Some Striking Sentences from Hoke Smith's Speech," *Atlanta Journal*, 29 June 1905, 1.

1. "In Race Riot Many Negroes Are Killed and Scores of Both Races Are Injured; Atlanta under Control of State Militia," *Atlanta Journal*, 23 September 1906, 1.

2. See Rosen, "'Not That Sort of Women,'" 268–72, 285, for a discussion of white male identity under assault in the urban South by black definitions of freedom including access to public space and the violent white response by workingmen.

3. "In Race Riot Many Negroes Are Killed"; Roediger, *Wages of Whiteness*, 5, 7–10, 12–13, 20–21; Rosen, "'Not That Sort of Women,'" 267–76; Zipf, "'The WHITES shall rule the land or die.'"

4. Kuhn, "'A Full History,'" 89; Newby, *Plain Folk in the New South*, 32, 119, 182–83, 198–99, 206–29, 233–45, 322–23, 448, 460, chap. 5; Roediger, *Wages of Whiteness*, 8–14, 170–72. Factory work involved give and take between the employer and employee, despite these restrictions on workers. For an example of white working-class paternalism during the first two decades of the twentieth century, see MacLean, "Gender, Sexuality, and the Politics of Lynching." For a comparison with another New South City and black-white labor and political relations over time, see McKiven, *Iron and Steel*.

5. Newby, *Plain Folk in the New South*, 7–8, 39–46, 56, 64–67, 84–111; Ayers, *The Promise of the New South*, 62–65; Maclachlan, "Women's Work," 2, 4, 6, 8–13, 16, 22, 26; Hopkins, "Status, Mobility, and the Dimension of Change in a Southern City," 221–29; Rabinowitz, "Southern Urban Development," 116.

6. Inman, *Inman Diary*, 1:5, 33; Goodson, "'This Mighty Influence for Good or for Evil,'" 28–29; Dittmer, *Black Georgia in the Progressive Era*, 12; White, "The Black Sides of Atlanta," 209–12; Watts, "Black Political Progress in Atlanta, 1868–1895," 286; Dorsey, "To Build Our Lives Together," 13–16, 182–83.

7. Grable, "The Other Side of the Tracks: Cabbagetown," 52–54; Maclachlan, "Women's Work," chap. 6; Russell, *Atlanta, 1847–1890*, 187–99, 250–60; Doyle, *New Men, New Cities, New South*, 189–97; Spencer, "Decatur Street: A Natural Area," 25–26, 28–29.

8. Bolden, "The Political Structure of Charter Revision Movements," 74–75, 210–11; Dittmer, *Black Georgia in the Progressive Era*, 12; Galishoff, "Germs Know No Color Line," 33–36, 40–41; Doyle, *New Men, New Cities, New South*, 263, 278; Russell, *Atlanta, 1847–1890*, 216–17, 222, 228; Maclachlan, "Women's Work," 2–6, 16, 24–27, 46, 55, 60, 76; "In Race Riot Many Negroes Are Killed."

9. Watts, *Social Bases of City Politics*, chaps. 2–6; McKiven, *Iron and Steel*; Governor's

Correspondence, Executive Department Correspondence, 1–1–5, 2740–13, 1868, Georgia Department of Archives and History, Atlanta; Foner, *Nothing but Freedom*, chap. 1.

10. Watts, *Social Bases of City Politics*, 18–22, 49–50, 53, 78, 160–69; Russell, *Atlanta, 1847–1890*, 179; Dorsey, "To Build Our Lives Together," 177.

11. Russell, *Atlanta, 1847–1890*, 178–79; Watts, *Social Bases of City Politics*, 73.

12. Russell, *Atlanta, 1847–1890*, 179–82; Watts, *Social Bases of City Politics*, 21–23, 54, 73; Walton, *Black Republicans*, chap. 3.

13. Watts, *Social Bases of City Politics*, 23–25; Russell, *Atlanta, 1847–1890*, 181–82.

14. Watts, *Social Bases of City Politics*, 24–25, 170; Russell, *Atlanta, 1847–1890*, 181, 186–87; Garrett, *Atlanta and Environs*, 1:874, 903; Watts, "The Police in Atlanta," 166–67, 175–80. For William Brotherton's influence, see "A New City Committee," *Atlanta Journal*, 16 November 1892, 4.

15. Watts, *Social Bases of City Politics*, 36.

16. Ibid., 26–28. For Judge John L. Hopkins's comments, see "Judge Hopkins," *Atlanta Constitution*, 23 August 1892, 4.

17. Dorsey, "To Build Our Lives Together," 179–85.

18. Ibid., 185–86; Watts, *Social Bases of City Politics*, 27–29; Russell, *Atlanta, 1847–1890*, 210–13; Bacote, "The Negro in Atlanta Politics," 334–36. The evolution of Walter Brown's candidacy is the result of combining the narratives from Bacote and Russell. For Woodward's election history, see "A Primary or Not?" *Atlanta Constitution*, 27 August 1892, 4.

19. Russell, *Atlanta, 1847–1890*, 213.

20. "Endorse Mr. Broyles," *Atlanta Constitution*, 6 September 1892, 5; "A Primary or Not?"; "Woodward Will Run," *Atlanta Constitution*, 4 September 1892, 16; "Woodward's Record," *Atlanta Journal*, 17 October 1892, 2.

21. "A White Primary," *Atlanta Constitution*, 18 October 1892, 4; "A Primary November 14," *Atlanta Journal*, 18 October 1892, 3; Watts, *Social Bases of City Politics*, 30. Two days before the 18 October 1892 meeting, Judge John L. Hopkins and the city executive committee projected that the "result of its deliberations will either be a white primary, an appeal to the ballot box or a committee of one hundred elected from the wards." See "To the People," *Atlanta Constitution*, 16 October 1892, 14. For Dave M. Vining, see "It's a Primary," *Atlanta Constitution*, 21 October 1892, 2; Bacote, "The Negro in Atlanta Politics," 333–39. Bacote discounts the power of labor in this process and attributes the white primary to "the bitterness resulting from the campaign of 1891" among the "anti-barroom group."

22. "A White Primary"; "A Primary November 14"; Bacote, "The Negro in Atlanta Politics," 337–39; "A New City Committee," *Atlanta Journal*, 16 November 1892, 4; Russell, *Atlanta, 1847–1890*, 213; "How It Looks," *Atlanta Constitution*, 14 November 1892, 1. Thompson's name was also spelled Thomson by the *Atlanta Constitution*.

23. Watts, *Social Bases of City Politics*, 30–35; Bacote, "The Negro in Atlanta Politics," 333–39.

24. Kuhn, "'A Full History,'" 33–36, 38–39, 41–43, 65, 82–87, 113–14; Newby, *Plain Folk in the New South*, 168–73, 182; Lichtenstein, "'Through the Rugged Gates of the Penitentiary,'" 14–15; Rosen, "'Not That Sort of Women,'" 267–74; Simon, "The Appeal of Cole

Blease of South Carolina," 374–76. Lichtenstein provides a regional look at labor instability with convict labor being an alternative that negatively impacted black labor.

25. D'Avino, "Atlanta Municipal Parks, 1882–1917," 1–2, 7, 9, 44, 56–57, 65, 96, 103–5; Hickey, "Visibility, Politics, and Urban Development," chap. 5 and pp. 292–93, 245–47. See also MacLean, "Gender, Sexuality, and the Politics of Lynching"; Fink, *The Fulton Bag and Cotton Mills Strike,* chap. 2.

26. McLeod, *Workers and Work Place Dynamics,* 33–34, 37–42, 54, 62–63, 73, 85, 87, 113–16; Deaton, "Atlanta during the Progressive Era," 185–86. Fulton Bag would lose some of its mastery over labor and the industry in the 1890s and 1910s due to excessive turnover that transcended the norm and isolation from the commercial-civic elite. See Fink, *The Fulton Bag and Cotton Mills Strike,* chap. 2.

27. Newby, *Plain Folk in the New South,* 463–67, 472, 475; Mathias and Anderson, *Horse to Helicopter,* 41–42; *Atlanta Constitution,* 1 March 1901; Deaton, "Atlanta during the Progressive Era," 148–49, 162, and chap. 4; *Atlanta Constitution,* 26 August 1906; Roediger, *Towards the Abolition of Whiteness,* 131, 133–38; Letwin, "Interracial Unionism, Gender, and 'Social Equality,'" 519–54; Simon, "The Appeal of Cole Blease of South Carolina," 57–86. Deaton, Roediger, and Letwin also note interracial unionism in Atlanta and across the South that failed when southern political leaders called for white solidarity. Simon provides reasons for the failure to transcend race.

28. Newby, *Plain Folk in the New South,* 462–90; Hickey, "Visibility, Politics, and Urban Development," 31–39; Kuhn, "'A Full History,'" 114, 139, 143, 145–46, 165, 464–65, 467–69, 474–92; Fink, *The Fulton Bag and Cotton Mills Strike,* 13–14. Fink defines carpetbagger less pejoratively. Elsas "was more Savior than salvager of that benighted region." For a discussion of racial violence spanning this important decade, see Williamson, *The Crucible of Race,* 180–223; Prather, *We Have Taken a City;* Gilmore, *Gender and Jim Crow,* 92, 96–98, 106–17; Edmonds, *The Negro and Fusion Politics in North Carolina,* chaps. 10 and 11.

29. Hickey, "Visibility, Politics, and Urban Development," 33, 35–37, 39; Newby, *Plain Folk in the New South,* 478; Woodward, *Origins of the New South,* 312–20, 379–93. Hickey also argues that male "respectability" was an issue.

30. Kuhn, "'A Full History,'" 169–70, 153–54; Newby, *Plain Folk in the New South,* 479. Grantham establishes Smith's involvement with the *Journal,* but there is no mention of the 1897 Strike and Smith's role in it. Grantham, *Hoke Smith,* 18, 114.

31. Haygood, "Immigration," *Journal of Labor,* 23 November 1906, 3; "Law and Order League," *Journal of Labor,* 14 December 1906, 3; "Our Sanitary Force," *Journal of Labor,* 6 July 1906, 2; Watkins, "The City Sanitary Department," *Journal of Labor,* 16 November 1906, 3; "A Word to Police Commissioners," *Journal of Labor,* 17 August 1906, 2; "As to Politics and the Union," *Journal of Labor,* 14 September 1906, 2; "The Forces That Have Fought for the Children," *Journal of Labor,* 13 July 1906, 2.

32. "Negro Made Attempt to Kill Kirkwood Citizen," *Atlanta Journal,* 11 November 1905, 5; "Negro Is Arrested for Frightening Little Girl," *Atlanta Journal,* 21 November 1905, 1; "Says Negroes Robbed Him of Money," *Atlanta Journal,* 20 November 1905, 3; R. L. Cureton Robbed by Negro Highwayman," *Atlanta Journal,* 8 December 1905, 9; "Ne-

gro Made Threats to Whip Policeman," *Atlanta Journal,* 5 December 1905, 3.

33. "Lanterns of Brakemen Shot Out by Negroes, Trainmen Seek Safety," *Atlanta News,* 9 July 1906, 1; "Lady Is Injured, Her Buggy Hit by Wagon," *Atlanta News,* 17 July 1906, 1; "Negro Ran Wagon against Light Buggy," *Atlanta Journal,* 6 September 1906, 7.

34. "Gov. Northen in His Inaugural . . . ," *Savannah Tribune,* 5 November 1892, 2; "The Atlanta Conference," *Savannah Tribune,* 19 November 1892, 2; "Colored Men in Conference," *Savannah Tribune,* 26 November 1892, 2; "Blacks on Back Seat," *Atlanta Constitution,* 26 July 1896, 17; "The Race Loving . . . ," *Savannah Tribune,* 29 August 1896, 2; "In Atlanta the Colored People . . . ."

35. Martin, *Mule to Marta,* 2:14–15; Baker, *Following the Color Line,* 31–32; "According to Bishop Turner . . . ," *Atlanta Independent,* 28 January 1904, 4; "The Boycott and Bishop Turner," *Atlanta Independent,* 6 February 1904, 4. Councilman Thomas Longino restated state law in a city ordinance in 1900 intended to reduce racial tension. The boycott spanned February to December 1900. The white press ignored the protest, but black newspapers provided coverage.

36. Baker, *Following the Color Line,* 30–32; Kuhn, Joye, and West, *Living Atlanta,* 72; Martin, *Mule to Marta,* 2:14–15. Kuhn, Joye, and West note that by 1910s Georgia Railway and Power hired only white men born and reared in the country, believing that these employees would not join unions. See also Hunter, *To 'Joy My Freedom,* 146–47. Employees received "police powers" from the state and city to enforce segregation.

37. Baker, *Following the Color Line,* 32.

38. "Fight Occurred on Trolley Car," *Atlanta Constitution,* 16 July 1905, 5C; Martin, *Mule to Marta,* 2:15.

39. "Letters from the People—Separate Cars for Negroes," *Atlanta Constitution,* 19 July 1905, 6; "Jim Crow Cars before Senate," *Atlanta Constitution,* 8 July 1905, 7; Martin, *Mule to Marta,* 2:14–17; Baker, *Following the Color Line,* 30–31; Matthews, "Studies in Race Relations in Georgia, 1890–1930," 126–32; "Put Off Car, Negro Man Tries to Shoot Conductor," *Atlanta Journal,* 11 November 1905, 3. For Senator Strange, see Journal of the Senate of the State of Georgia 1905, 5, Georgia Department of Archives and History, Atlanta. It is not clear if this legislation passed due to the fact that a segregation statute existed which legislators in 1890 ratified. Most of the reform measures proposed in 1905 went down to defeat. See *Atlanta Constitution,* July and August 1905.

40. "Put Off Car, Negro Man Tries to Shoot Conductor"; "Negro Calls Conductor a Liar and Is Knocked from His Street Car," *Atlanta News,* 21 July 1906, 7.

41. "Negro Insults Girl on St. Car," *Atlanta News,* 8 July 1906, 1.

42. "Atlanta Street Car System," *Journal of Labor,* 31 August 1906, 6; "The Initiatory of Municipal Ownership," *Journal of Labor,* 14 September 1906, 2; "Organized Labor and Municipal Ownership," *Journal of Labor,* 5 October 1906, 3; Kuhn, "1906 Riot: Atlanta Papers Kindle Racist Violence," *Great Speckled Bird,* 28 August 1975, 8–9.

43. "North Carolina's Evidence," *Atlanta Journal,* 3 December 1905, 6; Milt Saul, "Hon. Josepheus Daniels, Able Editor and National Democratic Committeeman of North Carolina, Makes Ringing Statement about Negro Disfranchisement 'The Delay in Adopting the Amendment Caused a Revolution,'" *Atlanta Journal,* 3 December 1905, 6; "Georgia Editors Comment on the Gubernatorial Campaign; Editor Comfort Dis-

cusses Disfranchisement Issue," *Atlanta Journal*, 10 December 1905, 9; "Negro Disfranchisement," *Atlanta Journal*, 25 November 1905, 6; "Shall White Supremacy Be Destroyed?" *Atlanta Journal*, 12 November 1905, 8; "A Nigger in the Wood Pile," *Atlanta Journal*, 10 November 1905, 8; "Honorable T. W. Hardwick, in Ringing Letter to White Voters of Georgia, Presents in Eloquent Phrases and Unanswerable Argument the Question of Disfranchisement," *Atlanta Journal*, 26 November 1905, 7; Ralph Smith, "Voters Like Mr. Smith's Talk," *Atlanta Journal*, 7 December 1905, 5.

44. "The Free White Men of Georgia Are Fit to Rule Themselves and Will Prove It at the Polls Wednesday," *Atlanta Journal*, 21 August 1906, 7.

45. "Fulton County Police System," *Atlanta Journal*, 8 September 1906, 6; "Many Negroes Fall Victim to Mob Which Holds Uptown in Grasp," *Atlanta Journal*, 23 September 1906, 1.

Chapter 3. African Americans in Atlanta

Epigraph. Hope, "Negro Suffrage," 54.

1. For the Rucker family's evolution, see "Hon. Henry A. Rucker," 259–62, Long-Rucker-Aiken Family Papers, Atlanta History Center, folder Henry A. Rucker Personal Correspondence (1904–8) biographies (n.d.) newspaper clippings 1970, 1979; "Rucker Goes In: Downs Maj. Smyth," *Atlanta Constitution*, 27 July 1897, 5; "Rucker to Land; Likewise Smyth," *Atlanta Constitution*, 21 July 1897, 3. Rucker's mother moved to Atlanta in the late 1850s, and poverty forced Rucker to go to work on his own. For the biographies used in this chapter, see L. M. Hershaw, "On the Death of Henry Allen Rucker," *New York Age*, and Chet Fuller, "Henry A. Rucker," both in Henry A. Rucker vertical file, Archives Department, Woodruff Library, Atlanta University Center. See Miggins, "Between Spires and Stacks," 192–93, 196–99, for a discussion of first-generation migrants as leaders and the city building capabilities of black migrants. Rucker also obtained positions in the federal government between the 1870s and 1890s while still practicing his trade as a barber.

2. For a detailed biography of J. W. Dobbs, see Pomerantz, *Where Peachtree Meets Sweet Auburn*, 17–21, 62, 69–71, 81, 92.

3. For Rucker's federal career, see Mixon, "Politics and Race." For the black central business district, see Spencer, "Decatur Street: A Natural Area," 26–28.

4. Dorsey, "To Build Our Lives Together," 44–62, 104, 121, 136–40, 241–43, appendix; Carter, *The Black Side*; Thomas, *Life for Us Is What We Make It*, xi–xiv, 10–17, 21–23, 35–36; Hunter, *To 'Joy My Freedom*, viii, 4, 13–14, 20–21, 28, 31–33, 48–52, 57–60, 62; Porter, "Black Atlanta: An Interdisciplinary Study," 32, 46–61; Deaton, "Atlanta during the Progressive Era," 168–70. See one example of black resistance to convict labor in "Life-Time Convict Shot to Death in Midnight Rush to Gain Liberty," *Atlanta Constitution*, 4 August 1906, 1–2. For the impact of federal employment on black economic stability, see Gamble, *Making a Place for Ourselves*, 71, 85, 90, 101.

5. Higginbotham, *Righteous Discontent*, chaps. 1 and 2; Henderson, *Atlanta Life Insurance Company*, chap. 1; Gilmore, *Gender and Jim Crow*, xviii–xix.

6. Davis, "An African American Dilemma: John Hope and Black Leadership in the

Early Twentieth Century," 33; Franklin, *My Life and an Era*, chaps. 4–6; Gilmore, *Gender and Jim Crow*, chaps. 1–3.

7. Gilmore, *Gender and Jim Crow*, xviii–xix; Gaines, *Uplifting the Race*, 2–3, 6, 9, 12, 16–17, 20, 31, 35; Bederman, *Manliness and Civilization*, chap. 2.

8. "The Past as a Problem Solver," *Atlanta Constitution*, 3 October 1906, B4; "Rev. C. O. Jones of St. Mark's," *Atlanta Constitution*, 5 October 1906, 5; Cell, *The Highest Stage of White Supremacy*, 16–17, 19; see also 119, 130, 133, 143, 146–48, 153, 161, 179, 193, 214, 230–34; Higginbotham, *Righteous Discontent*, 26–27, 40–46; Wheeler, *Uplifting the Race*, xiv–xv, xvii. Cell notes that African Americans helped create the crisis in white supremacy by migrating to southern towns and cities, seeking political participation, and "growing uppityness" (234).

9. Penn and Bowen, eds., *The United Negro*, 6–11 August 1902, v–vi, xiv, 3, 5–6. For a discussion of the Congress and broader implications of the African American dilemma, see Mixon, "'Good Negro–Bad Negro.'"

10. Baker, *Following the Color Line*, 242, 267.

11. Hunter, *To 'Joy My Freedom*, 30–35; Goings and Smith, "'Unhidden' Transcripts," 372–78; Kelley, "We Are Not What We Seem," 76–89.

12. Dorsey, "To Build Our Lives Together," 20, 22, 24, 28, 45–46, 68; Department of Commerce and Labor, Bureau of the Census, Special Reports Supplementary Analysis and Derivative Tables 1900 (Washington, D.C.: Government Printing Office, 1904), 199; Census Reports, vol. 1, lxxiv, 612, 650; Russell, *Atlanta, 1847–1890*, 71.

13. Dittmer, *Black Georgia in the Progressive Era, 1900–1920*, 12–22; Lewis, *W.E.B. Du Bois: Biography of a Race*, 197–98, 386; Galishoff, "Germs Know No Color Line"; Stuart Galishoff, "The Health of Black Atlantans," 4–6; Porter, "Black Atlanta: An Interdisciplinary Study," 203; Rouse, *Lugenia Burns Hope*, chap. 4.

14. Galishoff, "Germs Know No Color Line." For segregation as a regional and national trend tied to industrialization, see Greenwood, *Bittersweet Legacy*, chaps. 3–6; Hanchett, *Sorting Out the New South City*, chaps. 3–6; Miggins, "Between Spires and Stacks," 192–93, 196–97, 199; Kusmer, "Black Cleveland and the Central-Woodland Community, 1865–1930," 266–69.

15. Rouse, *Lugenia Burns Hope*, 57–65; Kuhn, Joye, and West, *Living Atlanta*, 32–40; Galishoff, "Health of Black Atlantans," 4; Russell, *Atlanta, 1847–1890*, 218–21, 224, 226, 229; Hunter, *To 'Joy My Freedom*, chap. 9; "'Neglected Negro Menaces South's Civilization'—Powerful Plea by Judge Hopkins, Dean of Jurists," Hopkins Family Collection, 1852–1943, Atlanta History Center.

16. Spencer, "Decatur Street: A Natural Area," 26–28; Walton, *Black Republicans*, 50–51, 52, 57–61. European immigrants as well as white southerners also served black customers on Decatur Street. Their shops became gathering places for African Americans. At Decatur and Piedmont, the wholesale clothing store built by "old man Mahoney" had black customers "from the local as well as the rural communities." Working-class blacks "found it economical to buy bolts of cloth there."

17. Hunter, *To 'Joy My Freedom*, 163, 168–71, 179–86; Harris, *The Rise of Gospel Blues*, xx, 30–44.

18. Pleck and Pleck, introduction to *The American Man*, 26–27; Kingsdale, "The 'Poor Man's Club': Social Functions of the Urban Working-Class Saloon," 257, 259–69, 271, 273–77; Rouse, *Lugenia Burns Hope*, 64–65; Atlanta Chamber of Commerce, *Atlanta: A Twentieth-Century City*, 10, 39–40; Atlanta Chamber of Commerce, *Souvenir Album*, 2, 20–22; Dorsey, "To Build Our Lives Together," 50–51, 58–59, 61–62, see chaps. 3 and 4 on the church and benevolent societies; Hunter, *To 'Joy My Freedom*, 62, 65–66, 67–73. Men such as Jacob McKinley rose to elite status and construction contractor from his working-class position as a grocery cart operator. Telephone conversation with Allison G. Dorsey, 29 November 1999.

19. White, *A Man Called White*, 9–12; Porter, "Black Atlanta: An Interdisciplinary Study," 17, 32, 41, 69, 90, 106–9; Rouse, *Lugenia Burns Hope*, 58–64; Slade, "The Evolution of Negro Areas in the City of Atlanta," 24–25; Deaton, "Atlanta during the Progressive Era," 68–69, 168–70. For the role the working-class plays in urban development, see Thomas, *Life for Us Is What We Make It*, xi–xiv; Hunter, *To 'Joy My Freedom*, 25–28, 43, chap. 4.

20. Hunter, *To 'Joy My Freedom*, 151–53, 156–59, 161–67, 169–71, 183–86; "Rev. C. O. Jones of St. Mark's"; "Rev. Dr. C. E. Dowman on the 'Problem,'" *Atlanta Constitution*, 9 October 1906, 5; "The Past as a Problem Solver"; "Ministers Discuss the Problem," *Atlanta Constitution*, 17 October 1906, 6; "'Redeem the Bad Negro,' Says Rev. Crawford Jackson," *Atlanta Constitution*, 10 October 1906, 8; "Views of Rev. A. C. Ward on 'Problem,'" *Atlanta Constitution*, 8 October 1906, 4.

21. "One Hundred German Servant Girls to Be Brought Here from Chicago," *Atlanta Constitution*, 9 January 1906, 6; "Let Southern Whites Teach Negroes," *Atlanta Constitution*, 15 October 1906, 4; "Rev. John E. White Writes in Regard to Negro Problem," *Atlanta Constitution*, 10 October 1906, 8; "The Past as a Problem Solver."

22. Baker, *Following the Color Line*, 45–46; Galishoff, "Health of Black Atlantans," 3, 17; Garrett, *Atlanta and Environs*, 2:542–43; Dittmer, *Black Georgia in the Progressive Era, 1900–1920*, 12–13; *Annual Reports of the Chief of Police of the City of Atlanta, Georgia* for years ending 1896, 1897, 1900, 1901, 1902, 1903, 1904, Subject Collection, Atlanta History Center; Atlanta University Conference no. 9, pp. 49–50; see *Atlanta Constitution* and *Atlanta Journal*, January 1906 and 1907, for summarizations of *Annual Reports of the Chief of Police*, 1905, 1906, 1907.

23. "One Hundred German Servant Girls"; Higginbotham, *Righteous Discontent*, 101; Hunter, *To 'Joy My Freedom*, chap. 4; Cell, *The Highest Stage of White Supremacy*, 125–30, 141–42; "The Past as a Problem Solver." For examples of articles in the *Constitution* from 1903 to 1906, see Mixon, "The Atlanta Riot of 1906," 439–54.

24. Hunter, *To 'Joy My Freedom*, 51, 58–60, 98–100, 105–9; Higginbotham, *Righteous Discontent*, 101; Mixon, "'Good Negro–Bad Negro,'" 617–20; Roediger, *Towards the Abolition of Whiteness*, 137–38, 161; Hunter, "Household Workers," 146, 150, 169–70, 188. See also McLeod, *Workers and Work Place Dynamics*, 1–2, 113–16; Cell, *The Highest Stage of White Supremacy*, 17–20, 47–50, 57–58, 101–2, 114–15, 126–27, 138–40, 149–51, 234; Maclachlan, "Women's Work," 339–42; Newby, *Plain Folk in the New South*, 464–91.

25. Adams, *A History of Atlanta University*, 23–24; Bacote, *The Story of Atlanta University*, 101; Mother to Linton C. Hopkins, 20 August 1904, 15 April 1905, Hopkins Family Collection, 1852–1943, Atlanta History Center, box 1, folder 6, Correspondence 1904–12. Judge John L. Hopkins, like his son Charles, supported Clark Howell's gubernatorial effort. See "'I Am for Howell,' Says Judge Hopkins in Great Tribute," *Atlanta Constitution*, 19 May 1906, 9; Hunter, *To 'Joy My Freedom*, 28, 31, 58–61, 204–9, and chap. 9. Hunter's longevity study of Atlanta suggests that personal control overcame white tendencies for state regulation. For examples of black insistence upon the freedom to control their work life, see Jenkins, *Seizing the New Day*, 42–44. See also white complaints: "The Past as a Problem Solver"; "Neglected Negro Menaces South's Civilization," as well as "Religion as a Race Problem Solution," 2 October 1906, and "Warning Given to the Negroes," 27 October 1906, all in ARVF October 1906 Aftermath.

26. Gilmore, *Gender and Jim Crow*, 1–3, 12–13, 15, 21, 24; Hunter, *To 'Joy My Freedom*, 51, 58–60, 98–100, 105–8, 124–29; Special Report Occupations at the Twelfth Census, 486–88; Thirteenth Census, vol. 4, Population, 1910 Occupation Statistics, 536; Higginbotham, *Righteous Discontent*, 101; Mixon, "'Good Negro–Bad Negro,'" 617–20.

27. Maclachlan, "Women's Work," 199–200, 342–45.

28. "The South and North," *Atlanta Constitution*, 2 January 1905, 6; "Georgia Awaits Coming Immigration Stream," *Atlanta Constitution*, 2 January 1905, 3; "Initial Batch of Immigrants," *Atlanta Constitution*, 6 February 1903, 7; "Immigration and the Labor Problem," *Atlanta Constitution*, 5 February 1905, 4B; "The Negro and Immigration," *Atlanta Constitution*, 15 February 1905, 6; "Immigration and the Negro," *Atlanta Constitution*, 26 March 1906, 4.

29. "Speech to Atlanta Society of the National German-American Alliance," Robert Foster Maddox Papers, MS 143, Private Collection, Atlanta History Center, box 1, folder Robert Maddox Speeches; Louis B. Magid, "Thoughtful Study of Immigrant: The Imperative Need of Georgia," *Atlanta Constitution*, 15 October 1905, 2B. See "Immigration and Health," *Atlanta Journal*, 5 January 1904, 6, for a voice against immigration; Higham, *Strangers in the Land*, 165–82; Iorizzo, "The Padrone and Immigrant Distribution," 44–49, 70; Norrell, "Steelworkers and Storekeepers"; Nelli, "Italians in Urban America." The *Constitution* declared that Englishmen, Poles, Slavs, Germans, and other European immigrants would be useful in meeting Georgia's agricultural needs and developing the New South. Italians were especially suited for cotton culture because of their work ethic, reliability, and "conservative" political philosophy. The southern crusade to tap European immigration failed to materialize in 1905 or 1906, even though the press encouraged open debate on the issue. Immigrants did not flock to Atlanta or the South, despite isolated colonies of immigrants appearing in the region.

30. "Italian v. Negro Field Labor," *Atlanta Constitution*, 22 January 1906, 6; "Italians Are Enroute to Form Large Colony," *Atlanta Journal*, 10 January 1904, 11; "Sell the Land to Immigrants," *Atlanta Constitution*, 14 February 1906, 11; "Police Faced a Negro Riot," *Atlanta Constitution*, 17 September 1905, 1C.

31. Davis, "An African American Dilemma: John Hope and Black Leadership in the

Early Twentieth Century," 33; Franklin, *My Life and an Era*, chaps. 4–6; Gilmore, *Gender and Jim Crow*, chaps. 1–3.

32. Bacote, "The Negro in Atlanta Politics," 333–41; Dorsey, "To Build Our Lives Together," chaps. 5 and 6. For an examination of class and culture divisions between the black elite and working class, see Greenwood, *Bittersweet Legacy*, chap. 3.

33. Bacote, "The Negro in Atlanta Politics," 333–41. See Bayor, *Race and the Shaping of Twentieth-Century Atlanta* for the realization of many of these urban services from the 1940s into the 1990s.

34. "Go Vote Today Early," *Atlanta Constitution*, 3 December 1890, 4; "The People's Ticket," *Atlanta Constitution*, 4 December 1890, 5; Garrett, *Atlanta and Environs*, 2:226; Cooper, *Official History of Fulton County*, 633–36, 719–20. See Dorsey, "To Build Our Lives Together," 245–92, for a list of affluent African Americans in Atlanta between 1880 and 1900 and the source of the "grocers' slate." Lovinggood, Palmer, and Render were not listed, and their status is undetermined.

35. Bacote, "The Negro in Atlanta Politics, 333–41; Walton, *Black Republicans*, 45–61; Shapiro, "The Populist and the Negro: A Reconsideration," 27–36; Abramowitz, "The Negro in the Populist Movement," 281; Harlan, *Booker T. Washington: The Making of a Black Leader, 1865–1901*, 291–92.

36. Penn and Bowen, *The United Negro*, v–vi, 5; Wheeler, *Uplifting the Race*, 26–30, 50–83, 97–99, 127–29; "Thousands of Negroes to Meet in Washington," *Atlanta News*, 18 July 1906, 7. The panelists included Penn and Bowen's wives, who addressed the convention about motherhood, social purity, and child marriage. Other sessions focused on public school teaching, social elevation of the race, and morality and citizenship.

37. Penn and Bowen, *The United Negro*, xiv, 6; Wheeler, *Uplifting the Race*, 97–99, 127–29.

38. Penn and Bowen, *The United Negro*, 3. John Hope reported the warning of an unnamed white cleric that "colored people [needed] to be good Negroes." They must be people who refrained from getting "mad about 'Jim Crow' cars and . . . slow to urge their rights," since it was "a heavy task when you attempt to reform the Anglo-Saxon." Hope, "Negro Suffrage," 59.

39. Hope, "Negro Suffrage," 59; Penn and Bowen, *The United Negro*, 2–5; Higginbotham, *Righteous Discontent*, 18; Wheeler, *Uplifting the Race*, xv–xvii.

40. Proctor, *Between Black and White*, 91–92; Rodney, "Henry Hugh Proctor," 40–42. See also Barton, *The Church That Saved a City*, concerning First Congregational Church and Proctor.

41. Proctor, *Between Black and White*, 93, 105–6, 120–21. Proctor reinforced his convictions with two credos acquired while a student at Fisk and Yale Universities. At Fisk, he internalized his lifelong credo: "To live that prejudice against one would be unreasonable." Yale caused him to realize that "the only fault . . . found of me was my color."

42. Proctor, *Between Black and White*, 93, 120–21; Rodney, "Henry Hugh Proctor," 48–64; Higginbotham, *Righteous Discontent*, 173.

43. Proctor, *Between Black and White*, 58–60; Harris, *The Rise of Gospel Blues*, 11–13.

44. Proctor, *Between Black and White*, 97, 121; "Will Oppose Dance Halls," *Atlanta Constitution*, 19 February 1905, sec. D; "No Dance Halls Given Licenses," *Atlanta Constitution*, 21 February 1905, 6; "The Negro Problem and Other Subjects Discussed by Georgia Readers," *Atlanta Georgian*, 1 September 1906, 9. Rucker did not specifically name the New York City riot of 1900 in this quotation. For a description of the 1900 riot and its impact on members of the black elite and their social behavior goals, see Lorini, *Rituals of Race*, chaps. 5 and 6.

45. "Will Oppose Dance Halls."

46. "Negroes Want Man on Board," *Atlanta Constitution*, 7 January 1905, 2"; Petition of Negroes to Use the Carnegie Library," Correspondence 1877–1910, series 1, reel 1, frame 143, W.E.B. Du Bois Papers, microfilm collection, University of Cincinnati; Garrett, *Atlanta and Environs*, 2:375–78.

47. Proctor, *Between Black and White*, 94–95, 101, 113; "Will Oppose Dance Halls;" "The Negro Problem and Other Subjects Discussed by Georgia Readers," *Atlanta Georgian*, 1 September 1906, 9. First Congregational Church's elite membership grew, and white elite support in raising funds built the present First Congregational Church in 1908. Allison G. Dorsey notes that Proctor left Atlanta in the early 1920s thoroughly fed up with Atlanta's white elite and the obstacles they constructed to constrain black advancement. See Dorsey, "To Build Our Lives Together," epilogue.

48. Proctor, *Between Black and White*, 19–22, 39–40; Bacote, "The Negro in Georgia, 1880–1908," 350, 354; Kathleen Redding Adams, interview held in her apartment at 899 Park Street S.E., Atlanta, 13 August 1985. Mrs. Adams was ninety-five years old in 1985 and still serving as historian for First Congregational Church. A teenager in 1906, she attended First Church during Proctor's tenure and participated in its uplift programs following the riot.

49. Atlanta University, "Some Notes on Negro Crime," 49–58, 65; Lane, *Roots of Violence in Black Philadelphia*, 1–6, 37–43, and chaps. 1, 5, and 6; Higginbotham, *Righteous Discontent*, chap. 7.

50. Atlanta University, "Some Notes on Negro Crime." Lane demonstrates that similar strains of poverty, absence of jobs, and calculated discrimination led to crime in the North. Lane, *Roots of Violence in Black Philadelphia*, 1–6, chaps. 5 and 6. Carl Harris notes that municipal authorities in Birmingham arrested blacks and used the courts to control as well as force them into convict labor. Harris, *Political Power in Birmingham*, 198–207. Both Orr and Gilmore note that white politicians fabricated rape and crime charges against African Americans to create an antiblack atmosphere that resulted in violence. Orr, *Charles Brantley Aycock*, 141–42; Gilmore, *Gender and Jim Crow*, 71–84.

51. Hope, "Negro Suffrage," 56–60.

Chapter 4. "Sowing Dragon's Teeth": Watson, Hardwick, and Progressive Reform, 1904–1906

Epigraph. Watson, editorial, *Tom Watson's Magazine* 2 (October 1905): 397–98.

1. For a discussion of southern Progressivism, see Grantham, "The Promise of

Southern Progressivism," 235–37, 240; Link, "The Paradox of Southern Progressivism," 243–45, 253; Link, *The Paradox of Southern Progressivism, 1880–1930*, 59–60, 62–67, 75–78; Senechal de la Roche, "The Sociogenesis of Lynching," 61–63.

2. Cummings, "Thomas William Hardwick," 2, 6–14; Hicks, "Watson and Hardwick in Georgia Politics," 72–74, 88, 100–102, 131–32, 135–36, 138–42, 148, 152–74. Hicks chronicled the fragmenting of the coalition between Watson, Hardwick, and Smith.

3. Watson, "Down in Georgia—Editorials," *Tom Watson's Magazine* 4 (March 1906): 1; Watson, "The Ungrateful Negro from a Newspaper—Editorials," *Tom Watson's Magazine* 4 (April 1906): 165–69, 170–71, 173. Turner and Lyons attended a convention in Macon, Georgia, dealing with black rights. Turner spoke at the conference. This was at least the third time in Turner's career that he condemned the United States. Only in 1906 did whites respond. See Redkey, *Respect Black*, 60, 172–74, 184–85, 196; Redkey, *Black Exodus*, 41, 171, 245, 252; Angell, *Bishop Henry McNeal Turner*, 242–45.

4. Watson, "The Ungrateful Negro," 168–69, 173; "Editorial Notes," *Jeffersonian*, 29 November 1906, 5. My thanks to the staff of the Library of Congress and the Interlibrary Loan staffs at the University of North Carolina at Charlotte and University of North Carolina at Chapel Hill in unearthing the *Jeffersonian*.

5. "Editorial Notes"; "The Negro Problem Once More," *Jeffersonian*, 4 October 1906, 4; "Negro Secret Societies," *Jeffersonian*, 11 October 1906, 5.

6. "Drifting towards Niagara," *Jeffersonian*, 29 November 1906, 4. For accusations against T. Thomas Fortune and a black Los Angeles newspaper, *Liberator*, see "The Negro Question Once More." Notably, Benjamin Davis, editor of the *Atlanta Independent*, was not listed as an antiwhite editor.

7. "The Negro Problem Once More"; "Negro Secret Societies"; Watson, "The Ungrateful Negro," 165–68, 170–71; Wattles, "The Municipal Boss," *Tom Watson's Magazine* 4 (March 1906): 91–92; Ruppenthal, "Election Reforms: The Trend toward Democracy," *Tom Watson's Magazine* 4 (March 1906): 76–84; "Down in Georgia—Editorials"; E. B. Holly to Watson, 14 November 1906, TEWPR, reel 6, series I, Correspondence, November/December 1906, folder 70–93.

8. Woodward, *Tom Watson*, 15, 24–29, 35, 51; Bryan, *Henry Grady or Tom Watson?* 34–35, 37, 64; Coleman, *A History of Modern Georgia*, map: "Counties and County Seats."

9. Bryan, *Henry Grady or Tom Watson?* 64–67, chaps. 1–3; Woodward, *Tom Watson*, 44, 75–77, 84, 114, 119, 125–28, 132–35, 147, 219–22; Leuchtenburg, *A Guide to the Microfilm Edition of the Thomas E. Watson Papers*, xviii; Cook, *The Governors of Georgia*, 193–95, 200–205; Carageorge, "An Evaluation of Hoke Smith and Thomas E. Watson as Georgia Reformers," 23; Shaw, *Wool-Hat Boys*, 77–90; Matthews, "Studies in Race Relations in Georgia, 1890–1930," 126–27; 132–33, 143, 154–55; Shapiro, "The Populist and the Negro: A Reconsideration," 27–36; Abramowitz, "The Negro in the Populist Movement," 264–66, 271, 281.

10. Shaw, *Wool-Hat Boys*; Korobin, "The Politics of Disfranchisement in Georgia," 23–24, 27; Gravlee, "Tom Watson: Disciple of 'Jeffersonian Democracy,'" 85–111; Thos E. Watson to J. H. Smyth, 26 April 1900, TEWPR, reel 3, series I, Correspondence 1898–1903, folder 45-52.

11. Thomas E. Watson to Rebecca L. Felton, 27 June 1902, Rebecca L. Felton Collection 1902, MS 81, box 4, Special Collections, University Libraries, University of Georgia, Athens. See also Woodward, *Tom Watson*, 5–6, 114–35, 220–23; Gravlee, "Tom Watson: Disciple of 'Jeffersonian Democracy,'" 93, 106–7; Shaw, *Wool-Hat Boys*, 171–72; Fingerhut, "Tom Watson, Blacks, and Southern Reform," 335–36. Herbert Aptheker argues that Thomas Watson and the Populists were one of the white groups that opposed racism in the United States. Watson, however, was ambitious and compromised race advocacy for political office and power within the Democratic Party. Discussion with Herbert Aptheker, 1 May 1985, Cincinnati, Ohio.

12. Watson to Felton, 27 June 1902, Rebecca L. Felton Collection, Special Collections, University Libraries, University of Georgia, Athens. See "Henry C. People's Powerful Speech on Disfranchisement of the Negro," *Atlanta Journal*, 18 August 1906, 6, for confirmation of these themes in the Hoke Smith gubernatorial campaign. See also Woodward, *Tom Watson*, 371–72; Grantham, "Georgia Politics and the Disfranchisement of the Negro," Grace T. Sherry Collection, Atlanta History Center, 77–136–10, MS 226, p. 3; Shaw, *Wool-Hat Boys*, 21, 200–201; Kousser, *The Shaping of Southern Politics*, 220–21.

13. Hooper Alexander to Watson, 1 August 1904, TEWPR, reel 3, series I, Correspondence 1898–1903 (1904), folder 53–153.

14. Watson to Felton, 27 June 1902, Rebecca L. Felton Collection, Special Collections, University Libraries, University of Georgia, Athens; Bryan, *Henry Grady or Tom Watson?* 66–67, 77–81; "Tom Watson Declares That He Will Support the People's Candidate," *Atlanta Journal*, 4 August 1906, 4; "Good Workers in a Good Cause," *Atlanta Journal*, 23 August 1906, 8; "Overwhelming Majority for Hoke Smith Says Hardwick," *Augusta Herald*, 2 July 1905, Clippings 1905–6, Scrapbook 60, p. 49, HSC, box 78; Grantham, *Southern Progressivism*, xvi–xvii.

15. Hunter, *To 'Joy My Freedom*, 212–13; Grantham, *Southern Progressivism*, 111–12, 421. Southern Progressivism extended beyond the eleven states of the former Confederacy. The South took a leading role in initiating reforms that northerners implemented. New municipal governmental structures formulated in Texas introduced commission governance across the country. Federal, domestic, and foreign policies on race were modeled after restrictions that white southerners imposed upon blacks. See Woodward, *Origins of the New South*, 388–89 and chap. 14; Crawford, "The Warriors of Civilization," 5–9; Wiebe, *The Search for Order*, chaps. 6 and 9; Bederman, *Manliness and Civilization*, 21–30, 70–75.

16. Grantham, *Southern Progressivism*, xvii, 10–12; Grantham, "The Promise of Southern Progressivism," 235–37; Link, *Paradox*, pt. 1.

17. Wiebe, *The Search for Order*, 155–57; Bederman, *Manliness and Civilization*, 10–12, 20–29; Orr, *Charles Brantley Aycock*, 107–11; Gilmore, *Gender and Jim Crow*, 3–4.

18. Grantham, "The Promise of Southern Progressivism," 240; Link, *Paradox*, 59–60, 62, 75–78.

19. Watson to Felton, 27 June 1902, Rebecca L. Felton Collection, Special Collections, University Libraries, University of Georgia, Athens; "Good Workers in a Good Cause," *Atlanta Journal*, 23 August 1906, 8; "Overwhelming Majority for Hoke Smith Says

Hardwick," *Augusta Herald*, 2 July 1905, Clippings 1905–6, Scrapbook 60, p. 49, HSC, box 78. For a brief discussion concerning the contradictions within Populism and Progressivism and the parallel activities of both movements, see Greenberg, "Twentieth-Century Liberalism: Transformation of an Ideology," 59–60.

20. Hicks, "Watson and Hardwick in Georgia Politics," 14–15; Cummings, "Thomas William Hardwick," 1; Orr, *Charles Brantley Aycock*, 81, 101–11, 121–24, 132–35; Gilmore, *Gender and Jim Crow*, 62–74, 96–98; Doyle, *Nashville in the New South*, chap. 6; Cummings, "Thomas William Hardwick," 2–3; Kousser, *The Shaping of Southern Politics*, 217.

21. Cummings, "Thomas William Hardwick," 3, 5; Hicks, "Watson and Hardwick in Georgia Politics," 20–21; Wells, *Southern Horrors and Other Writings*, 141–43; Grantham, "Some Letters," 336–37, Hardwick to Watson, 18 September 1905. The corruption, however, in the Black campaign was so obvious that Black resigned only to win the position again after a special election provided a more honest result.

22. Cummings, "Thomas William Hardwick"; Hicks, "Watson and Hardwick in Georgia Politics," 6, 18–22; Grantham, "Some Letters," 333–35, Hardwick to Watson, 26 June 1905.

23. Cummings, "Thomas William Hardwick," 5–6; Hicks, "Watson and Hardwick in Georgia Politics," 43–45; T. J. Holmes to W. H. Fleming, 19 May 1902, 1–2, TEWPR, reel 3, series I, Correspondence 1898–1903, folder 45–52.

24. Hardwick to Watson, 12 April 1904, 1–3, and 25 July 1904; J. Max Barber to Watson, 1 April 1904, 26 May 1904, and 8 June 1904, Booker Washington to Arthur Brisbane, 8 June 1904, and J. R. Gray to Watson, 13 April 1904, all in TEWPR, reel 3, series I, Correspondence 1898–1903 (1904), folder 53–153. For the exchange between Cleveland and Watson, see "Negro Not His Guest, Says Mr. Cleveland," *New York Times*, 4 March 1904, 5; "Attack Cleveland's Veracity," *New York Times*, 13 April 1904, 5; "Cleveland Repeats Denial," *New York Times*, 4 April 1904, 7; "Watson Rebuked by Mr. Cleveland," *New York Herald*, 4 April 1904, 1. Clark Howell and James R. Gray did not publish Watson's attacks on Grover Cleveland. According to Hardwick, the two editor/owners had a hard time explaining their actions to Watson.

25. Woodward, *Tom Watson*, 370–71; "Tom Watson Declares That He Will Support the People's Candidate"; Hicks, "Watson and Hardwick in Georgia Politics," 46.

26. Grantham, "Some Letters," 330–31, Hardwick to Watson, 6 December 1904, and 336, Hardwick to Watson, 18 September 1905; "Hardwick Seeks No Senate Seat," *Atlanta Constitution*, 17 January 1905, 3; Crowe, "Racial Violence and Social Reform," 234–39.

27. Hicks, "Watson and Hardwick in Georgia Politics," 49–50; Baker, *Following the Color Line*, 68; see also 69, 72–74, 88–90; Grantham, *Hoke Smith*, 133; Kousser, *The Shaping of Southern Politics*, 219. Brown supervised an operation employing 540 blacks and 60 whites. A paternalist, he endeavored to keep his charges docile and loyal by maintaining better accommodations, medical care, food, and some social affairs.

28. "Hoke Smith to Pope Brown and Reply of Mr. Brown," *Atlanta Journal*, 4 June 1905, 1; Grantham, "Some Letters," 332, 334, Hardwick to Watson, 4 May 1905 and 26 June 1905; "Pope Brown's Withdrawal," *Atlanta Journal*, 9 June 1905, 8.

29. M. L. Myrick to Clark Howell, "Confidential," 3 March 1905, CHPUGA, folder

1905 Gubernatorial Campaign; Grantham, "Some Letters," 332–33, Hardwick to Watson, 4 May 1905.

30. J. R. Gray to Clark Howell, 22 May 1905, CHPUGA, folder 1905 Gubernatorial Campaign; "Announcement for Governor of Hon. Hoke Smith and his correspondence with Hon. Pope Brown," HSC, box 51, folder Undated—Miscellaneous; Grantham, *Hoke Smith,* 134–40; Woodard, *Tom Watson,* 372–74.

31. Fort, "History of the *Atlanta Journal,*" 38–47; Grantham, *Hoke Smith,* 132–33.

32. "The Clansman," *Atlanta Journal,* 6 June 1905, 8; Aldine Chambers to Ewall Jones, 13 April 1905, ACP, box 25, folder "Personal" 1903–8. For a discussion of Thomas Dixon's influence and the South's impact on him, see Williamson, *The Crucible of Race,* 140–80; "The Clansman," *Atlanta Journal,* 6 June 1905, 8. The press in Charlotte, North Carolina, endorsed *The Clansman* and rallied behind Dixon's criticism of President Theodore Roosevelt's egalitarian assertions about blacks and whites. See Hanchett, *Sorting Out the New South City,* 119–20.

33. L. D. McGregor to Watson, 11 March 1904, and Ben E. Rufaell (?) to Watson, 26 May 1904, 1–3, both in TEWPR, reel 3, series I, Correspondence 1898–1903 (1904), folder 53–153.

34. John S. Cohen to Watson (Personal & Confidential), 21 July 1904, TEWPR, reel 3, series I, Correspondence 1898–1903 (1904), folder 53–153. By the end of the campaign Watson would complain to Gray that the *Journal* treated him with "bitter vindictiveness." Gray was at first "surprised" by the assertion and denied the claim, calling it "unjust and unwarranted." As a parting shot he wrote, "It is not likely that we shall ever agree politically, but as long as we have no reason to doubt your sincerity of purpose I see nothing that would justify our pursuing you in a vindictive way, and I certainly see nothing that justifies you in entertaining such feelings toward us." See Gray to Watson, 14 November 1904, TEWPR, reel 4, series I, Correspondence 1898–1903 (1904), folder 53–153.

35. Grantham, *Hoke Smith,* 136, 138–39; "Tom Watson Declares That He Will Support the People's Candidate"; "Troup County Citizens Form Hoke Smith Club," *Atlanta Journal,* 4 June 1905, 2. Grantham suggests that Smith was placed under considerable pressure to compete for governor.

36. Grantham, "Some Letters," 333–35, Hardwick to Watson, 26 June 1905. Hardwick's 9 August 1905 letter to Watson indicated that the *Atlanta Journal* and Hoke Smith had complied. See p. 335.

37. Grantham, *Hoke Smith,* 3, 11, 13–14, 20–39, 67–71, 147–48; Hoke Smith to Fulton Colville, 20 May 1902, Letterbook 10 May 1902–27 August 1902, p. 56, HSC, box 63, Letterbooks 10 May 1902–5 March 1903; "Hon. Hoke Smith Then and Now," *Atlanta Independent,* 3 March 1906, 4; *Atlanta Constitution,* 1 January 1904, 7; Cooper, *Official History of Fulton County,* 450.

38. Hoke Smith to Rev. Horace Bumstead, 13 September 1902, 1–2, Atlanta University Collection, folder 7, box 2, Auburn Avenue Research Library on African American Culture and History, Archives Division, Atlanta-Fulton Public Library System. See "That Negro Reformatory," *Atlanta Journal,* 11 June 1905, 4; "Negro Fined for Being in Wrong

Place at New Depot," *Atlanta Journal,* 24 June 1905, 3; "Aycock Begged Mob to Spare His Life," *Atlanta Journal,* 29 June 1905, 1; "Negro Defies Well Known Cities," *Atlanta Journal,* 18 June 1905, 6; "This Feud, Red with Children's Blood," *Atlanta Journal,* 19 June 1905, 1, 2; "Negro Given Seven Years for Shooting an Inspector," *Atlanta Journal,* 15 June 1905, 7; "The Clansman," *Atlanta Journal,* 10 June 1905, 6; "Alleged Ku Klux Unearthed near Dalton," *Atlanta Journal,* 15 June 1905, 2; "Some Letters from the People—Richard H. Earle Writes of Disfranchisement Laws," *Atlanta Journal,* 24 June 1905, 7; "Let the People Select a Governor," *Atlanta Journal,* 19 June 1905, 6; "Troup County Citizens Form Hoke Smith Club"; "Georgia Editors Talk about the Governorship—The Reform Movement," *Atlanta Journal,* 25 June 1905, 5; "'No Quarter for Railroad and Ring Rule,' the Key Note of Hoke Smith's Initial Speech," *Atlanta Journal,* 29 June 1905, 3.

39. "State Press Comment about Governorship—The Editor Raps Both," *Atlanta Journal,* 13 June 1905, 8; J. A. B. Mahaffey to Richard B. Russell Sr., 20 October 1905; W. D. Griffith to Russell, 28 December 1905; Walter R. Brown to Russell, 13 July 1905; H. C. Anderson to Russell, 18 July 1905; and W. I. Hayward to Russell, 18 November 1905, all in the Richard B. Russell Sr. Papers, series iv, subseries B, box 18, Political Campaign 1906 folders, Russell Memorial Library, University of Georgia, Athens. For information on the three additional gubernatorial candidates, see Garrett, *Atlanta and Environs,* 2:499, and for James M. Smith, see Oshinsky, *"Worse than Slavery,"* 64–66.

40. "State Press Comment about Hoke Smith—Plain Statesmanlike Document," *Atlanta Journal,* 7 June 1905, 5; Woodward, "Tom Watson and the Negro in Agrarian Politics," 54; W. P. Boggs to L. G. Hardman, 1 August 1906, 1–2, Hardman to Mr. Editor, 2 April 1906, 1–2, and Thomas S. Johnson to Hardman, 26 May 1906, 1–3, all in Lamartine G. Hardman Collection, series iv, subseries A, box 2, folder Legislative 1906, 1907, Russell Memorial Library, University of Georgia, Athens.

Chapter 5. "The Seeds of Incendiarism": The Gubernatorial Campaign of 1905–1906

Epigraph. Watson, editorial, *Tom Watson's Magazine* 2 (October 1905): 397–98.

1. "State Press Comment about Governorship—The Editor Raps Both," *Atlanta Journal,* 13 June 1905, 8; Emory Speer to Clark Howell, 27 July 1905, CHPUGA, folder 1906-9.

2. "Terrell Renominated for 2nd Term; Celebration Erupts," *Atlanta Constitution,* 2 June 1904, 3. Ten years later as Senate president, Howell had attempted to reform the franchise with the Australian ballot.

3. "One Duty of the Convention," *Atlanta Constitution,* 1 June 1904, 4. For the impact of the Australian ballot on black voting rights, see Niswonger, *Arkansas Democratic Politics, 1896–1920,* 17–24, and Doyle, *Nashville in the New South,* 135–42.

4. "Clark Howell vs Hoke Smith Hoke Smith vs Clark Howell," 1–2, ACP, box 5, folder 3 (74–19) Correspondence re: Statewide Political Campaigns, 1903–1926; "History Is Human Howell: A Great Editor," *Atlanta Constitution,* 2 February 1962, CHF; Jones, "The Administration of Governor Joseph M. Terrell Viewed in the Light of the Progres-

sive Movement," 271–77; Grantham, "Georgia Politics and the Disfranchisement of the Negro," Grace T. Sherry Collection, Atlanta History Center, 77–136–10, MS 226, pp. 3–4.

5. Thos. W. Loyless to Clark Howell, 25 January 1905, 1–3, CHPUGA, folder 1905 Gubernatorial Campaign; Loyless to Richard B. Russell, 13 February 1905, and Walter R. Brown to Russell, 30 June 1905, both in Richard B. Russell Sr. Papers, Russell Memorial Library, University of Georgia, series iv, subseries B, box 18, folder Russell Political Campaign 1906.

6. "State Press Comment about Governorship—The Editor Raps Both"; Sherman, *The Republican Party and Black America,* 7; Grantham, *Hoke Smith,* 140–48; "Judge Calloway on Negro Disfranchisement," *Augusta Herald,* 8 July 1905; Crowe, "Racial Violence and Social Reform," 240–41; Bacote, "The Negro in Georgia Politics," 405, 427. Clark Howell made similar appointments of African Americans to patronage positions as Senate president in Georgia. See also September 1905 *Atlanta Journal,* esp. 15 September. Turner supported Howell in 1905 and continued his work for emigration. Turner eventually had no use for Howell or Smith except to promote emigration to Africa.

7. "Georgia's Tranquility for Few Votes," *Atlanta Constitution,* 1 June 1906, 6; "As to the End Justifying the Means," *Atlanta Constitution,* 3 June 1906, 6; "The Interest of the Farmer in 'Disfranchisement' Agitation and Its Price to the Farmer: Strife," *Atlanta Constitution,* 1 August 1906, 1, 6; Joel Chandler Harris to Clark Howell, 17 May 1906, "At the Sign of the Wren's Nest," series I, subseries 3, Personal Correspondence: General 1906, box 6, folder 6, item 2, Joel Chandler Harris Collection, Woodruff Library, Emory University, Atlanta. The Aldine Chambers Papers include informal rural polls taken by Chambers's father and other individuals in 1906 also suggesting a Howell defeat. Pike County had "every District in the county represented" with a 75 to 5 margin in favor of Smith. James W. English Jr. was a member of Smith's campaign. See Meansville, Ga., letter from Thomas Z. Jones to Chambers, 9 August 1906, box 25, folder 1906; Dear Colonel, 9 July 1905, box 5, folder 3 (74–19) Correspondence re: Statewide Political Campaigns 1903–1926; Thos. Jones to Col. Aldine Chambers, 23 April 1906, box 25 (74–19) Personal; and Aldine Chambers to A.J.W. Culpepper, 24 May 1906 and 23 August 1906, box 25, folder 1906, all in ACP, MS 70.

8. "The Issue That Failed and Its Successor," *Atlanta Constitution,* 3 January 1906, 6. For a broader description of the newspaper battle during the campaign, see Grantham, *Hoke Smith,* 144, and Crowe, "Racial Violence and Social Reform," 236–46; "Fight to Divide Democracy," *Atlanta Constitution,* 7 January 1906, B5. This assault upon Smith continued in the *Constitution* throughout January and February 1906.

9. "State Press Comment on Gubernatorial Campaign—Fight to Divide Democracy," and "Borrowing Trouble," *Atlanta Constitution,* 7 January 1905, B5; "Impartial Papers of the State on Joint Debate at Columbus—"Negro Not a Political Menace," *Atlanta Constitution,* 12 January 1906, 4.

10. "Address of Clark Howell Candidate for the Democratic Nomination for Governor as Delivered in Joint Debate at Columbus, Georgia with Hoke Smith," 3–9, Clark Howell Collection, Woodruff Library, Emory University, Atlanta; "Not the Atlanta Way," *Journal of Labor,* 29 May 1905, 1.

11. Sam Jones, "Sam Jones Writes about Coming Session of Legislature," *Atlanta Journal*, 17 June 1905, 7. See also "The Free White Men of Georgia Are Fit to Rule Themselves and Will Prove It at the Polls Wednesday," *Atlanta Journal*, 21 August 1906, 7; "Georgia's Patriotic Weekly Editors," *Atlanta Journal*, 22 August 1906, 6; "State Press Comment about Hoke Smith—The Ishmaelite for Hoke Smith," *Atlanta Journal*, 11 June 1905, 4; "State Press Comment about Hoke Smith—Editor Farmer for Hoke Smith," *Atlanta Journal*, 11 June 1905, 4; "The People Must Organize," *Atlanta Journal*, 11 June 1905, 4; Emory Speer to Howell, 27 July 1905, CHPUGA, folder 1906–9.

12. Wattles, "The Municipal Boss," *Tom Watson's Magazine* 4 (March 1906): 91–92; Ruppenthal, "Election Reforms: The Trend toward Democracy," *Tom Watson's Magazine* 4 (March 1906): 76–84; Watson, "Down in Georgia—Editorials," *Tom Watson's Magazine* 4 (March 1906): 1; Watson, "The Ungrateful Negro from a Newspaper—Editorials," *Tom Watson's Magazine* 4 (April 1906): 165–68, 170–71. *Tom Watson's Magazine* included articles penned by other reformers. These authors criminalized populations who gambled, drank to excess, brawled in the streets, and got "into trouble with the police." This class was "susceptible" to "manipulation" by the "boss regime" or the "criminal rich" who operated "the saloons, dives, and all the hosts of graft and shady business, [who] hold the balance of power." See also Griewank, "Emergence of the Concept of Revolution," 56–59; Thomas, *The Confederacy as a Revolutionary Experience*, 1–2, 56, 137; Gilmore, *Gender and Jim Crow*, 61–71. Griewank suggests that the crossing over of the term "revolution" from the European scientific community to the political definition constructed a word that set patterns for defining such political revolutions as the 1688 Glorious Revolution that returned a state to its previous "stable" status with its institutions modified to function again as they had before. Southern Progressive reform sought to reaffirm whiteness and race relations, as they had existed before Reconstruction.

13. "'No Quarter for Railroad and Ring Rule,' the Key Note of Hoke Smith's Initial Speech," *Atlanta Journal*, 29 June 1905, 3; "'No Quarter for Railroad and Ring Rule,'" *Atlanta Journal*, 30 June 1905, 2; "Speech of Hoke Smith Delivered at Madison, Georgia, June 29, 1905," 3, 5, HSC, box 51, folder Undated: Miscellaneous; Quick, "Hoke Smith and the Revolution in Georgia," *Reader* 10 (1907): 241–48; Grantham, *Hoke Smith*, 139–40; Woodward, *Tom Watson*, 373. Thomas E. Watson also emphasized in September 1905 that he and Smith embarked upon a mission to circumvent the power of Georgia's Democratic Party executive committee. To achieve this end, black people had to be disfranchised to guarantee the white primary and wrest control of the party from the executive committee. See Watson, "Mr. Watson and the Georgia Campaign," *Tom Watson's Magazine* 3 (December 1905): 131–32.

14. Quick, "Hoke Smith and the Revolution in Georgia," 245–46.

15. "Speech of Hoke Smith," 20–24; Smith, "Black Militia in Savannah, Georgia," 9–18, 25–27, 59, 67–74; Adjutant-General Letterbook, 1902–6, 2972–04 (22–1), Georgia Department of Defense, Georgia Department of Archives and History, Atlanta, 31; Muskat, "The Last March: The Demise of the Black Militia in Alabama," 23, 27–34; Diamond and Baylen, "The Demise of the Georgia Guard Colored, 1868–1914," 311–13; Colby, *The Na-*

tional Guard of the United States, chap. 2; Johnson, *African American Soldiers in the National Guard,* chap. 1; Clippings and Speeches 1906, Scrapbook 62, p. 2, HSC, box 79; "Want Negro Troops Disbanded in Georgia," *Atlanta Journal,* 1 January 1904, 2; *Atlanta Journal,* August 1905; Bacote, "The Negro in Georgia Politics," 411; Gilmore, *Gender and Jim Crow,* 63–72. The federal government sought to centralize and standardize state militias so that they could be better integrated within the regular armed forces during wartime emergencies. Georgia objected to elevating its black militia companies up to national requirements that equalized their readiness and authority with white militia units. Militia leadership questioned whether black militiamen would prevent black disturbances. Nevertheless, federal reorganization threatened to increase black power with federally sanctioned social equality.

16. "Speech of Hoke Smith," 20–28; Bacote, "The Negro in Georgia Politics," 402–4; Smith, "Voters Like Mr. Smith's Talk," *Atlanta Journal,* 7 December 1905, 5; "Petition to Run for Governor," 25 May 1905, HSC, box 18. This petition, reputed to be the first request for Smith to run, comes from Coweta County. Merchants and farmers made up 67 percent of those listed on the petition. For parallels on the scope of reform in other southern states, see Williamson, *The Crucible of Race,* 414–59; Dailey, "Deference and Violence," 562–64, 575, 583–88.

17. Clippings and Speeches 1906, Scrapbook 62, p. 28; Bacote, "The Negro in Georgia Politics," 402–3; Smith, Voters Like Mr. Smith's Talk," 5.

18. *Atlanta Journal,* 1 October 1905, 4; *Atlanta Journal,* 26 November 1905, 6.

19. "Booths in Maryland Crowded with Voters," *Atlanta Journal,* 7 November 1905, 1; "Negro Ballot Won Out in Maryland," *Atlanta Journal,* 8 November 1905, 1; "Maryland's Lesson to Georgia," *Atlanta Journal,* 8 November 1905, 6; "Negro Disfranchisement," *Atlanta Journal,* 21 November 1905, 6; "A Lesson for Georgia," *Atlanta Journal,* 23 November 1905, 6. See also "Maryland's Lesson to Georgia," *Atlanta Journal,* 9 November 1905, 6; "Vote of Negro Target for Maryland," *Atlanta Journal,* 5 November 1905, 3; "Letters from the People on Timely Topics—Result in Maryland Indeed Justifies Georgia Reformers," *Atlanta Journal,* 18 November 1905, 7; "Prepare for War in Time of Peace," *Atlanta Independ*ent, 10 March 1906, 4.

20. *Atlanta Journal,* 26 November 1905, 6; *Atlanta Journal,* 1 October 1905, 4. For the Wilmington riot, see Prather, *We Have Taken a City,* and Gilmore, *Gender and Jim Crow.*

21. *Atlanta Journal,* 24 November 1905, 6. For an examination of North Carolina's attempt to create a New South through white supremacy, see Billings, *Planters and the Making of the "New South,"* 38–42, 52–54, 75–92, 121–26, 129, 131, 136–42, 189–92, 203–7.

22. Milt Saul, "U.S. Senator Simmons of North Carolina in Showing How Amendment Has Worked Annihilates Howell's Platform Declarations Regarding Negro Disfranchisement," *Atlanta Journal,* 27 November 1905, 6.

23. "Disfranchisement Convincingly Discussed—Colonel Afendel, of North Carolina," *Atlanta Journal,* 27 November 1905, 7; Milt Saul, "Senator Overman, of North Carolina, in Graphic Terms, Shows the Results North Carolina Has Obtained from Amendment Disfranchising the Negro," *Atlanta Journal,* 30 November 1905, 6.

24. Saul, "Simmons"; "North Carolina's Governor on Disfranchisement," *Atlanta*

Journal, 22 November 1905, 8; "Shall White Supremacy Be Destroyed," *Atlanta Journal*, 12 November 1905, 8; Branch, "Negro Disfranchisement as Seen in North Carolina—Interesting Letters from the People," *Atlanta Journal*, 2 December 1905, 9.

25. "Hon. T. W. Hardwick, in Ringing Letter to White Voters of Georgia, Presents in Eloquent Phrases and Unanswerable Argument the Question of Disfranchisement," *Atlanta Journal*, 26 November 1905, 7.

26. Saul, "Those Who Are Scheming to Divide White People of Georgia Are Warming the Negro into Political Life Again Says Benjamin Tillman of South Carolina," *Atlanta Journal*, 11 December 1905, 6; *Atlanta Journal*, 24 November 1905, 6.

27. "The White Vote Will Not Be Divided," *Atlanta Journal*, 6 May 1906; "Hon J. Bryan Grimes, North Carolina's Leading Farmer, and Twice Elected Secretary of State Tells of Beneficial Effects of Disfranchisement, *Atlanta Journal*, 29 June 1906, 6; "Negro Disfranchisement Has Saved the Honor of Virginia," *Atlanta Journal*, 3 June 1906, 1, 3; "What the Ring Candidate Stands For," *Atlanta Journal*, 5 June 1906, 8; "Greatest Ovation Ever Recorded," *Atlanta Journal*, 9 June 1906, 1.

28. James L. Anderson, "Negro Disfranchisement," *Atlanta Journal*, 2 July 1906, 4.

29. "Editor Beasley's Eloquent Plea for Disfranchisement Citing North Carolina Experience," *Atlanta Journal*, 2 July 1906, 4.

30. "Congressman T. W. Hardwick Makes Able Speech on the Subject of Disfranchisement of the Negro," *Atlanta Journal*, 14 July 1906, 4.

31. Dailey, "Deference and Violence," 559–64, 575, 583–86, 588; Saul, "Those Who Are Scheming to Divide White People of Georgia . . . Again Says Benjamin Tillman of South Carolina"; Governor's Correspondence, 1868–69, Georgia Department of Archives and History, Atlanta. See also *Savannah Tribune* 1876–89.

Chapter 6. Summer of 1906

Epigraph. Thomas Martin, *Atlanta and Its Builders: A Comprehensive History of the Gate City of the South* (Atlanta: Century Memorial, 1902).

1. For a similar pattern and a different interpretation, see Senechal, *The Sociogenesis of a Race Riot*, 73–78, 80–86. See also Waldrep, *Roots of Disorder*, for the ongoing debate and use of legal and extralegal means to control black people both in the South and nationally.

2. See Bauerlein, *Negrophobia*, 45–49, 61–71, for discussions of crime, white powerlessness, failure of the legal system, and one newspaper editor's role in defining institutional failure in Atlanta in 1906. Also see Waldrep, *Roots of Disorder*, for broader patterns.

3. See Brown, *Strain of Violence*, chap. 7; Grimshaw, *Racial Violence in the United States*, 17–23, 254–55, 287–92, 402–7; Waldrep, *Roots of Disorder*, introduction.

4. Winston, "Disfranchisement Makes Subject-Citizens Targets of the Mob," 4–10, in Fitts, *A History of Black Baptists*, 258. Winston served as president of Northern University in Long Branch, N.J. Hope, "Negro Suffrage," 56–57. See also Davis, "An American Dilemma," 41 and 27–48, for Hope's early militancy in Atlanta and the fine line he

walked between radicalism and responsibilities as the leader of Atlanta Baptist College. My thanks goes to Andy Ambrose for bringing this article to my attention.

5. Cottrol, *The Afro-Yankees,* chaps. 2 and 3; Du Bois, *The Philadelphia Negro,* 26–32; Winch, *Philadelphia's Black Elite,* chap. 7.

6. Brown, *Strain of Violence,* 189–90, 205–12; Grimshaw, *Racial Violence in the United States,* 402–7.

7. Dorr, "Black-on-White Rape," 713–20; Dailey, "Deference and Violence."

8. "Strongly in Favor White Supremacy, *Atlanta Journal,* 2 June 1906, 2; Hall, "'The Mind That Burns in Each Body,'" 328–30; Waldrep, *Roots of Disorder,* 4–5, 23.

9. Emory Speer to Howell, 27 July 1905, CHPUGA, folder 1906–9. South Carolina's "Pitchfork" Ben Tillman targeted Speer in January 1906 as a judge who was too lenient with black criminals. In his defense, Speer contended that the law tied his hands.

10. "Judge George Hillyer Firmly Sustains Well-Known Views," *Atlanta Georgian,* 29 August 1906, 6; "Negro Criminal Enemy of Race," *Atlanta Constitution,* 26 October 1905, 1. See *Georgian* for some discussion of 1894. For a scholarly examination of the "good ole days," see Waldrep, *Roots of Disorder,* esp. chap. 2.

11. Hall, "'The Mind That Burns in Each Body,'" 328–35, 347; Dailey, "Deference and Violence"; "Strongly in Favor White Supremacy," *Atlanta Journal,* 2 June 1906, 2; Dyer, *Theodore Roosevelt and the Idea of Race,* 113–14, chap. 5; Waldrep, *Roots of Disorder.*

12. Barber, "The Atlanta Tragedy," *Voice of the Negro,* November 1906, 477, from folder Riot 1906, Atlanta History Center.

13. Ibid., 477; *Atlanta News,* 20 October 1905–8 December 1905. The *Atlanta Constitution* and *Atlanta Journal* chronicled the same story. See esp. "Negro Brice Pleads Guilty; Will Hang on December 8," *Atlanta News,* 13 November 1905, 1, 7; "The Unusual Case of the Negro Brice," *Atlanta News,* 14 November 1905, 6. Jim Walker was also called Will Brice by the white press.

14. Baker, *Following the Color Line,* 5. For other discussions on the "assaults," see Barber, "The Atlanta Tragedy," 477–78; Rainey, "The Race Riot of 1906 in Atlanta," 10; McKelway, "The Atlanta Riots—A Southern Point of View." Rainey cites another assault on 13 July 1906 when an eighteen-year-old lady walking in a field was "ambushed."

15. Barber, "The Atlanta Tragedy," 477–78; Crowe, "Racial Violence and Social Reform," 252.

16. Barber, "The Atlanta Tragedy," 477. One of the articles in the *Atlanta Georgian,* 24 September 1906, 3 was entitled "Cause of Trouble Was 4 Attempts on Women—None Was a Real Case of Criminal Assault."

17. "Protest Made Against Ku Klux Klan by the Best Citizens of the City and County," *Atlanta Journal,* 31 August 1906, 9; "Ku Klux Klan to Be Revived Again," *Atlanta Journal,* 28 August 1906, 1; "Ku Klux Klan to Protect Women Is Now Proposed," *Atlanta News,* 25 August 1906, 1; "Let the Women Arm Themselves," *Atlanta Journal,* 23 August 1906, 8.

18. "Let the Women Arm Themselves"; "Protect Our Women at Any Cost," *Atlanta Journal,* 25 August 1906, 6; "Protection for the Women of the Community," *Atlanta Journal,* 26 August 1906, 6; "Atlanta's Vigilance Committee," *Atlanta Journal,* 29 August 1906, 6.

19. For a partial history concerning Daniel and Graves, see Fort, "History of the *Atlanta Journal*," 37–44. See "Directors of the Atlanta News—Col. English Accepts News Presidency," *Atlanta News*, 21 August 1906, 4 for English and Hopkins financial involvement. See "'Ku Klux Klan' to Protect Women Is Now Proposed," *Atlanta News*, 25 August 1906, 1; "By All Means Organize the 'Ku Klux Klan,'" *Atlanta News*, 26 August 1906, 6; "Vigilance Committee Is Being Organized," *Atlanta News*, 26 August 1906, 1–2; "$1,600 Reward to Capture Negro," *Atlanta News*, 26 August 1906, 1; "Reward of $1,650 for This Negro Assailant," *Atlanta News*, 26 August 1906, 6; "A Reward of $1,000 to Guarantee Protection to the White Women of Fulton County," *Atlanta News*, 17 August 1906, 6; "The News' Reward for Assailants," *Atlanta News*, 20 August 1906, 6 for antiblack editorials and articles.

20. "The Career of the Atlanta News," Robert Foster Maddox Papers, MS 143, Private Collection, Atlanta History Center, MS 143, box 1, folder Robert Maddox Speeches; Barber, "The Atlanta Tragedy," 477; Fort, "History of the *Atlanta Journal*," 36–38, 41–42, 44–47; John Temple Graves to Thomas E. Watson, 22 May 1906, TEWPR, reel 5, series I, Correspondence 1898–1903 (1906), folder 53–153.

21. "Fourth National Is 10 Years Old," *Atlanta News*, 17 July 1906, 5; "Hon. Joseph Hirsch, Director of the Atlanta News," *Atlanta News*, 22 August 1906, 6; "Directors of the Atlanta News Publishing Company—Col. English Accepts News Presidency"; "Colonel James W. English Jr. President of the Atlanta News Publishing Company," *Atlanta News*, 21 August 1906, 1, 4, 5; "Reorganization of the News," *Atlanta News*, 21 August 1906, 6. For the economic reach of the English family, see "The Fourth National Bank," *Atlanta News*, 7 August 1906, 6.

22. "Continue Crusade," *Atlanta News*, 24 August 1906, 7; "The News Official Organ of Fulton County," *Atlanta News*, 2 July 1906, 6; "Charles Daniel Appointed by Dr. Helms a Special Deputy Sheriff in Fulton County," *Atlanta News*, 26 August 1906, 1; "By All Means Organize the 'Ku Klux Klan,'" *Atlanta News*, 26 August 1906, 6; "Vigilance Committee Is Being Organized," *Atlanta News*, 26 August 1906, 1–2; "Stop the Sale of Firearms to Negroes at Once," *Atlanta News*, 28 August 1906, 6; Rouse, *Lugenia Burns Hope*, 42–43.

23. "'Ku Klux Klan' to Protect Women Is Now Proposed"; "By All Means Organize the 'Ku Klux Klan;'" "Vigilance Committee Is Being Organized"; "$1,600 Reward to Capture Negro"; "Reward of $1,650 for This Negro Assailant"; "A Reward of $1,000 to Guarantee Protection to the White Women of Fulton County"; "The News' Reward for Assailants"; Barber, "The Atlanta Tragedy," 477; "Continue Crusade."

24. "The Peril of Negro Intimacies," *Atlanta News*, 13 July 1906, 6; "Negro Insults Girl on St. Car," *Atlanta News*, 8 July 1906, 1; "A Duty for Dixie's Sons," *Atlanta News*, 18 August 1906, 6; "An Appeal to Our Noble Southern Women," *Atlanta News*, 16 August 1906, 6; Hickey, "Visibility, Politics, and Urban Development," 42–44 esp. 43–44, see also 5–18, 26–27; 30–31.

25. "Women Indorse the News for Its Efforts in Their Behalf," *Atlanta News*, 22 August 1906, 6. Lithia Springs was patterned after the Chautauqua institutions begun nationally in 1874 to train Sunday School teachers. Henry W. Grady in 1888 founded Atlanta's Piedmont Chautauqua with 200 other elite citizens. Lithia Springs was a

small resort town twenty-one miles outside Atlanta. Classrooms for 1,000 and a tabernacle seating 7,000 were planned by Grady's group. The main purpose of Lithia Springs and Chautauquas was to distribute knowledge. See Garrett, *Atlanta and Environs,* 2:167–69.

26. "Stop the Sale of Firearms to Negroes at Once"; Rouse, *Lugenia Burns Hope,* 42–43.

27. "The 'Reign of Terror' Must End"; "Protecting Assault Victims," *Atlanta Constitution,* 6 February 1906, 6.

28. "Continue Crusade," *Atlanta News,* 24 August 1906, 7.

29. "The 'Reign of Terror' Must End," "From a Strong Man in South Georgia," "Stop It at Any Cost," and "The Protection of Our Homes," *Atlanta Georgian,* 24 August 1906, 6; "The Reign of Terror: The Georgian's Crusade Indorsed by Strong Men All Over the South—One of Georgia's Ablest Business Men," *Atlanta Georgian,* 27 August 1906, 6.

30. "The Negro Dives Must Go," *Atlanta Journal,* 30 August 1906, 6; "The 'Reign of Terror' Must End"; "Protest Made against Ku Klux Klan by the Best Citizens of the City and County," *Atlanta Journal,* 31 August 1906, 9; Mathias and Anderson, *Horse to Helicopter,* 39, 41–43, 46–47, 51–52.

31. "Drive Out the Dives!" *Atlanta Constitution,* 31 August 1906, 6; "For Protection of White Women," *Atlanta Constitution,* 27 August 1906, 5; "Vagrant Negroes Fill Streets and Saloons at All Hours of Day," *Atlanta Constitution,* 25 August 1906, 1; "Decatur Street Alive with Idling Negroes," *Atlanta Constitution,* 26 August 1906, 7C; "Decatur Street Was Undismayed until 9 O'clock When Threatened Riot Cleared the Whole Street," *Atlanta Journal,* 23 September 1906, 2; "Police Court Celebrities at Monday Morning Session," *Atlanta Constitution,* 28 August 1906, 3; "Dives Are Run as Restaurants," *Atlanta Constitution,* 30 August 1906, 4.

32. "No Room for Negro Soldiers," *Atlanta Constitution,* 25 August 1906, 6; "Negro Soldiers Are Removed," *Atlanta Constitution,* 26 August 1906, 5C; Taylor, *In Search of the Racial Frontier,* 176–79; Mathias and Anderson, *Horse to Helicopter,* 46, 51–52; "Rioting Negro Troops Spread Terror in Texas," *Atlanta News,* 15 August 1906, 1; "Negro Soldiers Riot Because They Couldn't Drink at Bar with Whites," *Atlanta News,* 15 August 1906, 4. Taylor also argues that tensions in Brownsville included black-white and Latino-black with both whites and Latinos mutually objecting to black soldiers.

33. "Minister's Union Would Break Up Negro Dives," *Atlanta Journal,* 30 August 1906, 4.

34. "Wants Loafers to Work," *Atlanta Constitution,* 28 August 1906, 4. For similar expressions, see "Law Breaking Negroes Worst Menace to Race," *Atlanta Constitution,* 30 August 1906, 4; "Negro Minister Writes of Existing Conditions," *Atlanta Journal,* 30 August 1906, 4.

35. "Negro Minister Writes of Existing Conditions"; "Drive Out the Dives!"

36. "Police Force Is Increased by Twelve Men," *Atlanta Constitution,* 29 August 1906, 1; "Council Will Investigate Municipal Ownership of Gas and Electric Plants," *Atlanta Journal,* 18 September 1906, 13; "Drive Out the Vagrants," *Atlanta Constitution,* 26 August 1906, 4B; "Crusade against Negro Dives by Police Has Begun in Dead Earnest," *Atlanta Journal,* 22 September 1906, 1; "22 Negro Restaurants Are Refused Licenses," *Atlanta Journal,* 22 September 1906, 1; "Decatur Street Was Undismayed."

37. "Drive Out the Vagrants"; "Police Force Is Increased by Twelve Men."
38. Mathias and Anderson, *Horse to Helicopter*, 46, 51–52.
39. "Police Force Is Increased by Twelve Men"; "Drive Out the Vagrants."

Chapter 7. Riot

Epigraph. Voice of the Negro, November 1906, 473.

1. See "Trial of George Blackstock," ARVF October 1906 Aftermath; Crowe, "Racial Massacre," 158–59; Williamson, *The Crucible of Race*, 217. For comparisons of targeting by white rioters, see Senechal, *The Sociogenesis of a Race Riot*, 129–46.

2. *Atlanta Constitution*, 23 September 1906, 1. This barbershop was not the one owned by Alonzo Herndon. None of his employees were lost to the riot. See Barbershop Ledgers, 66 Peachtree, vol. December 1903–July 1906 (includes records for August 1906–February 1907), Alonzo Herndon Papers, Alonzo Herndon House and Museum, Atlanta.

3. Crowe, "Racial Massacre," 152–57; Rainey, "The Race Riot of 1906 in Atlanta," 70 (note that this document is not paginated; therefore, the page numbers are only approximate); "Many Negroes Fall Victim to Mob Which Hold Uptown in Its Grasp," *Atlanta Journal*, 23 September 1906, 1; McKelway, "The Atlanta Riots—A Southern Point of View," 559–60. The *Atlanta Journal* suggested that the riot started with a black man stabbing a white man. McKelway indicated that rumors heightened racial tensions. For a similar pattern of white violence, see Hall, "'The Mind That Burns in Each Body,'" 330.

4. Crowe, "Racial Massacre," 152–57; "Here Are 'Extras' Issued Saturday," *Atlanta Georgian*, 29 September 29, 1906, 11; "Many Negroes," and "In Race Riot Many Negroes Are Killed and Scores of Both Races Are Injured," *Atlanta Journal*, 23 September 1906, 1; "Facts of Last Night's Reign of Terror," *Atlanta Constitution*, 23 September 1906, 1; WRFG Radio, "Atlanta Race Riot of 1906," side 1, LAS.

5. *Atlanta News*, 23 September 1906, 2; "Crowd Begins to Mobilize," *Atlanta Journal*, 23 September 1906, 4; Crowe, "Racial Massacre," 154, 156–63; Rainey, "The Race Riot of 1906 in Atlanta," 71; Dittmer, *Black Georgia in the Progressive Era 1900–1920*, 95–97; "Cars Riddled by Bullets of Negroes," *Atlanta Journal*, 23 September 1906, 3; "Facts," *Atlanta Constitution*, 23 September 1906, 1; "In Race Riot Many Negroes Are Killed," 1; "Mob Ruled Gate City Last Night," *Atlanta Constitution*, 23 September 1906, 2C; "Chased Negroes All the Night," 1, 3; Williamson, *The Crucible of Race*, 217.

6. Crowe, "Racial Massacre," 156; "What Threw Mob into Wild Frenzy," *Atlanta Constitution*, 23 September 1906, 1; "Chased Negroes All the Night," *Atlanta Constitution*, 23 September 1906, 3; "Many Negroes Fall Victim to Mob," 3; "Crowd Begins to Mobilize"; "Too Much Talk Was His Doom," ARVF 23–30 September 1906; WRFG Radio, "Atlanta Race Riot of 1906," sides 1 and 2, LAS; White, *A Man Called White*, 9–10; "In Race Riot Many Negroes Are Killed."

7. "Mob Ruled Gate City Last Night."

8. *Atlanta News*, 23 September 1906, 1; *Atlanta Journal*, 23 September 1906, 4; "Hospital Is Crowded with Dead and Wounded," *Atlanta Journal*, 23 September 1906, 5; "Injured Blacks Crowd Hospital," *Atlanta Constitution*, 23 September 1906, 3C.

9. "Effects of Water Maddened Mob," *Atlanta Constitution,* 23 September 1906, 3; "In Race Riot Many Negroes Are Killed," 1, 4; Crowd Begins to Mobilize"; "Hospital Is Crowded with Dead and Wounded."

10. "In Race Riot Many Negroes Are Killed"; "Mob Ruled Gate City Last Night."

11. "In Race Riot Many Negroes Are Killed"; "Many Negroes Fall Victim to Mob," 4.

12. "Riot Reviewed by Police Board," *Atlanta Constitution,* 29 September 1906, "Investigations of the Police Department," *Atlanta Constitution,* 30 September 1906, and "Mounted Police Save Property," 24 September 1906, all in ARVF 23–30 September 1906; Crowe, "Racial Massacre," 156–57, 162; "Mayor Orders All Saloons Closed Today," *Atlanta Constitution,* 24 September 1906, 1; Godshalk, "In the Wake of Riot," 127; WRFG Radio "Atlanta Race Riot of 1906," side 2, LAS.

13. "In Race Riot Many Negroes Are Killed"; "Many Negroes Fall Victim to Mob"; "Mob Demanded Jones' Horses," *Atlanta Constitution,* 23 September 1906, 4C; "Smashed Open Big Pawn Shop," *Atlanta Constitution,* 23 September 1906, 4C.

14. For arrests, see *Atlanta Constitution,* 23 September 1906, 1. For A. C. Moore, see "Many Killed, Many Injured," *Atlanta Constitution,* 24 September 1906, 1; and "Riot Calls Were Sounded and Militia Called Out," *Atlanta Journal,* 23 September 1906, 3. According to the *Journal,* Moore lived at 130 Julian, but the *Constitution* placed him at 117 Julian.

15. "Many Negroes Fall Victim to Mob"; "In Race Riot Many Negroes Are Killed," 1, 4; "Stern Justice by Recorder for Rioters," *Atlanta Georgian,* 24 September 1906, 1; "Recorder Hands Out Summary Decisions," *Atlanta Georgian,* 24 September 1906, 4. The recorder labeled T. F. Clements a riot leader. Clements was arrested for throwing a brick at a police officer during the riot. Clements lived at 82 Plum Street. See *Atlanta Constitution,* 23 September 1906, 3. See also Atlanta City Directory 1906, 582, 600, Atlanta History Center; Atlanta City Directory 1907, 612, Atlanta History Center, for the addresses of other white people who were arrested. My thanks go to Dr. Bobby Donaldson for helping compile the list of forty white people arrested.

16. "Negro Insults Girl on St. Car," *Atlanta News,* 8 July 1906, 1; "Women Indorse the News for Its Efforts in Their Behalf," *Atlanta News,* 22 August 1906, 6; "Atlanta's Street Car System," *Journal of Labor,* 31 August 1906, 6; "The Initiatory of Municipal Ownership," *Journal of Labor,* 14 September 1906, 2; "Organized Labor and Municipal Ownership," *Journal of Labor,* 5 October 1906, 3; Kuhn, "1906 Riot: Atlanta Papers Kindle Racist Violence," *Great Speckled Bird,* 28 August 1975, 8–9; "Many Negroes Fall Victim to Mob," 4.

17. "Attack by Mobs on Street Cars," and "Fierce Fight on Street Car," *Atlanta Constitution,* 23 September 1906, 4C.

18. *Atlanta Constitution,* 23 September 1906, 1; Rainey, "The Race Riot of 1906 in Atlanta," 71–73; McKelway, "The Atlanta Riots—A Southern Point of View," 557–59; Gibson, "Anti-Negro Riots in Atlanta." According to WRFG's re-creation, car no. 207 operated on the Auburn Avenue Line that night.

19. *Atlanta Constitution,* 23 September 1906, 1; WRFG Radio, "Atlanta Race Riot of 1906," side 1, LAS; "Many Negroes Fall Victim to Mob," 3; Godshalk, "In the Wake of Riot," 13–16; "Fierce Fight on Street Car."

20. "Frank Smith Stabbed to Death," *Atlanta Journal*, 23 September 1906, 4; "In Race Riot Many Negroes Are Killed,"

21. "Hospital Is Crowded with Dead and Wounded."

22. "Cars Riddled by Bullets of Negroes," 4.

23. Henderson, *Atlanta Life Insurance Company*, 24; "Atlanta Massacre," *Independent*, 4 October 1906, 799; barbershop ledgers, 1902–3, December 1903–July 1906 (includes August 1906–February 1907), Alonzo Herndon Papers, Alonzo Herndon House and Museum, Atlanta.

24. "In Race Riot Many Negroes Are Killed," 3.

25. "Many Negroes Fall Victim to Mob," 3.

26. "Greek's Store Wrecked by Mob," *Atlanta Constitution*, 23 September 1906, 3C; "Fierce Fight on Street Car," 4C; "In Race Riot Many Negroes Are Killed," 4.

27. "In Race Riot Many Negroes Are Killed," 1, 4; *Atlanta News*, 23 September 1906, 1; *Atlanta Constitution*, 23 September 1906, 1; Crowe, "Racial Massacre," 158–59.

28. "Peters Street Raided by Mob after Negroes," *Atlanta Journal*, 23 September 1906, 1; "Smashed Open Big Pawn Shop," *Atlanta Constitution*, 23 September 1906, 4C; "Three Stores Are Rifled," *Atlanta Constitution*, 23 September 1906, 4C; Garrett, *Atlanta and Environs*, 2:423–24. The *Atlanta Journal* claimed that Brown attempted to enter a house after being shot but fell at the door.

29. "In Race Riot Many Negroes Are Killed," 4; "Two Riot Calls Were Rung for First Time in Atlanta," *Atlanta Constitution*, 23 September 1906, 3C.

30. "Chased Negroes All the Night," 3; *Atlanta News*, 23 September 1906, 2.

31. Crowe, "Racial Massacre," 158–59.

32. Ibid., 162; White, *A Man Called White*, 9–10; "The Atlanta Riot," 7–8; Franklin, *From Slavery to Freedom*, 134; "Forty Arrests for Rioting," *Atlanta Constitution*, 23 September 1906, 1; "All in Prison to Stay There," *Atlanta Constitution*, 24 September 1906, 3; "Thirty Days and No Fine," *Atlanta Constitution*, 25 September 1906, 2; "Many Killed Many Injured," *Atlanta Constitution*, 24 September 1906, 1; Atlanta City Directory 1906, 1907, Atlanta History Center; "In Race Riot Many Negroes Are Killed," 1; Godshalk, "In the Wake of Riot," chap. 3. Charles Crowe defined the defense of black employees as "paternalism." The attitude or conception allowed "even violent Negrophobes to 'do favors' for '[a] deserving' Negro dependant."

33. "Stern Justice by Recorder for Rioters"; "Recorder Hands Out Summary Decisions"; "Thirty Days and No Fine"; "All in Prison to Stay There," ARVF 23–30 September 1906; Crowe, "Racial Massacre," 164–65; Godshalk, "In the Wake of Riot," 121–24, 131–48, 179–82. The six women were Anna Hawkins, Savannah Patrick, Lucile Rixey, Blanche Sims, Sallie Walker, and Jane Simon.

34. "Negroes Attack Inman Park Car," and "Negroes Fired into the Cars," *Atlanta Constitution*, 23 September 1906, 3C; "Rocks Are Hurled at All Street Cars," *Atlanta News*, 24 September 1906, 1; *Atlanta News*, 23 September 1906, 2. The militia did not mobilize until well after 1 a.m.

35. WRFG Radio, "Atlanta Race Riot of 1906," sides 1 and 2, LAS; White, *A Man Called White*, 9–10; "In Race Riot Many Negroes Are Killed," 1; "Greek's Store Wrecked by Mob." For further evidence of disregard for federal property, see "Two Riot Calls Were Rung

for First Time in Atlanta." For the Democratic state convention, see "Platform Adopted by Convention," *Atlanta Journal,* 5 September 1906, 6; "Mid Scenes of Great Enthusiasm Hoke Smith Was Nominated Governor," 5 September 1906, 3.

36. Lucy Rucker Aiken, interview, 17 August 1985, Atlanta; Porter, "Black Atlanta: An Interdisciplinary Study," 16–17; "Rucker Makes His New Bond," *Atlanta Constitution,* 2 August 1905, 3.

37. Kathleen Redding Adams, interview, 13 August 1985, Atlanta.

38. *Atlanta Journal,* 23 September 1906, 1; *Atlanta Constitution,* 23 September 1906, 1; Atlanta City Directory 1906, 1907 Atlanta History Center; "Forty Arrests for Rioting"; "All in Prison to Stay There"; "Many Killed; Many Injured"; "Thirty Days and No Fine."

Chapter 8. "Off the Streets"

Epigraph. "Two Riot Calls Were Rung for First Time in Atlanta," *Atlanta Constitution,* 23 September 1906, 3C.

1. See chapter 5.

2. "Only Words of Praise for the Boys in Khaki," *Atlanta Constitution,* 26 September 1906, 3; Aldine Chambers to J. W. Cavender, 27 September 1906, ACP, box 25, folder 1906; "Col. Anderson and His Men," *Atlanta Georgian,* 27 September 1906, 6; "Troops Called Out to Disperse Mob," *Atlanta Journal,* 23 September 1906, 1; "Governor Calls All Troops Out," *Atlanta Constitution,* 23 September 1906, 1. For militia training, see "Report of the Adjutant-General of the State of Georgia from January 1, 1906 to December 31, 1906," *Georgia Adjutant-General Report, 1903–1906* (Atlanta: Franklin-Turner, 1907), 100–101, 106–9, 135–36; "Riot Duty," Annual Report Adjutant-General, January 1905.

3. "Continue Crusade," *Atlanta News,* 24 August 1906, 7; "Governor Calls All Troops Out"; "Martial Law If Riots Continue," *Atlanta Constitution,* 24 September 1906, 4.

4. "Report of the Adjutant-General," 136; Crowe, "Racial Massacre," 167; "Facts of Last Night's Reign of Terror," *Atlanta Constitution,* 23 September 1906, 1; "In Race Riot Many Negroes Are Killed and Scores of Both Races Are Injured," *Atlanta Journal,* 23 September 1906, 1; Rainey, "The Race Riot of 1906 in Atlanta," 80.

5. "Report of the Adjutant-General," 137; "Tech Surgeon Badly Beaten," ARVF 23–30 September 1906.

6. "Report of the Adjutant-General," 137; "City Patrolled by Militiamen," *Atlanta Constitution,* 23 September 1906, 4C; McKelway, "The Atlanta Riots—A Southern Point of View," 560–61; "Big Crowd Attacked Company of Militia," ARVF 23–30 September 1906.

7. "Report of the Adjutant-General," 137; "City Patrolled by Militiamen," *Atlanta Constitution,* 23 September 1906, 4C; "General Resume of Today's News," *Atlanta News,* 24 September 1906, 1.

8. McKelway, "The Atlanta Riots—A Southern Point of View," 560–61; "Report of the Adjutant-General," 137; "Tech Surgeon Badly Beaten; "Big Crowds Attacked Company of Militia," *Atlanta Constitution,* 24 September 1906.

9. "Report of the Adjutant-General," 127–29, 137.

10. Major Jas. A. Thomas to Colonel William G. Obear, 30 September 1906, and letter to Major Jas. A. Thomas, 3 October 3 1906, both in Adjutant-General Letterbook, 1902–6, box 9, 2971–08, Georgia Department of Defense, Georgia Department of Archives and History, Atlanta. For a list of staff officers who served in Atlanta during the riot, see "Troops and Officers on Duty in Atlanta," ARVF 23–30 September 1906; Mixon, "The Atlanta Riot of 1906," 562–63.

11. "Law-Abiding Citizens," ARVF 23–30 September 1906; Crowe, "Racial Massacre," 167; Baker, "The Atlanta Riot," 8.

12. "Law-Abiding Citizens," ARVF 23–30 September 1906; "Gate City under Guard All Sunday," *Atlanta Constitution*, 24 September 1906, 1–2; "Report of the Adjutant-General," 128–29; Garrett, *Atlanta and Environs*, 2:423–24. For a view across Georgia, see Walter A. Harris to Col. A. J. Scott, 27 September 1906, and Dr. W. B. Burroughs to Capt. W. H. Harrison, 17 July 1906, both in Adjutant-General Letterbook, 1902–6, box 9, 2971-08 0922, series 13, Georgia Department of Defense, Georgia Department of Archives and History, Atlanta; Brundage, *Lynching in the New South*, chap. 4.

13. "Law-Abiding Citizens"; "Gate City under Guard All Sunday"; "No Extras Were Issued at Request of Militia," *Atlanta Constitution*, 24 September 1906, 2; "When Riot Stops Riots Will Cease," *Atlanta Constitution*, 24 September 1906, 3; "Riot's End All Depends on Negroes," *Atlanta Constitution*, 25 September 1906, 1.

14. "Law-Abiding Citizens"; "Dives Raided and Vagrants Sent to Jail," *Atlanta Constitution*, 23 September 1906, 4C; "Mayor Orders All Saloons Closed Today," *Atlanta Constitution*, 24 September 1906, 1; "Gate City under Guard All Sunday"; "No Extras Were Issued at Request of Militia."

15. "Wire Cutters Isolated Nelms," *Atlanta Constitution*, 23 September 1906, 4C; "Cut Wires to Sheriff's House," *Atlanta Journal*, 23 September 1906, 5; "25 New Deputies Sworn in Monday by Ordinary," *Atlanta Georgian* 24 September 1906, 4.

16. "Negro Suspect Makes Escape," *Atlanta Constitution*, 24 September 1906, 2.

17. Pomerantz, *Where Peachtree Meets Sweet Auburn*, 75.

18. "Shot at Negro in Marion Hotel," *Atlanta Constitution*, 24 September 1906, 2; "Fain Arrested on Riot Charge," *Atlanta Constitution*, 21 November 1906, "'Not Guilty' Says L. E. Fain," *Atlanta Constitution*, 6 November 1906, and "Fain Acquitted on Riot Charge," all in ARVF November 1906 Aftermath.

19. "Quiet Day Is Passed in Atlanta," *Atlanta Constitution*, 24 September 1906, 1; "Calm Is Now Restored after Wild Rioting; No Trouble Is in Sight," *Atlanta Georgian*, 24 September 1906, 1; "Negro Help Was Scarce," *Atlanta Constitution*, 24 September 1906, 2.

20. "City Streets Are in Need of Cleaning," *Atlanta Constitution*, 30 September 1906, 6C; "Says Negroes Will Not Work," *Atlanta Constitution*, 2 October 1906, 4; "Board Wants White Laborers," *Atlanta Constitution*, 29 September 1906, 7.

21. "Cars Stopped Running," *Atlanta Constitution*, 24 September 1906, 2; "Rumors, Riots, Fires Kept the Police Busy," *Atlanta Constitution*, 24 September 1906, 1; "Shots Are Fired into Streetcar," *Atlanta Constitution*, 24 September 1906, 2.

22. "Many Negroes Were Armed," *Atlanta Constitution*, 24 September 1906, 4; "Lynch Negro at East Point Sunday Night," *Atlanta Georgian*, 24 September 1906, 1.

23. Mixon, "The Atlanta Riot of 1906," 580; Kathleen Redding Adams, interview, 13 August 1985, Atlanta.

24. Pomerantz, *Where Peachtree Meets Sweet Auburn,* 69–71, 76.

25. WRFG Radio, "Atlanta Race Riot of 1906," sides 1 and 2, LAS; White, *A Man Called White,* 9–10.

26. White, *A Man Called White,* 11–12. For a discussion of the place of racism in American life at the turn of the century, see Kramer, "Empires, Exceptions, and Anglo-Saxons," and Lorini, *Rituals of Race.* Walter White biographer Kenneth R. Janken notes that there were no firearms in the White household during this episode of the Atlanta riot. Janken confirms that rioters did march on the White household. Conversation with Janken, 8 November 2003, at the Southern Historical Association, Houston.

27. White, *A Man Called White,* 11–12.

28. Ibid., 9–10; Porter, "Black Atlanta: An Interdisciplinary Study," 17.

29. Torrence, *The Story of John Hope,* 153.

30. Proctor, *Between Black and White,* 95–96; Lewis, *W.E.B. Du Bois: Biography of a Race,* 333–37, 350–54; Capeci and Knight, "Reckoning with Violence: W.E.B. Du Bois and the 1906 Atlanta Race Riot."

31. "Negroes Hold Up Whites," *Atlanta Constitution,* 25 September 1906, 2; "Atlanta Quiet during Day; Night Brought Bloodshed," *Atlanta Constitution,* 25 September 1906, 2; "Driven from Home by Armed Negroes," *Atlanta Constitution,* 25 September 1906, 1.

32. Baker, "The Atlanta Riot," 8, 17; WRFG Radio, "Atlanta Race Riot of 1906," side 2, LAS. Kathleen Redding Adams also confirms the problems with the two communities.

33. Baker, "The Atlanta Riot," 8, 17; WRFG Radio, "Atlanta Race Riot of 1906," side 2, LAS; Torrence, *The Story of John Hope,* 153.

34. "Vicious Blacks Are Sounding the Doom of Their Race," *Atlanta News,* 23 September 1906, 4; "An Appeal to Reason," *Atlanta Constitution,* 24 September 1906, 2, 6; "Obey the Law and Get Back to Business," *Atlanta Journal,* 24 September 1906, 6; "Mayor Woodward Appeals for Reign of Law," *Atlanta Georgian,* 24 September 1906, 1; "Stern Justice by Recorder for Rioters," *Atlanta Georgian,* 24 September 1906, 1.

35. "Obey the Law and Get Back to Business," 1, 3, 5, 6; "Assaults upon Women Must Stop," *Atlanta News,* 6 October 1906, 6; Aldine Chambers to M. L. Chambers, 28 September 1906, ACP, box 25, folder 1906; "The Battle of San Juan Hill," *Atlanta Constitution,* 17 July 1905, 4.

36. "Atlanta Quiet during Day, Night Brought Bloodshed."

37. "Two Negroes Are Indicted," *Atlanta Constitution,* 25 September 1906, 2; "280 Deputies Aid Officers," *Atlanta Constitution,* 25 September 1906, 2.

38. "Federal Troops Ready to Help," *Atlanta Constitution,* 25 September 1906, 1.

39. "Seventeenth at Newnan," *Atlanta Constitution,* 23 September 1906, 8A; "17th Regiment to Reach Atlanta Home Tuesday," *Atlanta Constitution,* 23 September 1906, 5C; "Did Not Report Regiment's Arrival," *Atlanta Georgian,* 26 September 1906, 7; "Taft Prepares to Leave Cuba," *Atlanta Constitution,* 9 October 1906, 1.

40. Edward Young Clarke, "When Raping Stops Riots Will Cease," *Atlanta Constitu-*

tion, 24 September 1906, 3; "Riot's End All Depends on Negroes," *Atlanta Constitution*, 25 September 1906, 1.

41. "Officer Killed in Night Fight," *Atlanta News*, 25 September 1906, 1; "Officer Heard Killed; Four Others Are Hurt in Brownsville Raid," 25 September 1906, ARVF 23–30 September 1906; "He Used a Dead Body to Ward Off Bullets," ARVF 23–30 September 1906; "State Militia Arrests 260 Negroes at Brownsville Restoring Order," *Atlanta News*, 25 September 1906, 1; Baker, "The Atlanta Riot," 8; Crowe, "Racial Massacre," 168; Torrence, *The Story of John Hope*, 153; "Blood in the Suburbs," *Atlanta Journal*, 25 September 1906, 1; "Disarm the Negroes," *Atlanta Journal*, 25 September 1906, 6; Garrett, *Atlanta and Environs*, 2:503. The Fulton County force consisted of Officers James Heard (killed), A. C. Eubanks, Frank Jordan, M. E. Odum (wounded), Poole (commander), Shockley, Cox, Oliver, and two others. There were "half a dozen citizens of the neighborhood," including Ernest Smith and J. E. Hicks.

42. "Two Negroes Killed in Battle with Officers after Desperate Figtt," "2 Blacks Riddled by Posse," "Mrs. Robert P. Thompson Died Suddenly of Fright When Negroes Were Shot," *Atlanta Journal*, 25 September 1906, and "Two Negroes Shot by an Angry Mob on R. Manley's Porch," all in ARVF 23–30 September 1906.

43. "Report of the Adjutant-General," 137–38.

44. Ibid.; "Officer Heard Killed; Four Others Are Hurt in Brownsville Raid," *Atlanta Journal*, 25 September 1906, and "Town of Brownsville Is Taken by Militia," both in ARVF 23–30 September 1906; WRFG Radio, "Atlanta Race Riot of 1906," side 2, LAS; Baker, "The Atlanta Riot," 8. The *Journal* noted that three companies of infantry were sent under Captain Dishman accompanying the governor's horse guard.

45. Baker, "The Atlanta Riot," 8; Williamson, *The Crucible of Race*, 218. For another description of the shooting, see Bauerlein, *Negrophobia*, 200.

46. "Two Negroes Killed in Battle with Officers after Desperate Figtt," ARVF 23–30 September 1906; "State Militia Arrests 260 Negroes at Brownsville Restoring Order" and "5 Blacks Dead for Sure; 12 Believed Killed," both in *Atlanta News*, 25 September 1906, 1.

47. "Peace and Order Restored by Authorities," *Atlanta Journal*, 25 September 1906, 1; Aldine Chambers to J. W. Chambers, 26 September 1906, ACP, box 25, folder 1906; "Saloons Remain Closed," ARVF 23–30 September 1906.

Chapter 9. Reconstruction: The Illusion of Hope

Epigraph. Diefendorf, "Prologue to a Massacre: Popular Unrest in Paris, 1557–1572," 1067.

1. Inman, *Inman Diary*, 1:5, 7, 33, 43–51, 56, 61, 64–67; Emory Speer to Clark Howell, 27 July 1905, CHPUGA, folder 1906–9; "Last Night's Riot and Its Lesson," *Atlanta Journal*, 23 September 1906, 1; Hunter, "Domination and Resistance," 167, 169, 182; Harris, "Etiquette, Lynching, and Racial Boundaries," 390–91; Goldfield, *Black, White, and Southern*, chap. 1.

2. Capozzola, "The Only Badge Needed Is Your Patriotic Fervor," 1358–59, 1364–69, 1374–77; Waldrep, *Roots of Disorder*, esp. chaps. 3–7; Davis, *Rumor of Revolt*; Winch, *Philadelphia's Black Elite*, chap. 7; Cottrol, *The Afro-Yankees*, 42–57; Diefendorf, "Pro-

logue to a Massacre," 1067, 1069–70, 1074, 1076–77, 1083–85, 1090; Brown, *Strain of Violence,* 205–14.

3. See Bauerlein, *Negrophobia,* 177–231, for a parallel interpretation of the riot's aftermath and black elite goals.

4. T. J. Eady, "Open Letters from the People—Atlanta and Other Cities," *Atlanta Georgian,* 29 September 1906, 6. See also Ruffins, "Sites of Memory, Sites of Struggle: The Materials of History," 32–33 for a discussion of the conflict between black and white visions of United States and African American history and the question of class within the black experience in defining the "well qualified, [and] deserving" African Americans in white eyes over time.

5. Myrta Lockett Avary, "Open Letters from the People: The Georgian Strikes the Right Chord," *Atlanta Georgian,* 29 September 1906, 6.

6. John Temple Graves, "A Word Personal and Otherwise," *Atlanta Georgian,* 28 September 1906, 6; John Temple Graves, "Saturday Evening," *Atlanta Georgian,* 29 September 1906, 6.

7. "A Voice for Law and Order," *Atlanta Georgian,* 25 September 1906, 1; "Prominent Atlantans Attend Mass Meeting," *Atlanta Constitution,* 26 September 1906, 2; "Law and Order Pledged by Thousand Atlantans," ARVF 23–30 September 1906; "Reputable Negroes of the City Beseech Protection of Law," *Atlanta Georgian,* 25 September 1906, 7; "Late News," *Atlanta Georgian,* 25 September 1906, 1; "Hundreds of Negroes Are Leaving Atlanta," *Atlanta Georgian,* 25 September 1906, 1.

8. "Committee of Ten Seeks Punishment of All Rioters," *Atlanta Georgian,* 26 September 1906, 1; Baker, "The Atlanta Riot," 15.

9. "Prominent Atlantans Attend Mass Meeting"; "Committee of Ten Seeks Punishment of All the Rioters"; Atlanta City Council Minutes, Atlanta History Center, vol. 21, September 26, 1906, 125–28; "What Georgian Readers Have to Say on a Variety of Interesting Questions—Some Strong Pointed Questions," *Atlanta Georgian,* 17 October 1906, ARVF October 1906; Baker, *Following the Color Line,* 14–16; Williamson, *The Crucible of Race,* 219–22.

10. "The Atlanta Riot," *Bulletin of Atlanta University,* October 1906, 1; "20 Atlantans Are Indicted for Rioting," *Atlanta Constitution,* 13 October 1906, ARVF October 1906 Aftermath; "Fain Acquitted on Riot Charge," ARVF November 1906 Aftermath.

11. "Negro Business' Ordered Closed," *Atlanta News,* 25 September 1906, 5; "Business Places of All Negroes Now Closed Up," *Atlanta Georgian,* 25 September 1906, 3; "Close Up Dives Say Citizens," *Atlanta News,* 25 September 1906, 7; "Churches Asks Negroes Not to Resist Arrest," *Atlanta Journal,* 25 September 1906, 1.

12. For J. Max Barber's commitment to the Atlanta Spirit along with other African Americans, see "Reputable Negroes Beseech Protection of Law." For a detailed examination of Barber's tenure in Atlanta and with the *Voice of the Negro* along with his militancy, see Bullock, "Profile of a Periodical: *The Voice of the Negro,*" 95–114. Barber was a member of the Niagara Movement including fellow Atlantans John Hope, W.E.B. Du Bois, and Alonzo Herndon. See Lewis, *W.E.B. Du Bois: Biography of a Race,* 319; see

also 316–19, 321–22 concerning members and ideals of the Niagara Movement for Civil Rights.

13. "Separation of the Races Is the Inevitable Solution," *New York World*, 24 September 1906.

14. Barber, "Why Mr. Barber Left Atlanta," *Voice of the Negro*, November 1906, 470; Barber, "Why Barber Sees It as Organized," *Voice of the Negro*, November 1906, 478.

15. Barber, "Why Barber Sees It as Organized." For the details of Barber's exile from Atlanta, see Mixon, "The Atlanta Riot of 1906," 658–70. For responses to Barber's departure, see "Let Us Stand Pat," *Atlanta Independent*, 29 September 1906, 4, and "Voice of the Negro Stilled in Atlanta," *Atlanta News*, 9 October 1906, 11. For a definition of "star chamber," see "Star Chamber Session Held," *Atlanta Constitution*, 15 November 1906, ARVF November 1906 Aftermath.

16. Bauerlein, *Negrophobia*, 275–77; Tuttle, ed. ,"W.E.B. Du Bois' Confrontation with White Liberalism during the Progressive Era," *Phylon* 35 (September 1974): 241, 249.

17. Tuttle, "Du Bois' Confrontation," 243, 245–52, 256; Bauerlein, *Negrophobia*, 275–77.

18. Tuttle, "Du Bois' Confrontation," 243, 245–52, 256; Bauerlein, *Negrophobia*, 275–77. For the discrediting of Du Bois, see Rev. C. B. Wilmer to Ray Stannard Baker, 19 November 1907, PRSB, reel 26, no. 105; Wilmer to Baker, 31 January 1908, PRSB, reel 26, nos. 210–11. For additional letters addressing the "servant problem" or attacking Du Bois, see Clark Howell to George Foster Peabody (servant question), 10 November 1906, PRSB, reel 25, no. 471; John E. White to Baker, 23 April 1908, PRSB, reel 26, nos. 337–38.

19. J. Max Barber, "The Atlanta Tragedy," *Voice of the Negro*, November 1906, 473.

20. "Saturday Night Will Be Quiet," *Atlanta Constitution*, 29 September 1906, 6; "Hundreds of Negroes Are Leaving Atlanta," *Atlanta Georgian*, 25 September 1906, 1; "Scores of Negroes Fleeing Atlanta," *Atlanta Georgian*, 25 September 1906, 2; Williamson, *The Crucible of Race*, 219–20, 535n.44.

21. "White Laborers Are Wanted by Board of Health," *Atlanta Georgian*, 29 September 1906, 8; "Board Wants White Laborers," *Atlanta Constitution*, 29 September 1906, 7; "City Streets Are in Need of Cleaning," *Atlanta Constitution*, 30 September 1906, 6C; "Says Negroes Will Not Work," *Atlanta Constitution*, 2 October 1906, 4; "Streets Still Need Cleaning," *Atlanta Constitution*, 3 October 1906, 3; 28 September 1906 and 9 January 1907, Board of Health 1905–7 Minutes, 98–111, City of Atlanta Collection, Atlanta History Center. Ninety of the black sanitation workers drove "trash carts," and sixty swept streets. The remainder's duties were not discussed in any of the sources. Benson would be reelected president on 9 January 1907, but there was no further discussion concerning replacing African Americans.

22. Benjamin J. Davis, "Among Our Enemies, We Are in Midst of Friends, and They Predominate," *Atlanta Georgian*, 26 September 1906, 6.

23. "Let Us Stand Pat," *Atlanta Independent*, 29 September 1906, 4; "Lawyer Crane Points at the Causes," *Atlanta Independent*, 29 September 1906, 3; "Our City Authorities Should Go One Round Further," *Atlanta Independent*, 6 October 1906, 4; "Mob Violence

Rape—Their Baneful Consequences," *Atlanta Independent*, 6 October 1906, 4; "Downright Hypocrites," *Atlanta Independent*, 13 October 1906, 4; "The Problem Solver Much in Evidence," *Atlanta Independent*, 13 October 1906, 4; "Let Us Admit Our Inferiority," *Atlanta Independent*, 20 October 1906, 4; "Negro Enterprises," *Atlanta Independent*, 27 October 1906, 4; "Some Telling Effects of Mob Violence," *Atlanta Independent*, 27 October 1906, 4; "What Has Northern Criticism of the South Profited Us?" *Atlanta Independent*, 3 November 1906, 4.

24. "Hundreds of Negroes Are Leaving Atlanta"; "Saturday Night Will Be Quiet," *Atlanta Constitution*, 29 September 1906, 6; Rodney, "Henry Hugh Proctor," 127; letters from parents, box 1, 1906, Papers of John and Lugenia Hope, ed. Alton Hornsby Jr. (Morehouse College, Atlanta University Center, Woodruff Library Archives Department, Atlanta; Firestone Library, Princeton University, 1984), microfilm.

25. Tuttle, "Du Bois' Confrontation," 248.

26. "Sixty Indicted for Murdering Officer Heard," "Heard Murder Again in Court," "Negroes Freed in Murder Case," and "Forty Negroes Will Be Tried," *Atlanta Constitution*, 22 October 1906, all in ARVF October 1906 Aftermath; "Life Term Given to Alex Walker," *Atlanta Constitution*, 1 November 1906, ARVF November 1906 Aftermath; "Murder Trial Goes to Jury," *Atlanta Constitution*, 12 December 1906, ARVF December 1906–January 1907; Garrett, *Atlanta and Environs*, 2:621–22.

27. J. Max Barber, "The Atlanta Tragedy," *Voice of the Negro*, November 1906, 474, 477.

28. Baker, "The Atlanta Riot," 16.

29. Williamson, *The Crucible of Race*, 220; Johnson and Roark, "Strategies of Survival," 89–91, 94, 97. For Wilmer, see Tuttle, "Du Bois' Confrontation."

30. "Christian League Formed to Solve the Race Problem," *Atlanta Constitution*, 22 November 1906, ARVF November 1906 Aftermath; Godshalk, "In the Wake of Riot," 210–19, 222–26; Baker, "Atlanta Riot," 27–28. The Business Men's Gospel Union officers in Atlanta were W. J. Northen (president), D. I. Carson, E. S. Gray, and W. H. Patterson (vice presidents), Dr. J. D. Turner (secretary), Marion M. Jackson (assistant secretary), John A. Brice (treasurer), J. W. Patterson (chairman, devotional committee), and John J. Eagan (chairman, finance committee). See also "Christian League Formed to Solve the Race Problem," *Atlanta Constitution*, 22 November 1906, ARVF November 1906 Aftermath.

31. Godshalk, "In the Wake of Riot," 168–79; Harlan, *Booker T. Washington: The Wizard of Tuskegee, 1901–1915*, 301–2; Baker, "The Atlanta Riot," 15; Garrett, *Atlanta and Environs*, 2:503; Proctor, *Between Black and White*, 96; "Civic League Planned by Committee of Ten," *Atlanta Constitution*, 20 November 1906, ARVF November 1906 Aftermath; Dittmer, *Black Georgia in the Progressive Era*, 167; Bauerlein, *Negrophobia*, 275–77. Godshalk lists Rev. E. R. Carter and W. F. Penn as two other members of the Colored Cooperative League. Harlan credits Hopkins as being a "hero" during the postriot period for his leadership in racial cooperation with Proctor. Dittmer provides a more detailed examination of Proctor's postriot career. See also Rodney, "Henry Hugh Proctor," 121–25, 137, 144–45. See Bayor, *Race and the Shaping of Twentieth-Century Atlanta* for the postriot legacy of segregation as public policy. See "Southern Commission on the

Race Problem," PRSB, reel 26, nos. 152–53; John E. White to Ray Stannard Baker, October 7, 1907, PRSB, reel 26, no. 67; John E. White to Ray Stannard Baker, 23 April 1908, PRSB, reel 26, nos. 337–38.

32. "The Atlanta Riot," *Bulletin of Atlanta University;* Henry Hugh Proctor, "Interracial Co-operation in Georgia," *Bulletin of Atlanta University,* October 1906, 2; "New Era of Reconstruction," *Bulletin of Atlanta University,* February 1907, 1; Rodney, "Henry Hugh Proctor," 114–16, 121–23; Bayor, *Race and the Shaping of Twentieth-Century Atlanta,* chap. 5.

33. Bayor, *Race and the Shaping of Twentieth-Century Atlanta,* 93–107, 131; for details on the connections between political organizing and a black police presence, see Dulaney, *Black Police in America,* 38–44.

34. Bayor, *Race and the Shaping of Twentieth-Century Atlanta,* 129–31, 142–48.

35. Mack H. Jones, "Black Political Empowerment in Atlanta: Myth and Reality," 8:130–31, 140–41. For an examination of how the commercial-civic elite's paternalism evolved in the twentieth century, this article suggests that black elite aspirations, as well as all African Americans, is a struggle between whites bent on maintaining their position of dominance and blacks seeking to escape white dominance to carve out their own niche. This process is spelled out in detail in Ronald Bayor's examination of Atlanta.

36. Dorsey, "To Build Our Lives Together," epilogue.

Bibliography

Primary Sources

Pamphlets

Atlanta Chamber of Commerce. *Souvenir Album: Atlanta, Georgia*. Atlanta: Jamestown Exposition, 1907.
———. *Atlanta: A Twentieth-Century City*. N.p., November 1903.

Papers

Adjutant-General 22 Series 13. Georgia Department of Archives and History, Department of Defense, Atlanta.
Atlanta City Council minutes. Atlanta History Center.
Atlanta city maps 1902, 1906. Georgia Department of Archives and History, Atlanta.
Atlanta Riot of 1906 folder. Atlanta History Center.
Atlanta Riot vertical files. Special Collections, Robert W. Woodruff Library, Atlanta University Center.
Atlanta University Collection. Auburn Avenue Research Library on African-American Culture and History, Archives Division, Atlanta-Fulton Public Library System.
Baker, Ray S. Papers. Main Library, Microfilm, Ohio State University, Columbus.
Chambers, Aldine. Papers. Atlanta History Center.
City of Atlanta Collection. Atlanta History Center.
Du Bois, W.E.B. Papers. Central Library, Microfilm, University of Cincinnati.
Executive Branch Papers. Georgia Department of Archives and History, Atlanta.
Felton, Rebecca L. Collection. Special Collections, University Libraries, University of Georgia, Athens.
Fleming, William F. Papers. Special Collections, University Libraries, University of Georgia, Athens.
Hardman, Lamartine G. Collection. Richard B. Russell Memorial Library, University of Georgia, Athens.
Hardwick, Thomas W. Papers. Richard B. Russell Memorial Library, University of Georgia, Athens.

Harris, Joel Chandler. Collection. Special Collections, Robert W. Woodruff Library, Emory University, Atlanta.
Herndon, Alonzo. Papers. Alonzo Herndon House and Museum, Atlanta.
Hope, John and Lugenia Hope. Papers. Firestone Library, Microfilm, Princeton University.
Hopkins Family Collection, 1852–1943. Atlanta History Center.
Howell, Clark. Collection. Robert W. Woodruff Library, Emory University, Atlanta.
Howell, Clark. Folder. Atlanta History Center.
Howell, Clark. Papers. Special Collections, University Libraries, University of Georgia, Athens.
Long-Rucker-Aiken Family Papers. Atlanta History Center.
Maddox, Robert Foster. Papers. Atlanta History Center.
Northen, William J. Papers. Georgia Department of Archives and History, Atlanta.
Ovington, Mary White. Collection. Archives of Labor History and Urban Affairs, Wayne State University, Detroit.
Rucker, Henry A., vertical file. Archives Department, Robert W. Woodruff Library, Atlanta University Center.
Russell, Richard B., Sr. Papers. Richard B. Russell Memorial Library, University of Georgia, Athens.
Schomberg Clippings File, 1925–1974. New York Public Library, Schomberg Center, New York.
Sherry, Grace T. Collection. Atlanta History Center.
Slater, William F. Papers. Georgia Department of Archives and History, Atlanta.
Smith, Hoke. Collection. Richard B. Russell Memorial Library, University of Georgia, Athens.
Thomas E. Watson Papers: Research Collections in American Politics. Bethesda, Md.: University Publications of America, 1991.
Watson, Thomas E. Collection. Richard B. Russell Memorial Library, University of Georgia, Athens.

Published and Unpublished Reports—State and Local Government

Annual Reports of the Chief of Police of the City of Atlanta, Georgia, 1897–1904. Atlanta.
Atlanta City Council Minutes. September–December 1906. Atlanta.
"Some Notes on Negro Crime Particularly in Georgia." Report of a social study made under the direction of Atlanta University. Ninth Conference for Study of Negro Problems, 1904. Atlanta.
Adjutant-General Letterbook, 1902–1906. Atlanta.
Georgia Adjutant-General Report, 1903–1906. Atlanta: Franklin-Turner, 1907.
Roll of Liberty, Colored Militia Units. Georgia.
"The Atlanta Session of the Negro Business League." Washington, D.C.: National Business League, 1906.
Baker, Ray Stannard, "The Atlanta Riot." Jesse Moorland Collection, Moorland-Springarn Collection, Moorland-Springarn Research Center, Howard University, Washington, D.C.

Census Reports Volume 1, Twelfth Census of the United States Taken in the Year 1900, Population Part I. pp. lxxiv, 612, 650. Washington, D.C.
Department of Commerce and Labor, Bureau of the Census. Special Reports Supplementary Analysis and Derivative Tables 1900. Washington, D.C.: Government Printing Office, 1904, p. 199.
Special Report Occupations at the Twelfth Census, pp. 486–88. Washington, D.C.
Thirteenth Census, vol. 4, Population, 1910 Occupation Statistics, 536. Washington, D.C.

Articles and Books

Baker, Ray Stannard. "The Atlanta Riot." *American Magazine,* April 1907, 4–28.
———. *Following the Color Line: An Account of Negro Citizenship in the American Democracy.* 1904, 1905, 1907, 1908; reprint, Williamstown, Mass.: Corner House, 1973.
Barton, Bruce. *The Church That Saved a City.* N.p, 1914.
Candler, Allen D., and Clement A. Evans, eds. *Georgia: Comprising Sketches of Counties, Towns, Events, Institutions, and People, Arranged in Cyclopedic Form.* 4 vols. Atlanta: State Historical Association, 1906; reprint, Spartanburg, S.C.: The Reprint Company, 1972.
Carter, Rev. Edward R. *The Black Side.* 1894; reprint, Freeport, N.Y.: Books for Libraries Press, 1971.
Du Bois, W.E.B. "The Tragedy of Atlanta from the Point of View of the Negroes." *World Today* Hearst International combined with *Cosmopolitan* 11 (1906): 1173–75.
Gibson, Thomas. "The Anti-Negro Riots in Atlanta." *Harper's Weekly* 50 (July–December 1906): 1457–59.
Grady, Henry. *The New South: Writings and Speeches of Henry Grady.* Savannah: Beehive Press, 1971.
Grantham, Dewey W., Jr. "Some Letters from Thomas W. Hardwick to Tom Watson Concerning the Georgia Gubernatorial Campaign of 1906." *Georgia Historical Quarterly* 34 (December 1950): 328–40.
Harris, Joel Chandler, ed. *Life of Henry Grady Including His Writings and Speeches: A Memorial Volume.* 1890; reprint, New York: Haskell, 1972.
Hope, John. "Negro Suffrage in the States Whose Constitutions Have Been Specifically Revised." *American Negro Academy Occasional Papers,* no. 11. The Negro and Elective Franchise. 1905; reprint, New York: Arno Press and New York Times, 1969.
Inman, Arthur. *The Inman Diary: A Public and Private Confession.* Vol. 1. Edited by Daniel Aaron. Cambridge: Harvard University Press, 1985.
Martin, Thomas. *Atlanta and Its Builders: A Comprehensive History of the Gate City of the South.* Atlanta: Century Memorial, 1902.
McKelway, A. J. "The Atlanta Riots—A Southern Point of View." *Outlook* 84 (November 1906): 557–62.
Ovington, Mary White. "Letter to the Outlook—The Atlanta Riots." *Outlook* 84 (November 1906): 684.
Penn, Irvine Garland, and John Wesley Edward Bowen, eds. *The United Negro: His Problems and His Progress Containing the Addresses and Proceedings of the Negro Young People's Christian Educational Congress.* Atlanta: D. E. Luther, 1902.

"Pictures That Dishonor Women." *Golden Age,* 27 September 1906, 8.
Terrell, Russell Franklin. *A Study of the Early Journalistic Writings of Henry W. Grady.* George Peabody College Teaching Contributions to Education, no. 39. Nashville: George Peabody College for Teachers, 1927.
Tuttle, William M., Jr., ed. "W.E.B. Du Bois' Confrontation with White Liberalism during the Progressive Era." *Phylon* 35 (September 1974): 241–58.
Watson, Thomas. "Down in Georgia—Editorials." *Tom Watson's Magazine* 4 (March 1906): 1.
———. Editorial. *Tom Watson's Magazine* 2 (October 1905): 397–98.
———. "Is the Black Man Superior to the White?" *Thomas Watson's Magazine* l (June 1905): 393–98.
———. "The Ungrateful Negro from a Newspaper—Editorials." *Tom Watson's Magazine* 4 (April 1906): 165–69, 170–71, 173.
Wells, Ida B. *Southern Horrors and Other Writings: The Anti-Lynching Campaign of Ida B. Wells, 1892–1900.* Edited by Jacqueline Jones Royster. Boston: Bedford Books, 1997.

Secondary Sources

Dissertations, Theses, and Papers

Bacote, Clarence A. "The Negro in Georgia, 1880–1908." Ph.D. diss., University of Chicago, 1955.
Blalock, Jesse. "Social Political and Economic Aspects of Race Relations in Atlanta from 1890–1908." Master's thesis, Atlanta University, June 1969.
Bolden, William. "The Political Structure of Charter Revision Movements in Atlanta during the Progressive Era." Ph.D. diss., Emory University, 1978.
Carageorge, Ted. "An Evaluation of Hoke Smith and Thomas E. Watson as Georgia Reformers." Ph.D. diss., University of Georgia, 1963.
Crawford, Jim. "The Warriors of Civilization: U.S. Soldiers, American Culture, and White Supremacy, 1898–1902." Paper presented at annual meeting of the Organization of American Historians, April 1995, Washington, D.C.
Cummings, Josephine N. "Thomas William Hardwick: A Study of a Strange and Eventful Career." Master's thesis, University of Georgia, 1961.
D'Avino, Gail Anne. "Atlanta Municipal Parks, 1882–1917: Urban Boosterism, Urban Reform in a New South City." Ph.D. diss., Emory University, 1988.
Deaton, Thomas M. "Atlanta during the Progressive Era." Ph.D. diss., University of Georgia, 1969.
———. "James G. Woodward Atlanta's Colorful Labor Mayor." Class paper, Georgia State University, Atlanta, 1985.
Dorsey, Allison G. "To Build Our Lives Together: African American Community Formation in the Redeemed South, Atlanta, 1875–1906." Ph.D. diss., University of California, Irvine, 1995.
Fennell, Dwight. "A Demographic Study of Black Businesses, 1905–1908, with Respect to the Race Riot of 1906." Master's thesis, Atlanta University, 1977.

Fort, Randolph L. "History of the *Atlanta Journal*." Master's thesis, Emory University, 1930.
Galishoff, Stuart. "The Health of Black Atlantans and Its Effects on Business and Race Relations during the Progressive Era." Paper presented at the 1983 annual meeting of the Organization of American Historians, Cincinnati, 17 April 1983.
Godshalk, David F. "In the Wake of Riot: Atlanta's Struggle for Order, 1899–1919." Ph.D. diss., Yale University, 1992.
Hickey, Georginia Susan. "Visibility, Politics, and Urban Development: Working-Class Women in Early Twentieth-Century Atlanta." Ph.D. diss., University of Michigan, 1995.
Hicks, Alfred E. "Watson and Hardwick in Georgia Politics: A Study in Political Personality and Reform Tension." Honors thesis, Trinity College, Hartford, Conn., 1967.
Hunter, Tera W. "Household Workers in the Making: Afro-American Women in Atlanta and the New South, 1861–1920." Ph.D. diss., Yale University 1991.
Kuhn, Clifford M. "'A Full History of the Strike as I Saw It': Atlanta's Fulton Bag and Cotton Mills Workers and Their Representations through the 1914–1915 Strike." Ph.D. diss., University of North Carolina, Chapel Hill, 1993.
Maclachlan, Gretchen Ehrman. "Women's Work: Atlanta's Industrialization and Urbanization, 1879–1929." Ph.D. diss., Emory University, 1992.
Matthews, John Michael. "Studies in Race Relations in Georgia, 1890–1930." Ph.D. diss., Duke University, 1970.
McCombs, McClure Person. "Pittsburg: A Sociological Study of a 'Natural Area.'" Master's thesis, Atlanta University, 1951.
Porter, Michael Leroy. "Black Atlanta: An Interdisciplinary Study of Blacks on the East Side of Atlanta, 1890–1930." Ph.D. diss., Emory University, 1974.
Rainey, Glenn W. "The Race Riot of 1906 in Atlanta." Master's thesis, Emory University, 1929.
Rodney, Lester J. "Henry Hugh Proctor: The Atlanta Years, 1894–1920." Ph.D. diss., Clark-Atlanta University, 1992.
Slade, Dorothy. "The Evolution of Negro Areas in the City of Atlanta." Master's thesis, Atlanta University, 1946.
Smith, Frances. "Black Militia in Savannah, Georgia." Master's thesis, Georgia Southern College, 1981.
Spencer, John Merrill. "Decatur Street: A Natural Area." Master's thesis, Atlanta University, August 1952.
Thornberry, Jerry John. "The Development of Black Atlanta, 1865–1885." Ph.D. diss., University of Maryland, 1977.
Walden, Carolyn. "An Analysis of the Black Experience as Reflected in *Voice of the Negro*, 1904–1907." Master's thesis, Atlanta University, 1971.
Wingo, Horace C. "Race Relations in Georgia, 1872–1908." Ph.D. diss., University of Georgia, 1969.
WRFG. "Atlanta Race Riot of 1906." Produced and researched by Harlan Joy and Barbara Joy. Atlanta, Georgia.

Articles and Books

Abramowitz, Jack. "The Negro in the Populist Movement." *Journal of Negro History* 38 (July 1953): 257–89.
Adams, Kathleen Redding. Interview, Atlanta, 13 August 1985.
Adams, Myron W. *A History of Atlanta University.* Atlanta: Atlanta University Press, 1930.
Aiken, Lucy Rucker. Interview, Atlanta, 17 August 1985.
"Aldine Chambers." *History of Georgia,* 2:352–53. Atlanta: S. J. Clarke, 1926.
Ambrose, Douglas. *Henry Hughes and Proslavery Thought in the Old South.* Baton Rouge: Louisiana State University Press, 1996.
Anderson, James D. *The Education of Blacks in the South, 1860–1935.* Chapel Hill: University of North Carolina Press, 1988.
Angell, Stephen Ward. *Bishop Henry McNeal Turner and African-American Religion in the South.* Knoxville: University of Tennessee Press, 1992.
Aptheker, Herbert. Interview, Cincinnati, 1 May 1985.
Ayers, Edward L. *The Promise of the New South: Life after Reconstruction.* New York: Oxford University Press, 1992.
———. *Southern Crossing: A History of the American South.* New York: Oxford University Press, 1995.
Bacote, Clarence A. "The Negro in Atlanta Politics." *Phylon* 16 (1955): 333–50.
———. "Negro Officeholders in Georgia under President McKinley." *Journal of Negro History* 45 (July 1959): 217–39.
———. "Negro Proscriptions, Protests, and Proposed Solutions in Georgia, 1880–1908." *Journal of Southern History* 25 (1959): 471–98.
———. "Some Aspects of Negro Life in Georgia, 1880–1908." *Journal of Negro History* 43 (July 1958): 186–213.
———. *The Story of Atlanta University: A Century of Service, 1865–1965.* Atlanta: Atlanta University, 1969.
Bair, Barbara. "Remapping the Black/White Body: Sexuality, Nationalism, and Biracial Antimiscegenation Activism in 1920s Virginia." *Sex, Love, Race: Crossing Boundaries in North American History,* ed. Martha Hodes, 399–422. New York: New York University Press, 1999.
Bauerlein, Mark. *Negrophobia: A Race Riot in Atlanta, 1906.* San Francisco: Encounter Books, 2001.
Bayor, Ronald H. *Race and the Shaping of Twentieth-Century Atlanta.* Chapel Hill: University of North Carolina Press, 1996.
Beard, Rick. "From Suburb to Defend Neighborhood: The Evolution of Inman Park and Ansley Park, 1890–1980." *Atlanta Historical Journal* (Summer/Fall 1982): 113–40.
Bederman, Gail. *Manliness and Civilization: A Cultural History of Gender and Race in the United States, 1880–1917.* Chicago: University of Chicago Press, 1995.
Berlin, Ira. *Slaves without Masters: The Free Negro in the Antebellum South.* New York: Random House, 1974.
Billings, Dwight B., Jr. *Planters and the Making of the "New South": Class, Politics, and*

Development in North Carolina, 1865–1900. Chapel Hill: University of North Carolina, 1979.

Blassingame, John W. "Before the Ghetto: The Making of the Black Community in Savannah, 1865–1880." In *In Search of the Promised Land Essays in Black Urban History*, ed. Theodore Kornweibel Jr. Port Washington, N.Y.: National University Publications, Kennikat Press, 1981.

———. *The Slave Community Plantation Life in the Antebellum South.* Rev. ed. New York: Oxford University Press, 1979.

Brown, Richard Maxwell. *Strain of Violence: Historical Studies of American Violence and Vigilantism.* New York: Oxford University Press, 1975.

Brownell, Blaine A. *The Urban Ethos in the South, 1920–1930.* Baton Rouge: Louisiana State University Press, 1975.

———. "The Urban South Comes of Age, 1900–1940." *The City in Southern History: The Growth of Urban Civilization in the South*, ed. Blaine A Brownell and David R. Goldfield, 123–58. Port Washington, N.Y.: National University Publications, Kennikat Press, 1977.

Brundage, W. Fitzhugh. *Lynching in the New South: Georgia and Virginia, 1880–1930.* Urbana: University of Illinois Press, 1993.

Bryan, Ferald J. *Henry Grady or Tom Watson? The Rhetorical Struggle for the New South, 1880–1890.* Macon: Mercer University Press, 1994.

Bullock, Penelope. "Profile of Periodical: *The Voice of the Negro*." *Atlanta Historical Journal* (Spring 1977): 95–114.

Byrne, Anne DeRosa, and Dana F. White. "Atlanta University's 'Northeast Lot': Community Building for Black Atlanta's 'Talented Tenth.'" *Atlanta Historical Journal* (Summer/Fall 1982): 155–76.

Candler, Allen D., and Clement A. Evans, eds. *Georgia: Comprising Sketches of Counties, Towns, Events, Institutions, and Persons, Arranged in Cyclopedic Form.* 4 vols. Atlanta: State Historical Association, 1906; rpt., Spartanburg, S.C.: Reprint Company, 1972.

Candler, Charles Howard. *Asa Griggs Candler.* Atlanta: Emory University, 1950.

Capeci, Dominic J., Jr., and Jack C. Knight. "Reckoning with Violence: W.E.B. Du Bois and the 1906 Atlanta Race Riot." *Journal of Southern History* 62 (November 1996): 727–66.

Capozzola, Christopher. "The Only Badge Needed Is Your Patriotic Fervor: Vigilance, Coercion, and the Law in World War I America." *Journal of American History* 88 (March 2002): 1354–82.

Cell, John W. *The Highest Stage of White Supremacy: The Origins of Segregation in South Africa and the American South.* Cambridge: Cambridge University Press, 1982.

Colby, Elbridge. *The National Guard of the United States: A Half Century of Progress.* Manhattan: Military Affairs and Aerospace Historian, 1977.

Coleman, Kenneth, ed. *A History of Modern Georgia.* Athens: University of Georgia Press, 1977.

Cook, James F. *The Governors of Georgia, 1754–1995.* Rev. ed. Macon: Mercer University Press, 1995.

Cooper, Walter G. *Official History of Fulton County.* 1934; reprint, Spartanburg, S.C.: Reprint Company, 1978.
Cottrol, Robert J. *The Afro-Yankees: Providence's Black Community in the Antebellum Era.* Westport: Greenwood Press, 1982.
Crimmins, Timothy. "West End: Metamorphosis from Suburban Town to Intown Neighborhood." *Atlanta Historical Journal* (Summer/Fall 1982): 33–50.
Crowe, Charles. "Racial Massacre in Atlanta, September 22, 1906." *Journal of Negro History* 54 (April 1969): 150–76.
———. "Racial Violence and Social Reform—Origins of the Atlanta Riot of 1906." *Journal of Negro History* 53 (July 1968): 234–56.
Dailey, Jane. "Deference and Violence in the Postbellum Urban South: Manners and Massacres in Danville, Virginia." *Journal of Southern History* 63 (August 1997): 553–90.
Davis, Harold E. *Henry Grady's New South: Atlanta Brave and Beautiful City.* Tuscaloosa: University of Alabama Press, 1990.
———. "Henry W. Grady, Master of the Ring, 1880–1886." *Georgia Historical Quarterly* 69 (Fall 1985): 315–37.
Davis, Leroy. "An African American Dilemma: John Hope and Black Leadership in the Early Twentieth Century." *Atlanta History: A Journal of Georgia and the South* 41 (Spring 1997): 33.
Davis, T. J. *Rumor of Revolt: The "Great Negro Plot" in Colonial New York.* Amherst: University of Massachusetts Press, 1985.
DeCredico, Mary A. "Image and Reality: Ken Burns and the Urban Confederacy." *Journal of Urban History* 23 (May 1997): 387–405.
Diamond, B. I., and Baylen, J. O. "The Demise of the Georgia Guard Colored, 1868–1914." *Phylon* 45 (December 1984): 311–13.
Diefendorf, Barbara. "Prologue to a Massacre: Popular Unrest in Paris, 1557–1572." *American Historical Review* 90 (December 1985): 1067–91.
Dittmer, John. *Black Georgia in the Progressive Era, 1900–1920.* Urbana: University of Illinois Press, 1977.
Dorr, Lisa Lindquist. "Black-on-White Rape and Retribution in Twentieth-Century Virginia: 'Men, Even Negroes Must Have Some Protection.'" *Journal of Southern History* 65 (November 2000): 711–48.
Doyle, Don H. *Nashville in the New South, 1880–1930.* Knoxville: University of Tennessee Press, 1985.
———. *New Men, New Cities, New South: Atlanta, Nashville, Charleston, Mobile, 1860–1910.* Chapel Hill: University of North Carolina, 1990.
Du Bois, W.E.B. *The Philadelphia Negro: A Social Study.* 1899; reprint, Philadelphia: University of Pennsylvania Press, 1996.
Durrett, Dan, and Dana F. White. "An-Other Atlanta The Black Heritage A Bicentennial Tour." *The Bicentennial Commission.* Atlanta: The History Group, 1975 printed by Western Publishing Company.
Edmonds, Helen G. *The Negro and Fusion Politics in North Carolina.* Chapel Hill: University of North Carolina Press, 1951.

Edwards, Laura F. "The Disappearance of Susan Daniel and Henderson Cooper: Gender and Narratives of Political Conflict in the Reconstruction-Era U.S. South." In *Sex, Love, Race: Crossing Boundaries in North American History*, ed. Martha Hodes, 294–312. New York: New York University Press, 1999.

———. *Gendered Strife and Confusion: The Political Culture of Reconstruction*. Urbana: University of Illinois Press, 1997.

Fingerhut, Eugene R. "Tom Watson, Blacks, and Southern Reform." *Georgia Historical Quarterly* 60 (Winter 1976): 324–43.

Fink, Gary M. *The Fulton Bag and Cotton Mills Strike of 1914–1915: Espionage, Labor Conflict, and New South Industrial Relations*. Ithaca: Industrial and Labor Relations Press, Cornell University, 1993.

Fits, Leroy. *A History of Black Baptists*. Nashville: Broadman Press, 1985.

Franklin, Buck Colbert. *My Life and an Era: The Autobiography of Buck Colbert Franklin*, ed. John Hope Franklin and John Whittington Franklin. Baton Rouge: Louisiana State University Press, 1997.

Franklin, John Hope. *From Slavery to Freedom: A History of Negro Americans*. 5th ed. New York: Knopf, 1980.

Friedman, Lawrence J. *The White Savage: Racial Fantasies in the Postbellum South*. Englewood Cliffs, N.J.: Prentice-Hall, 1970.

Gaines, Kevin K. *Uplifting the Race: Black Leadership, Politics, and Culture in the Twentieth Century*. Chapel Hill: University of North Carolina, 1996.

Galishoff, Stuart. "Germs Know No Color Line: Black Health and Public Policy in Atlanta, 1900–1918." *Journal of the History of Medicine and Allied Sciences* 40 (January 1985): 22–41.

Gamble, Vanessa Northington. *Making a Place for Ourselves: The Black Hospital Movement, 1920–1945*. New York: Oxford University Press, 1995.

Garrett, Franklin M. *Atlanta and Environs: A Chronicle of Its People and Events*. 2 vols. 1954; reprint, Athens: University of Georgia Press, 1969.

Gaston, Paul M. *The New South Creed: A Study in Southern Mythmaking*. Baton Rouge: Louisiana State University Press, 1970.

Gilmore, Glenda E. *Gender and Jim Crow: Women and the Politics of White Supremacy in North Carolina, 1896–1920*. Chapel Hill: University of North Carolina Press, 1996.

———. "When Jim Crow Had Wings: White Southerners and the Cultural Politics of Black Representation." Paper delivered at "Works in Progress Seminar" African American Studies Department, Woodrow Wilson School Bowl 5, Princeton University, March 12, 1999.

Goings, Kenneth W., and Gerald L. Smith. "'Unhidden' Transcripts: Memphis and African American Agency, 1862–1920." *Journal of Urban History* 21 (March 1995): 372–94.

Goldfield, David R. *Black, White, and Southern: Race Relations and Southern Culture, 1940 to the Present*. Baton Rouge: Louisiana State University Press, 1990.

———. *Cotton Fields and Skyscrapers: Southern City and Region*. 1982; reprint, Baltimore: Johns Hopkins University Press, 1989.

Goodson, Steve. "'This Mighty Influence for Good or for Evil': The Movies in Atlanta,

1895–1920." *Atlanta History: A Journal of Georgia and the South* 39 (Fall/Winter 1995): 28–29.

Grable, Stephen W. "The Other Side of the Tracks: Cabbagetown—A Working-Class Neighbor in Transition during the Early Twentieth Century." *Atlanta Historical Journal* (Summer/Fall 1982): 51–66.

Grantham, Dewey W., Jr. "Georgia Politics and the Disfranchisement of the Negro." Grace T. Sherry Collection. Atlanta Historical Society.

———. *Hoke Smith and the Politics of the New South.* Baton Rouge: Louisiana State University Press, 1958, 1967.

———. "The Progressive Movement and the Negro." *South Atlantic Quarterly* 54 (1955): 461–77.

———. "The Promise of Southern Progressivism." In *Major Problems in the History of the American South,* vol. 2: *The New South,* 2d ed., ed. Paul D. Escott, David R. Goldfield, Sally G. McMillian, and Elizabeth Hayes Turner, 230–40. Boston: Houghton Mifflin, 1999.

———. "Southern Progressives and Racial Imperative." In Grantham, *The Regional Imagination: The South and Recent American History.* Nashville: Vanderbilt University Press, 1979.

———. *Southern Progressivism: The Reconciliation of Progress and Tradition.* Knoxville: University of Tennessee Press, 1983.

Gravlee, G. Jack. "Tom Watson: Disciple of 'Jeffersonian Democracy.'" In *The Oratory of Southern Demagogues,* ed. Carl M. Logue and Howard Dorgan, 85–111. Baton Rogue: Louisiana State University Press, 1981.

Greenberg, Cheryl. "Twentieth-Century Liberalism: Transformation of an Ideology." In *Perspectives on Modern America: Making Sense of the Twentieth Century,* ed. Harvard Sitkoff, 55–79. New York: Oxford University Press, 2001.

Greenwood, Janette Thomas. *Bittersweet Legacy: The Black and White "Better Classes" in Charlotte, 1850–1910.* Chapel Hill: University of North Carolina Press, 1994.

Griewank, Karl. "Emergence of the Concept of Revolution." In *Revolution in Modern European History,* ed. Henry Lubasz, 55–61. New York: Macmillan, 1966.

Grimshaw, Allen D. *Racial Violence in the United States.* Chicago: Aldine, 1969.

Hall, Jacquelyn Dowd. "'The Mind That Burns in Each Body': Women, Rape, and Racial Violence." In *Power of Desire: The Politics of Sexuality,* ed. Ann Snitow, Christine Stansell, and Sharon Thompson, 328–49. New York: Monthly Review Press, 1983.

Hall, Jacquelyn Dowd, Robert Korstad, and James Leloudis. "Cotton Mill People: Work, Community, Protest in the Textile South, 1880–1940." *American Historical Review* 91 (April 1986): 245–86.

Hanchett, Thomas W. *Sorting Out the New South City: Race, Class, and Urban Development in Charlotte, 1875–1975.* Chapel Hill: University of North Carolina Press, 1998.

Harlan, Louis R. *Booker T. Washington: The Making of a Black Leader, 1865–1901.* New York: Oxford University Press, 1975.

———. *Booker T. Washington: The Wizard of Tuskegee, 1901–1915.* New York: Oxford University Press, 1983.

———. *Separate and Unequal Public School Campaigns and Racism in the Southern Seaboard Status, 1901–1915.* Chapel Hill: University of North Carolina Press, 1958.
Harris, Carl V. *Political Power in Birmingham, 1871–1921.* Knoxville: University of Tennessee Press, 1977.
Harris, J. William. "Etiquette, Lynching, and Racial Boundaries in Southern History: A Mississippi Example." *American Historical Review* 100 (April 1995): 387–410.
Harris, Julia Collier. *The Life and Letters of Joel Chandler Harris.* Boston: Houghton Mifflin, 1918.
Harris, Michael W. *The Rise of Gospel Blues: The Music of Thomas Andrew Dorsey in the Urban Church.* New York: Oxford University Press, 1992.
Henderson, Alexa B. *Atlanta Life Insurance Company: Guardian of Black Economic Dignity.* Tuscaloosa: University of Alabama Press, 1990.
Hertzberg, Steven. "Southern Jews and Their Encounter with Blacks: Atlanta, 1850–1915." *Atlanta Historical Journal* (Fall 1979): 7–24.
Higham, John. *Strangers in the Land: Patterns of American Nativism, 1860–1925.* New Brunswick, N.J.: Rutgers University Press, 1955.
Holmes, William F. "The Southern Farmer's Alliance and the Georgia Senatorial Election of 1890." *Journal of Southern History* 50 (May 1984): 197–224.
Hopkins, Richard J, "Status, Mobility, and the Dimensions of Change in a Southern City." In *Cities in American History*, ed. Kenneth T. Jackson and Stanley K. Schultz, 216–31. New York: Knopf, 1972.
Hunter, Floyd. *Community Power Structure: A Study of Decision Makers.* Chapel Hill: University of North Carolina Press, 1953.
———. *Community Power Succession: Atlanta's Policy Makers Revisited.* Chapel Hill: University of North Carolina Press, 1980.
Hunter, Tera W. "Domination and Resistance: The Politics of Wage Household Labor in New South Atlanta. In *The New African American Urban History*, ed. Kenneth W. Goings and Raymond Mohl, 167–82. Thousand Oaks, Calif.: Sage, 1996.
———. *To 'Joy My Freedom: Southern Black Women's Lives and Labors after the Civil War.* Cambridge: Harvard University Press, 1997.
Iorizzo, Luciano J. "The Padrone and Immigrant Distribution." *The Italian Experience in the United States*, ed. Silvano M. Tomasi and Madeline H. Engel, 44–70. New York: 1977.
Jenkins, Wilbert L. *Seizing the New Day: African Americans in Post-Civil War Charleston.* Bloomington: Indiana University Press, 1998.
Johnson, Charles, Jr. *African American Soldiers in the National Guard: Recruitment and Development during Peacetime and War.* Westport: Greenwood Press, 1992.
Johnson, Michael P., and James L. Roark. "Strategies of Survival: Free Negro Families and the Problem of Slavery." In *In Joy and Sorrow: Women, Family, and Marriage in the Victorian South, 1830–1900*, ed. Carol Bleser, 88–102. New York: Oxford University Press, 1991.
Jones, Alton DuMar. "The Administration of Governor Joseph M. Terrell Viewed in the Light of the Progressive Movement." *Georgia Historical Quarterly* 48 (September 1964): 271–90.

Jones, Mack H. "Black Political Empowerment in Atlanta: Myth and Reality." *Annals of the American Academy of Political and Social Science* 439 (1978): 90–117; reprinted in *Black Communities and Urban Development in America, 1720–1990: A Ten-Volume Collection of Articles Surveying the Social, Political, Economic, and Cultural Development of Black Urban Communities,* vol. 8: *Progress versus Poverty, 1970 to the Present,* ed. Kenneth L. Kusmer, 128–55. New York: Garland, 1991.

Kelley, Robin D. G. "'We Are Not What We Seem': Rethinking Black Working-Class Opposition in the Jim Crow South." *Journal of American History* 80 (June 1993): 75–112.

Kingsdale, Jon M. "The 'Poor Man's Club': Social Functions of the Urban Working-Class Saloon." In *The American Man,* ed. Elizabeth H. Pleck and Joseph H. Pleck, 257–77. Englewood Cliffs: Prentice-Hall, 1980.

Knight, Lucian Lamar. *History of Fulton County Georgia: Narrative and Biographical.* Atlanta: A. H. Cawston, 1930.

Korobin, Russell. "The Politics of Disfranchisement in Georgia." *Georgia Historical Quarterly* 74 (Spring 1990): 23–24.

Kousser, J. Morgan. *The Shaping of Southern Politics: Suffrage Restriction and the Establishment of the One-Party South, 1880–1910.* New Haven: Yale University Press, 1974.

Kramer, Paul A. "Empires, Exceptions, and Anglo-Saxons: Race and Rule between British and United States Empires, 1880–1910." *Journal of American History* 88 (March 2002): 1315–53.

Kuhn, Clifford. "1906 Riot: Atlanta Papers Kindle Violence." *Great Speckled Bird,* 28 August 1975, 8–9.

Kuhn, Clifford M., Harlon E. Joye, and E. Bernard West. *Living Atlanta: An Oral History of the City, 1914–1948.* Atlanta and Athens: Atlanta Historical Society and University of Georgia Press, 1990.

Kusmer, Kenneth L. "Black Cleveland and the Central-Woodland Community, 1865–1930." In *Cleveland: A Metropolitan Reader,* ed. W. Dennis Keating, Norman Krumholz, and David C. Perry, 265–82. Kent: Kent State University Press, 1995.

Lane, Roger. *Roots of Violence in Black Philadelphia, 1860–1900.* Cambridge: Harvard University of Press, 1986.

Larsen, Lawrence. *The Rise of the Urban South.* Lexington: University of Kentucky Press, 1985.

———. *The Urban South: A History.* Lexington: University of Kentucky Press, 1990.

Letwin, Daniel. "Interracial Unionism, Gender, and 'Social Equality' in the Alabama Coalfields, 1878–1908." *Journal of Southern History* 61 (August 1995): 519–54.

Lewis, David Levering. *W.E.B. Du Bois: Biography of a Race, 1868–1919.* New York: Henry Holt, 1993.

Lichtenstein, Alex. "'Through the Rugged Gates of the Penitentiary': Convict Labor and Southern Coal, 1870–1900." In *Race and Class in the American South since 1890,* ed. Melvyn Stokes and Rick Halpern, 14–15. Providence: Berg, 1994.

Link, William A. *The Paradox of Southern Progressivism, 1880–1930.* Chapel Hill: University of North Carolina Press, 1992.

———. "The Paradox of Southern Progressivism." In *Major Problems in the History of the American South,* vol. 2: *The New South,* 241–53. Boston: Houghton Mifflin, 1999.
Lorini, Alessandra. *Rituals of Race: American Public Culture and the Search for Racial Democracy.* Charlottesville: University Press of Virginia, 1999.
MacLean, Nancy. "Gender, Sexuality, and the Politics of Lynching: The Leo Frank Case Revisited." In *Under Sentence of Death: Lynching in the South,* ed. W. Fitzhugh Brundage, 158–88. Chapel Hill: University of North Carolina Press, 1997.
Martin, Jean. *Mule to Marta.* Vol. 2. Atlanta: Atlanta Historical Society, 1977.
Mathias, William J., and Anderson, Stuart. *Horse to Helicopter: First Century of the Atlanta Police Department.* Atlanta: Community Life Publications: Criminal Justice Series School of Urban Life Georgia State University, Decatur, National Graphics, 1973 by Georgia State University.
McCurry, Stephanie. "The Politics of Yeoman Households in South Carolina." In *Divided Houses: Gender and the Civil War,* ed. Catherine Clinton and Nina Silber, 22–42. New York: Oxford University Press, 1992.
McKiven, Henry M., Jr. *Iron and Steel: Class, Race, and Community Birmingham, Alabama, 1875–1920.* Chapel Hill: University of North Carolina Press, 1995.
McLeod, Jonathan W. *Workers and Work Place Dynamics in Reconstruction-Era Atlanta: A Case Study.* Los Angeles: UCLA Center for Afro-American Studies Institute of Industrial Relations, 1989.
Meier, August, and David Lewis. "History of the Negro Upper Class in Atlanta, Georgia, 1890–1958." *Journal of Negro Education* 28 (Spring 1959): 128–39.
Miggins, Edward M. "Between Spires and Stacks: The People and Neighborhoods of Cleveland." In *Cleveland: A Metropolitan Reader,* ed. W. Dennis Keating, Norman Krumholz, and David C. Perry, 179–201. Kent, Ohio: Kent State University Press, 1995.
Miller, Randall M. *The Afro-American Slaves: Community or Chaos?* Malabar, Fla.: Robert E. Krieger, 1981.
Mixon, Gregory. "'Good Negro–Bad Negro': The Dynamics of Race and Class in Atlanta during the Era of the 1906 Riot." *Georgia Historical Quarterly* 81 (Fall 1997): 593–621.
———. "Henry McNeal Turner versus the Tuskegee Machine: Black Leadership in the Nineteenth Century." *Journal of Negro History* 89 (Fall 1994): 363–80.
———. "The Political Career of Henry A. Rucker: A Survivor in a New South City." *Atlanta History: A Journal of Georgia and the South* 45 (Summer 2001): 4–26.
———. "Politics and Race: Henry A. Rucker and Aldine Chambers during the Era of the Atlanta Riot." Paper presented at the Association for the Study of African American Life and History annual meeting, Washington, D.C., 27 September–1 October 2000, 15–31.
Muskat, Beth Taylor. "The Last March: The Demise of the Black Militia in Alabama." *Alabama Review* (January 1990): 23–34.
Nagel, Paul C. "Reconstruction, Adams Style." *Journal of Southern History* 52 (February 1986): 3–18.
Nelli, Humbert S. "Italians in Urban America." In *The Italian Experience in the United States,* ed. Silvano M. Tomasi and Madeline H. Engel, 77–103. New York: 1977.

Newby, I. A. *Jim Crow's Defense: Anti-Negro Thought in America, 1900–1930*. Baton Rouge: Louisiana State University Press, 1965.
———. *Plain Folk in the New South: Social Change and Cultural Persistence, 1880–1915*. Baton Rouge: Louisiana State University Press, 1989.
Niswonger, Richard L. *Arkansas Democratic Politics, 1896–1920*. Fayetteville: University of Arkansas Press, 1990.
Norrell, Robert J. "Steelworkers and Storekeepers: Social Mobility among Italian Immigrants in Birmingham." In *The Italian Americans: Through the Generations*, ed. Roco Caporate, 100–107. Staten Island: 1986.
Orr, Oliver H., Jr. *Charles Brantley Aycock*. Chapel Hill: University of North Carolina Press, 1961.
Orum, Anthony M. *City-Building in America*. Boulder: Westview Press, 1995.
Oshinsky, David M. *"Worse than Slavery": Parchman Farm and the Ordeal of Jim Crow Justice*. New York: Free Press, 1996.
Pleck, Elizabeth H., and Joseph H. Pleck, eds. Introduction to *The American Man*. Englewood Cliffs, N.J.: Prentice-Hall, 1980.
Pomerantz, Gary M. *Where Peachtree Meets Sweet Auburn: The Saga of Two Families and the Making of Atlanta*. New York: Scribner, 1996.
Prather, H. Leon, Sr. *We Have Taken a City: Wilmington Racial Massacre and Coup of 1898*. Cranbury, N.J.: Fairleigh Dickerson University Press, 1984.
Proctor, Henry Hugh. *Between Black and White: Autobiographical Sketches*. 1925; reprint, Freeport, N.Y.: Black Heritage Library Collection, Books for Libraries Press, 1971.
———. "Interracial Co-operation in Georgia." *Bulletin of Atlanta University*, October 1906, 2.
"Progressivism." In *Major Problems in the History of the American South, vol. 2: The New South Documents and Essays*, ed. Paul D. Escott and David R. Goldfield, 204–76. New York: D. C. Heath, 1990.
Quick, Herbert. "Hoke Smith and the Revolution in Georgia." *Reader* 10 (1907): 241–48.
Rabinowitz, Howard N. "Continuity and Change: Southern Urban Development, 1860–1900." In *The City in Southern History: The Growth of Urban Civilization in the South*, ed. Blaine A. Brownell and David R. Goldfield, 92–122. Port Washington, N.Y.: National University Publications, Kennikat Press, 1977.
———. *Race Relations in the Urban South, 1865–1890*. Urbana: University of Illinois Press, 1980.
———. "Southern Urban Development, 1860–1900." In *The City in Southern History: The Growth of Urban Civilization in the South*, ed. Blaine A. Brownell and David R. Goldfield. Port Washington: National University Publications, Kennikat Press, 1977.
Redkey, Edwin S. *Black Exodus: Black Nationalist and Back-to-Africa Movements, 1890–1910*. New Haven: Yale University Press, 1969.
———. *Respect Black: The Writings and Speeches of Henry McNeal Turner*. New York: Arno Press and New York Times, 1971.
Roediger, David R. *Towards the Abolition of Whiteness: Essays on Race, Politics, and Working-Class History*. New York: Verso, 1994.

———. *The Wages of Whiteness: Race and the Making of the American Working Class.* New York: Verso, 1991.
Rosen, Hanna. "'Not That Sort of Women': Race, Gender, and Sexual Violence during the Memphis Riot of 1866." In *Sex, Love, Race: Crossing Boundaries in North American History,* ed. Martha Hodes, 267–93. New York: New York University Press, 1999.
Rouse, Jacqueline A. *Lugenia Burns Hope: Black Southern Reformer.* Athens: University of Georgia Press, 1989.
Ruffins, Faith Davis. "Sites of Memory, Sites of Struggle: The Materials of History." In *Major Problems in African-American History, vol. 2: From Freedom to 'Freedom Now,' 1865–1990s Documents and Essays,* ed. Thomas C. Holt and Elsa Barkley Brown, 24–34. New York: Houghton Mifflin, 2000.
Russell, James Michael. *Atlanta, 1847–1890: City Building in the Old South and New.* Baton Rouge: Louisiana State University Press, 1988.
Senechal, Roberta. *The Sociogenesis of a Race Riot: Springfield, Illinois, in 1908.* Urbana: University of Illinois Press, 1990.
Senechal de la Roche, Roberta. "The Sociogenesis of Lynching." *Under Sentence of Death: Lynching in the South,* ed. W. Fitzhugh Brundage, 48–76. Chapel Hill: University of North Carolina Press, 1997.
Shapiro, Herbert. "The Populist and the Negro: A Reconsideration." In *The Making of Black America,* vol. 2, *The Black Community in Modern America,* ed. August Meier and Elliott Rudwick, 27–36. New York: Athenaeum, 1969.
Shaw, Barton C. *The Wool-Hat Boys: Georgia's Populist Party.* Baton Rouge: Louisiana State University Press, 1984.
Sherman, Richard B. *The Republican Party and Black America: From McKinley to Hoover, 1896–1933.* Charlottesville: University Press of Virginia, 1973.
Simon, Bryant. "The Appeal of Cole Blease of South Carolina: Race, Class, and Sex in the New South." *Journal of Southern History* 62 (February 1996): 57–86.
Stone, Charles F. *The Story of Dixie Steel: The First Fifty Years.* Atlanta: Atlanta Steel, 1951.
Thomas, Emory. *The Confederacy as a Revolutionary Experience.* 1971; reprint, Spartanburg: University of South Carolina Press, 1991.
Thomas, June Manning, and Marsha Ritzdorf. *Urban Planning and the African American Community: In the Shadows.* Thousand Oaks, Calif.: Sage, 1997.
Thomas, Richard W. *Life for Us Is What We Make It: Building Black Community in Detroit, 1915–1945.* Bloomington: Indiana University Press, 1992.
"Tom Watson: Disciple of 'Jeffersonian Democracy.'" In *The Oratory of Southern Demagogues,* ed. Carl M. Logue and Howard Dorgan, 85–111. Baton Rouge: Louisiana State University Press, 1981.
Torrence, Ridgely. *The Story of John Hope.* New York: Macmillan, 1948.
van den Berghe, Pierre L. *Race and Racism: A Comparative Perspective.* New York: Wiley, 1967.
Waldrep, Christopher. *Roots of Disorder: Race and Criminal Justice in the American South, 1817–80.* Urbana: University of Illinois Press, 1998.

Walton, Hanes, Jr. *Black Republicans: The Politics of the Black and Tan.* Metuchen: Scarecrow Press, 1975.
Watts, Eugene J. "Black Political Progress in Atlanta, 1868–1895." *Journal of Negro History* 59 (July 1974): 268–84.
———. "The Police in Atlanta, 1890–1905." *Journal of Southern History* 39 (May 1973): 165–82.
———. *The Social Bases of City Politics: Atlanta, 1865–1903.* Westport: Greenwood Press, 1978.
Wheeler, Edward L. *Uplifting the Race: The Black Minister in the New South, 1865–1902.* Lanham: University Press of America, 1986.
White, Dana F. "The Black Sides of Atlanta: A Geography of Expansion and Containment, 1970–1870." *Atlanta Historical Journal* (Summer/Fall 1982): 199–225.
White, Dana F., and Timothy J. Crimmins. "Urban Structure Atlanta: An Introduction." *Atlanta Historical Journal* (Summer/Fall 1982): 6–12.
White, Walter. *A Man Called White.* New York: Arno Press and New York Times, 1969.
Wiebe, Robert H. *The Search for Order, 1877–1920.* American Century series. David Donald, general editor. New York: Hill and Wang, 1967.
Williamson, Joel. *The Crucible of Race: Black-White Relations in the American South since Emancipation.* New York: Oxford University Press, 1984.
———. "Wounds Not Scars: Lynching, the National Conscience, and the American Historian." *Journal of American History* 83 (March 1997): 1221–53.
Wilmore, Gayraud S. *Black Religion and Radicalism: An Interpretation of Religious History of Afro-American People.* 2d ed. Maryknoll, N.Y.: Orbis Books, 1983.
Wilson, Bobby M. *America's Johannesburg: Industrialization and Racial Transformation in Birmingham.* Lanham: Rowman and Littlefield, 2000.
Winch, Julie. *Philadelphia's Black Elite: Activism, Accommodation, and the Struggle for Autonomy, 1787–1848.* Philadelphia: Temple University Press, 1988.
Woodward, C. Vann. *Origins of the New South, 1877–1913.* Baton Rouge: Louisiana State University Press, 1951, 1971.
———. *The Strange Career of Jim Crow.* 3d ed. New York: Oxford University Press, 1974.
———. *Tom Watson, Agrarian Rebel.* 1938; reprint, New York: Oxford University Press 1977.
———. "Tom Watson and the Negro in Agrarian Politics." In *The Negro in the South since 1865: Selected Essays in American Negro History,* ed. Charles E. Wynes, 54. New York: Harper and Row, 1968.
Wright, George C. "The Billy Club and the Ballot: Police Intimidation of Blacks in Louisville, Kentucky, 1880–1930." *Southern Studies: An Interdisciplinary Journal of the South* 23 (Spring 1984): 20–41.
Zipf, Karen. "'The WHITES shall rule the land or die': Gender, Race, and Class in North Carolina Reconstruction Politics." *Journal of Southern History* 65 (August 1999): 499–534.

Index

Page numbers in italics indicate maps.

Adair, Forrest, 118
Adams, Kathleen Redding, 95, 105
Adams, Mattie, 85, 92
African American elite. *See* Black elite
African American working class. *See* Working-class blacks
Alcoholic beverages. *See* Liquor trade; Prohibition issue
Alexander, Hooper, 57
Allen, Alma, 10, *112*
Alley dwellings, 41, 42
American Magazine, 7, 9
Anderson, Clifford L.: Committee of Ten and, 118–19; during riot, 102, 103–4, 106, 108, 109
Annexation, 24–25
Antiblack policies: in Atlanta, 16; of Democratic Party, 23, 29–30, 53–54; vagrancy, 34, 79. *See also* Disfranchisement; Segregation
Anti-Saloon League, 125
Arming of white civilians, 88–89, 102, 110
Arnold, Mrs. Frank (Mattie), 10, *99*, 104
Arnold, Reuben, 31
Arrests: of blacks, 44; in Brownsville, 109–10
Arthur, Chester, 23
Assaults: Baker on, 76; collisions depicted as, 7, 35; first alleged, 8, *96*; second alleged, 9, *98*; third alleged, 10, *114*; fourth alleged, 10, *99*; fifth alleged, 10, *112*; sixth alleged, 10; by Glenn, 123; newspapers on, 73; precipitating, 77; streetcars and, 35–37; of white women by black men, 75, 76–77

Atlanta Baptist College, 47, 106. *See also* Hope, John
Atlanta Constitution: antiblack attitude of, 80; "Culmination of Crime Was Reached in Atlanta," 9–10; delivery boys of, 94; on electoral system, 30; endorsement of riot by, 108; on negro labor trust, 45; policies advocated during Reconstruction by, 17; on Proctor, 48; racial issues and, 4; on riot calls, 101
Atlanta Georgian: antiblack attitude of, 78–79; endorsement of riot by, 108; founding of, 21; "Hundreds of Negroes Are Leaving Atlanta," 122; "The Reign of Terror for Southern Women," 77
Atlanta Independent, 40, 122
Atlanta Journal: on African Americans, 1; black crime crusade of, 77–78; *The Clansman* and, 21, 61; disfranchisement and, 37, 70–71; editors of, 137n. 28; endorsement of riot by, 108; founding of, 20; Hardwick letter in, 70; sensationalism of, 20–21; Smith and, 20
Atlanta Life Insurance Company, 40
Atlanta News: antiblack attitude of, 78–79, 80; endorsement of riot by, 108; J. English, Jr., and, 22; founding of, 21; public opposition to, 108
"Atlanta Spirit": Civil War veterans and, 15; commercial-civic elite and, 47; race relations and, 128; reconstruction after riot and, 120, 122

Atlanta University, 106, 119
Auburn Avenue, 43, 105, 126
Australian ballot, 65
Avary, Myrta Lockett, 117
Aycock, Charles B., 69

Baker, Ray Stannard: on arrests of blacks, 44; on assaults, 76; on J. Brown, 60; on Brownsville, 107; on collision, 7; on C. Hopkins, 125; interviews by, 9; on streetcars, 36
Barber, J. Max: assaults and, 76, 77; Committee of 1,000 and, 118; Committee of Ten and, 119, 121–22; cooperation with white elite, 120–21; exile of, 121; on riot, 85; *Voice of the Negro*, 40; Watson on, 55
Barbershops, 85–86, 91, 95
Barefield, Will, 35
Barnes, Sidney, 36
Beatle, James, 9
Beaverslide, 38
Bell, W. J., 8
Bellwood section, *99*, 104
Belsa, J. D., 93–94
Benevolent societies, 43
Benson, C. F., 122
Biracial meeting about riot, 119–20
Birmingham, Alabama, 15–16
Black, James C., 59
Black elite: clientele of, 38, 39; commercial-civic elite and, 117, 127; Committee of Ten and, 119–22; education and, 39; exclusion of, 126; fears of, 80–81; goals of, 3; political equality and, 45–46; Smith on, 40–41; working classes and, 40
Blackstock, George W., 85, 119
Black working class. *See* Working-class blacks
Blame for riot, 119, 120–21
Bowen, John Wesley Edward: Gammon Seminary and, 47, 107; house-to-house search and, 110; Negro Young People's Christian Education Congress and, 40, 46
Bradley, Aaron, 23
Branham, Robert, 108
Brantley, William M., 36
Briggs, J. W., 92
Brooks, Wiley, 109

Brotherton, William, 21–22, 30
Broughton, Len G., 125
Brown, Eustace, 92
Brown, H. Rap, vii
Brown, James Pope, 60–61
Brown, Leonard, 55
Brown, Milton, 92–93
Brownell, Blaine, 2
Brownsville, Texas, 80
Brownsville (suburb of Atlanta), 107–8, 109–10, *115*
Broyles, Nash R., 35, 118
Bryan, Orrie and Thomas L., 9, 108
Bullard, J. H., 36
Bulletin of Atlanta University, 119
Bullock, Rufus, 29
Business Men's Gospel Union, 117, 124

Calhoun, Andy E., 35, 101
Campbell, Mrs. J. W., 123
Candler, Asa D., 46, 118
Candler, Warren, 46–47
Carmichael, Frank, 76–77
Carnegie, Andrew, 48
Carson, Officer, 88
Chaffin, Mary "Lizzie," 10
Chambers, Aldine, 15, 61, 108
Charlotte, North Carolina, 15–16, 42
Chattahoochee Brick Company, 21–22
Chicago, Illinois, vii
Christianity, 44, 124
Citizens' Ticket, 31, 32
City charter, 14, 22, 24, 30
City executive committee, 30–31, 32, 45
Citywide elections, 29–30
Civic League, 117, 124–26
Civil War veterans, 15, 136n. 21
The Clansman (Dixon), 21, 61
Clark, Alicia, 35
Clark College, 107
Class. *See* Black elite; Commercial-civic elite; Working-class blacks; Working-class whites
Clements, T. F., 89, 108
Clergy: black, 46–49, 80; white, 108–9
Cleveland, Grover, 20, 60
Cleveland, J., 36
Cohen, John S., 61, 118

Colleges: black protection of, 106, 107; militia deployment around, 103, 106. *See also specific colleges*
Collier, M. Lamar, 118
Collisions, black with white, 7, 35
Colored Cooperative League, 117, 121, 124–26
Colquitt, Alfred, 136n. 21
Commercial-civic elite: ambivalent feelings about riot of, 124; beliefs of, 14; black elite and, 117, 127; city building by, 14–15; civic patriotism and, 13–14; control and, 48–49, 81; deputizing of, 104, 108, 110; dual role of, 73; economic dominance of, 126; electoral reforms of, 16, 22–26, 29–31, 32–33; fears of, 2–3, 11; leisure realm and, 33; newspaper support by, 78; as new white men, 2; press and, 116; Progressivism and, 57–58; punishment of rape and, 76; race relations and, 128; reconstructing dominance of, 2–3; segregation and, 110; white supremacy and, 22; working-class whites and, 3
Commission on Interracial Cooperation, 125
Committee of Forty-nine, 29–30
Committee of 1,000, 118
Committee of Ten, 110, 117, 118–22, 123
Convict lease labor, 21–22, 56
Cooper, J. Tyler, 32
Cooper, Walter, 17, 20, 21, 119
Copenhill, *82*
Crime: national survey of black, 48–49; newspapers and, 77–78; perceptions of, 74, 76; rape, 75–76. *See also* Assaults; Lynching
Crumbley, F. M., 45–46
Crumbly, H. H., 46

Dance halls, black, 47–48
Daniel, Charles, 21, 77, 78. *See also Atlanta News*
Danville, Virginia, 71, 74
Darktown, 43, 105
Davis, Benjamin, 40, 62, 91, 122–23
Davis, James, 91
Decatur Street: as focus of church and press, 44, 80; inspections of, 81; Marietta Street, intersection with, 42–43; riot and, 87, 88, 91, 95; working class and, 33, 44
Democratic National Committee, 19
Democratic Party: antiblack rhetoric of, 53–54; blacks in, 23–24; disfranchisement and, 63, 71–72; electoral reform and, 32–33; Grady, Howell, Smith, and, 20; Hemphill and, 46; primary of (1897), 25; violence and, 29, 71; white primary and, 23, 29–30. *See also* Hardwick, Thomas William; Watson, Thomas Edward
Detroit, Michigan, viii
Detroit Barbershop, 91
Diefendorf, Barbara, 116
Disfranchisement: black, 4, 25; Democratic Party and, 63, 71–72; Georgia Constitution and, 126–27; in gubernatorial campaign, 64–65; Howell on, 66–67; in Maryland, 69; in North Carolina, 69–70; riot and, 128–30; Smith and, 62, 68, 81; Watson, Hardwick, and, 53–54, 56–57, 59, 60; white, 32–33
Dives, 43, 80, 81, 104
Dixon, Thomas: *The Clansman,* 21, 61
Dobbs, John Wesley, 39, 105, 127
Dobbs, J. T. and Emmie, 81
Domestic servants, 44–45
Donaldson, C. L., 105
Douglass, Frederick, 60
Du Bois, W.E.B.: benevolent societies and, 43; Committee of Ten and, 119; conference report of, 48; departure of, 129; family of, during riot, 106–7; on C. Hopkins, 125; library committee and, 48; Niagara Movement and, 49; Wilmer and, 121; working-class blacks and, 40

Eady, T. J., 117
East St. Louis, vii
Edgewood Avenue, 94
Edwards, Rosa, 81
Electoral reform: commercial-civic elite and, 16, 22–26, 29–31, 32–33; Howell and, 65
Elite. *See* Black elite; Commercial-civic elite
Ellis, W. D., 118, 137n. 28
Elsas, Jacob, 33, 34
English, Harry, 21–22, 78
English, James W., Jr., 21–22, 78, 101

English, James W., Sr.: *Atlanta News* and, 78; Barber and, 121; as city builder, 15; Committee of Ten and, 110, 118–19; as police commissioner, 30; power of, 17, 21–22; riot and, 86–87
Entertainment district. *See* Leisure realm
Estill, John H., 62
Evans, M. T., 32
Ewing, Richard, 81
Exodus of black residents after riot, 122–23, 129

Farrow, Henry P., 122
Feagan, J. T., 36
Federal employment of blacks, 39, 55
Felton, Rebecca L., 56
Finch, William, 29
Fire hoses, 87
Forsyth Street viaduct, 93
Fortune, T. Thomas, 55
Fourth Ward, 43, 107
Frazier, Luther, 9, 108
Fulton Bag and Cotton textile mill, 33, 34

Gammon Theological Seminary, 46, 47, 107
Gender. *See* Masculinity; Women
Georgia Child Labor Committee, 24
Georgia Railway and Electric Company, 36
Glenn, Joe, 123, 125
Gordon, John B., 136n. 21
Grady, Henry W.: *Atlanta Constitution* and, 17; beliefs of, 18–19; as city builder, 15; Danville riot and, 71; Hillyer and, 22; home rule and, 17–18; Howell and, 65; political protégés of, 4, 19, 20
Graham, George, 29
Graham, J. M., 36
Grand jury, 108
Graves, John Temple: on "an illegal revolution," 72; *Atlanta Journal* and, 21; Barber on, 77; Committee of 1,000 and, 118; politics of, 61; on riot, 117; "Separation of the Races Is the Inevitable Solution," 120. *See also Atlanta Georgian*
Gray, James R.: on North Carolina, 69; political power and, 17; Progressivism and, 24; as reformer, 60–62; riot victims' fund and, 118; Watson and, 62; Wilmington model and, 63. *See also Atlanta Journal*
Green, Henry, 10
Griffin Farmer, 68
Grimes, J. Bryan, 69
Gubernatorial campaign (1905, 1906): candidates in, 62–63; Howell and, 64, 65–67; reform and, 64–65; Smith and, 37, 61–62

Hamburg, South Carolina, 71
Hammond, W. R., 76
Hanna, Marcus A., 39
Hardware stores, 88–89, 92
Hardwick, Thomas William: antiblack attitude of, 53; on black worker, 37; career of, 58–60; disfranchisement and, 54, 59, 60, 129; letter by, 70; politics of, 63; as Progressive, 58; Watson and, 59–60, 62; on white violence, 71
Harris, Walter, 103
Hawthorne, J. B., 71
Heard, James, 109, 123
Heard, John S., 109
Hearnshaw, Jim, 122
Hemphill, W. A., 17, 46
Herndon, Alonzo, 40, 91, 118, 168n. 12
Higher education, black institutions of, 38. *See also specific colleges*
Hill, Benjamin, 19–20
Hillyer, George: black crime crusade and, 77; career of, 22; Citizens' Ticket and, 31; as city builder, 15; city charter and, 14; Committee of 1,000 and, 118; Committee of Forty-nine and, 29–30; as Confederate veteran, 136n. 21; newspaper crusade of, 11; political power and, 17; Progressivism and, 24; on Smith, 19; violence and, 74, 75; Walker and, 76; as water systems expert, 42
Hines, James K., 15
Hirsch, Joseph, 77, 78
Hoffman, Arthur, 93
Holcombe, Martha, 10, *112*
Holderby, A. R., 108–9
Holmes, Nick, 45–46
Holsey, Lucius H., 118

Home rule, 13–14, 17–18, 129
Hope, John: Atlanta Baptist College and, 47; on capitalists, 38; education of, 40; on exodus, 123; Niagara Movement and, 49; on political equality, 45; during riot, 106; on violence, 74
Hope, Lugenia Burns, 79
Hopkins, Charles T.: *Atlanta News* and, 78; black elite and, 119; Civic League and, 117, 124–25; Colored Cooperative League and, 121; Committee of 1,000 and, 118; Committee of Ten and, 123, 124
Hopkins, John L., 29–30, 124
Hopkins, Linton, 77
Houston, Texas, vii
Howell, Clark: Committee of 1,000 and, 118; on disfranchisement, 72; Grady and, 4, 19, 20; as gubernatorial candidate, 64, 65–67; politics and, 15, 17, 25, 65; Progressives and, 24; Smith and, 66–67, 68
Howell, Evan P., 15, 17
Hurt, Joel, 105
Hurt, Nym, 91

Independence, black: attacks on, 80, 128–30; dives and, 43; McKinley nomination and, 23–24; working class and, 38
Industrialization, 130
Inman, Arthur and Samuel, 24
Institutional control, 44–45, 74–75
Investigation of riot, 119
Irish immigrants, vii

Jackson, T. W., 81
Jackson, W. A., 102
Jennings, Henry, 81, 88, 93, 120
Jentzen, John, 122
Jim Crow segregation, 24, 35, 36, 56
Johnson, H. L., 120
Johnson, T.H.M., 120
Johnson, Will, 123
Jones, Sam (Rev.), 67
Jones, Sam D., 118
Journal of Labor, 34, 37
Joyner, W. R., 87, 118, 119
Judicial reform, 75

Keith, P. A., 81
Kelley, Bishop, 109
Kimball House Hotel, 91
Kimmel, John, 8
Kimmel, Knowles, 7–8, 9, 85, *96*
King, Rodney, viii
Kline, R. R., 93
Knights of Labor, 31

Landrum, W. W., 109
Latham, T. W., 32
Laundresses, black, 23, 45
Lawrence, Mabel and Ethel, 77, *82,* 108
Lee, James, 44
Lee, L. L., 46
Leisure realm: dance halls, black, 47–48; dives, 43, 80, 81, 104; elite control of, 33; newspaper attacks on, 79–80; riot and, 89, 93, 104. *See also* Decatur Street
Library, public, for African Americans, 48
Liquor trade, 31, 104. *See also* Prohibition issue
Lithia Springs, Georgia, 159–60n. 25
Looting, 88–89, 92
Los Angeles, California, viii
Lovinggood, R. L., 46
Lynching, 20, 62, 76, 126

Macon, Georgia, 103
Madison, Georgia, 62
Magnolia and Vine Streets, intersection of, *112*
Manley, R., 109
Martin, Mrs. Eugene M., 106
Martin, Thomas, 73
Maryland, 69
Masculinity: helplessness/powerlessness and, 11, 37; Kimmel and, 9; punishment of rape and, 75, 76
Mayo, William, 88
McClelland, J. E., 123
McClure's Magazine, 9
McCord, H. Y., 118
McGhee, Luther, *99*
McGruder, Sam, 109
McHenry, Charles, 46

McHenry, Jackson, 23, 32, 45–46
McIntosh County, Georgia, 67
McKelway, A. J., 76, 102
McKinley, Jacob, 46
McKinley, William, 23, 39, 46
Mechanicsville, 38, 42
Middlebrooks, Jim, *99*
Militia: black volunteer companies, 68, 73, 80; federal government and, 156n. 15; federal troops and, 108; white, mobilization of, 95, 101–4, 109, *113*; white, ordered to Fort McPherson, 8–9. *See also* Anderson, Clifford L.
Miller, John, 36–37
Ministers Union of the African Episcopal Church, 80
Mississippi, 25
Mitchell, Margaret and Eugene, 104
Monday of riot, 108–10
Moore, A. C., 89
Moore, Eunice, 92
Mortality, black, 42
Moyer, I. P., 46
Murphy, John E., 118
Murphy, Willis, 46, 118
Muse, George, 77, 118, 119
Myers, Hiram, 107

Nashville, Tennessee, 15–16
Negro Young People's Christian Education Congress, 40, 46–47
Neighborhoods, black, 38, 94, 105. *See also specific neighborhoods*
Nelms, John W.: Committee of Ten and, 118–19; on Daniel, 78; deputizing of white civilians by, 104, 108, 110; riot and, 89; Troy and, 9; Walker and, 76
Nelson, Ben, 91
Nelson, C. K., 47
Newark, New Jersey, viii
New Bern, North Carolina, 70
New South: black labor in, 45; Grady and, 18; politicians in, 59; Progressivism in, 15–16; urbanization of, 2
Newspapers: antiblack violence and, 129; black crime crusade of, 77–78; black elite and, 80–81; delegation advising, 118; editorials in, 73; endorsement of riot by, 108; extra editions of, 7, 104; manipulation of, 116; political power and, 17; recreational sites, attacks on, 79, 81. *See also specific newspapers*
New York City, vii
New York World, 120
Niagara Movement, 49, 120
North Carolina: Charlotte, 42; disfranchisement in, 69–70; New Bern, 70; Wilmington, 63, 69, 70, 74
Northen, William J., 117, 119, 124, 136n. 21

Oakland City, *96*
Old South, 2
Overman, Lee S., 70
Owens, Ruby, 107, 109–10

Palmer, J. W., 46
Paris, France, 116
Paternalism, racial, 116–17, 123–24, 128
Peachtree Street, 85–86, 88, 91–92
Pearson and McCarley hardware store, 92
Pendleton, John T., 118, 119
Penn, Irvine Garland, 40, 46
People's Ticket, 31, 46
Peters Street, 92, 95, *97*
Philadelphia, vii, viii, 74
Piedmont Hotel, 45, 89, 94, *98*
Pittsburg: description of, 38, 43; map of, *100*; militia deployment around, 103; riot in, 35
Plantation: Grady on, 18–19
Plessy v. Ferguson, 35
Police commissioners, board of, 29–30
Police force: antivagrant policy and, 80; members of, 167n. 41; officers in, from working class, 37; political manipulation of, 30; during riot, 87–89, 103
Political parties. *See* Democratic Party; Populism; Republican Party
Poll tax, 29
Poole, Annie Laurie, 76–77
Population, 41
Populism (Populist Party), 46, 56, 57, 58

Power: access to, 128–29; political, 11, 17
Press. *See* Newspapers
Price, L. J., 107, 110
Primary, white, 4, 23, 29–30, 32
Proctor, Henry Hugh: advice of, 120; benevolent societies and, 43; Colored Cooperative League and, 125, 126; Committee of 1,000 and, 118; Committee of Ten and, 119; departure of, 129, 148n. 47; Du Bois and, 121; on exodus, 123; family of, during riot, 106–7; C. Hopkins and, 125; as right thinker, 47–49; sermons of, 80; working-class blacks and, 40
Produce Row, 43
Progressivism: commercial-civic elite and, 57–58; home rule and, 129; Smith, Hillyer, Gray, and, 24; in South, 15–16, 150n. 15
Prohibition issue, 23, 31, 125
Prosecution of rioters, 118, 119, 122, 123
Providence, Rhode Island, 74

Quick, Herbert, 67

Race riots: in Atlanta, overview of, 1–2, 74; causes of, 74–75; in 1800s, 74; in New York City and Philadelphia, vii; in 1900s, vii–viii; Watson on reasons for, 55. *See also* Violence
Radical Republicans, 29
Rape, 75–76
Reconstruction after Civil War, 17, 29
Reconstruction after riot. *See* Committee of Ten
Recorder's Court, 108
Recreational sites. *See* Leisure realm
Redding, Wesley C., 95
Render, J. D., 46
Republican Party: blacks and, 23–24, 49; disunity in, 29; Rucker and, 39, 46; Smith on, 68; whites in, 25
Residential areas, 28, 41–42, 43–44. *See also* Neighborhoods, black
Retaliation by blacks, fears of, 103, 104–5
Richardson, Will, 25
Right thinking, 47, 48
Riot relief fund, 119

Roan, Leonard S., 118, 123
Roosevelt, Theodore, 39
Rosler, E. M., 36
Rosser, Luther Z., 77, 118, 123
Rucker, Annie Eunice, 95
Rucker, Betsey, 39
Rucker, Henry A.: barbershop of, 91; career of, 39; as civic leader, 45–46; Davis and, 122; Republican Party and, 23, 46; during riot, 94–95
Rural migrants, 27–28
Russell, Richard B., Sr., 62–63
Ryan, Ed, 8

Saloons, 33, 38
Sanitation workers, 122
Saturday night of riot, 85–92
Saul, Milt, 69–70
Schloss, Ed, 107
Seely, F. L., 78, 118
Segregation: in aftermath of riot, 126; of Atlanta, 42; black elite and, 40; commercial-civic elite and, 110; "guardianship" through, 123–24; C. Hopkins and, 125; streetcars and, 35–37, 89. *See also* Jim Crow segregation
Shepard, W. G., 88
Shotgun houses, 42
Simmons, Furnifold, 69–70
Simon, Jane, 94
Skating rink, 87–88
Slaton, John, 104
Smith, Burton, 103
Smith, Frank, 90
Smith, Hoke: Barber and, 120–21; beliefs of, 20–21; on blacks, 1, 40–41, 67; in campaign speech, 27; in Cleveland administration, 20, 65–66; disfranchisement and, 81; Grady and, 4, 19, 20; Gray and, 21; as gubernatorial candidate, 37, 61–62, 64–65, 67–68; Howell and, 66–67, 68; organized labor and, 34; as political leader, 15; political power and, 17, 19–20, 25; Progressivism and, 24; riot and, 93, 94; on streetcars, 37; Watson on, 64. *See also Atlanta Journal;* Piedmont Hotel

Smith, James M., 63
Smithers's pawn shop, 92
South Atlanta, 105, 107–8, 109
Speer, Emory, 13, 64, 74–75
Spelman College, 106
Springfield, Illinois, vii
St. Bartholomew's Day Massacre, 116
Steele, A. R., 118
Storr's School, 39
Strange, H. B., 36
Streetcars: attacks on, 88, 89–91, 94, *100*; creation of system of, 14; segregation and, 35–37; suburban migration of elites and, 28; violence and, 105; women on, 79
Summerhill, 38, 43, 107, *114*
Sunday of riot, 92–95, 102–8

Taft, William Howard, 39
Talley, Herbert, 119
Taylor, C. H., 60
Terrell, Joseph: J. English, Jr., and, 22; and fund for apprehension of rioters, 118; Howell and, 65; militia and, 8–9, 102–3; riot and, 101
Third Ward, 44
Thomas, Roy, 91
Thompson, Mrs. Robert P., 109
Thompson, W. S., 32
Tillman, Ben, 70, 71
Tin Can Alley, 43
Tomlinson, G. C., 89
Tom Watson's Magazine, 53, 67
Troy (victim of mob), 8, 9
Tuesday of riot, 109–10, 118
Tulsa, Oklahoma, vii
Turner, Henry McNeal, 20, 23, 54, 66, 118

Union Station, 92, *98*
Urban culture, black, 11–12, 129–30
Urbanization, 2, 24, 130

Vagrancy, 34, 79
Van Epps, Howard, 76
Victims' fund, 118
Vine City, 42
Vining, Dave M., 32

Violence: antiminority urban, 116; black powerlessness and, 73–74; *The Clansman* and, 61; judges and, 74–76; Monday of riot, 108–10; political, during Reconstruction, 29; racial, before Civil War, 74; racial, benefits of, 69–70, 71; Saturday night of riot, 85–92; Sunday of riot, 92–95; Tuesday of riot, 109–10; white reformers and, 71. *See also* Race riots
Virginia, 71, 74
Voice of the Negro, 40

Walker, Alex, 123
Walker, C. N., 92
Walker, Jim, 75–76
Wanamaker, John, 68
Ward, A. C., 44, 109
Ward system, 24–25, 29, 30
Washington, Booker T., 45, 68
Watson, Ed, 91
Watson, Thomas Edward: antiblack attitude of, 53–55; beliefs of, 56–57; career of, 56, 57; disfranchisement and, 54, 56–57, 60, 129; Grady and, 136n. 17; Gray and, 61, 62; Hardwick and, 59–60, 62; Progressivism and, 57–58; on Smith, 64
Welch, Henry, 87
West End, *111*
Western and Atlantic Railroad, 33
White, John E., 109
White, Walter, 105–6
White elite. *See* Commercial-civic elite
White working class. *See* Working-class whites
Wilmer, Cary Breckenridge, 77, 121, 124
Wilmington, North Carolina, 63, 69, 70, 74
Wilson, Woodrow, 19
Wimbush, C. C., 23
Winn, Jerry, 35
Winston, W. J., 73–74
Women: streetcars and, 35–37; as transit riders, 79; white, assaults on, by black men, 75, 76–77; in workforce, 33, 34
Woodside, J. J., 88
Woodward, James G.: alarm declared by, 87; as city councilman, 31; Committee of Ten

and, 118–19; as mayoral candidate, 31–32; response to exodus by, 123; riot and, 86, 104; white primary and, 32
Work, Monroe N., 48
Workforce, management control of, 33–35
Working-class blacks: black elite and, 40; dive owners and, 81; in police force, 37; residential areas for, 28, 41–42, 43–44; Smith on, 41; urban culture of, 129–30; working-class whites and, 3–4, 33–34
Working-class whites: alignment with white elites by, 28–29; Decatur Street and, 44; People's Ticket of, 31; primary, white, and, 32; removal from electorate, 32–33; residential areas for, 28; in riot, 89, 95; as rural migrants, 27–28; working-class blacks and, 3–4, 33–34
Workplace: black attempts to determine rules of, 11, 38, 45
Work stoppages, 105, 122

Gregory Mixon is assistant professor of history at the University of North Carolina at Charlotte. This is his first book. He has contributed articles to the *Journal of Negro History, Atlanta History: A Journal of Georgia and the South,* and the *Georgia Historical Quarterly.*

www.ingramcontent.com/pod-product-compliance
Lightning Source LLC
Chambersburg PA
CBHW032252150426
43195CB00008BA/422